Sailing to Hemingway's Cuba

Sailing to Hemingway's Cuba

DAVE SCHAEFER

𝕊

SHERIDAN HOUSE

First published 2000 by
Sheridan House Inc.
145 Palisade Street
Dobbs Ferry, NY 10522
www.sheridanhouse.com

Library of Congress Cataloging-in-Publication Data

Schaefer, David, 1938-
　　Sailing to Hemingway's Cuba/Dave Schaefer.
　　　p. cm
　　Includes bibliographical references.
　　ISBN 1-57409-110-7 (alk. paper)
　　　1. Hemingway, Ernest, 1899-1961—Homes and
haunts—Cuba. 2. Schaefer, David, 1938—Journeys—
Cuba. 3. Cuba—Description and travel. 4. Literary
landmarks—Cuba. 5. Sailing. I. Title

　　PS3515.E37 Z8216 2000
　　813'.54—dc21
　　[B]　　　　　　　　　　　　　　　00-032207

Edited by Janine Simon
Design by Jesse Sanchez
Photos by the author unless otherwise noted

Printed in the United States of America

ISBN　　　1-57409-110-7

For Courtney, Dylan and Jackson
If you catch wanderlust, you can blame your grandfather.

Acknowledgments

The people who placed their safety and well-being at risk by signing on as DREAM WEAVER crew members on the many legs of this voyage made this book possible. Bob Platt, always supported and at times helped by his wife Thea, was on board more than anyone else, and was an excellent crew member and friend. Ed DesLauriers made his first ocean leg with pluck and a sense of humor. Dale Nichols Sutherland weathered the coldest, roughest legs of the trip with grace and good humor, and we are planning now for some of the good times. Gordon Tapsell and Enid Harrington Tapsell on WHIM OF ARNE were wonderful mentors and traveling companions. Ralph DesLauriers is fun to be around and was a constant positive force field even on the uncomfortable days and nights off the Georgia coast. Old friends Don and Gael Steffens and their friends in Vero Beach adopted a wayfaring sailor and turned what could have been a lonely Christmas into a warm memory. Phil Moizeka was game for everything, and I hope we'll get to cruise together again. The Cuba crew members, John Dupee and Fritz Horton, are exceptional sailors, delightful companions, and will probably never know how much their presence on board meant to me. Staff members for Vermont's two exceptional senators, Patrick Leahy and James Jeffords, made this book possible with their efforts on my behalf with the Treasury Department. Sue Stephenson and Robert Daniel on the catamaran TIGER LILY remained good pals to a lonely sailor who needed good pals. My son, Kurt, helped me keep my affairs glued together while I was off having an adventure and getting my pockets picked, and I regret he was not aboard for some of this odyssey.

A Word About Identities of Cubans and Sailors in Cuba

The names of all American sailors in Cuba and their boat names have been changed. I have changed the names of all the living Cubans mentioned except Rubén, Esperanza, Isadora, Eusebio Leal and, of course, Fidel Castro. The names of the Salvadorans accused of bombings have not been changed. The names of places, bars, restaurants, and names of foreigners who are not at risk by visiting Cuba have not been changed.

Sailing to Hemingway's Cuba

Contents

xi INTRODUCTION   *Searching for Pilar*

1 CHAPTER 1   *Southbound to Margaritaville*

47 CHAPTER 2   *The St. Tropez of the Poor*

71 CHAPTER 3   *Key West to Havana*

103 CHAPTER 4   *Marina Hemingway*

121 CHAPTER 5   *Tracking Papa in Old Havana*

151 CHAPTER 6   *Cuba Libre*

173 CHAPTER 7   *Dictators and Mobsters*

201 CHAPTER 8   *Hemingway at Home*

221 CHAPTER 9   *Finding Pilar*

231 CHAPTER 10   *Havana Nights*

249 CHAPTER 11   *Back into the Stream*

267 BIBLIOGRAPHY AND SOURCES

Searching for Pilar

An Introduction

The sound of swallows debating noisily just overhead dragged me from a deep sleep in the V-berth of DREAM WEAVER, my 32-foot sloop. The swallows were perched on the rim of the open hatch three feet above my face, facing outward, their tail feathers bobbing to the beat of their chirping in such a way that I expected a splat of bird lime on the forehead at any moment. Then they were off, drawn to breakfast on the mayflies rising from the surface of Lake Champlain.

It is good to start a July day on a boat, waking to swallows. I had gone to sleep re-reading Hemingway's *The Old Man and the Sea*, struggling along with the old Cuban against a nature that operates without remorse. The story begins near Havana, Cuba.

I was a senior in journalism school at the University of Wisconsin in 1959 when Fidel, Raúl and Che finally triumphed and tossed out Batista, his mob friends, gambling and other capitalistic vices. Cuba, embargoed and off limits to Americans for 40 years, but just 90 miles away. Key West is closer to Havana than to Miami. In the eyes of the U.S. government, going to Cuba is assumed to be "trading with the enemy" and the penalties can be severe.

Images from high school days returned, gleaned from *Time*, *Life*, *Colliers* and *True* magazine photos and stories. There was Hemingway, the larger-than-life writer and his cronies and women occupying a world I wanted to occupy. Scant mystery why I became a journalist: the Hemingway legend that still fascinates and frustrates writers to this very day. I had tried my hand at fiction, but to no avail. Close, but no cigar. The notion still haunted me, a ghost from a young man's dream that came in the night and said, "You gave up too easily."

Now, with Cuba struggling to recover from economic collapse and Castro growing both long in the tooth and long in the beard, it was beginning to crack open. What was there now? I had read that Hemingway's home there, Finca Vigía, had been preserved by the Castro government right down to the sports magazines on the bed and bottles of Campari on the table next to Hemingway's lopsided easy chair. His most precious possession, the 38-foot fishing boat, PILAR, was there at the finca, on the hard.

Working early in the morning, standing at a shelf in his bedroom, pecking at a portable typewriter propped up with a book, Hemingway put the finishing touches on another Pilar, the fiery female guerilla loyalist of the Spanish Civil War in *For Whom the Bell Tolls*. Like Fidel, Pilar's little band waged guerilla warfare from hideouts in the mountains. Unlike Fidel, they lost.

For the entire century, Cuba had been a stage for the glamorous and the powerful: Teddy Roosevelt's charge up San Juan Hill, the mob years under Meyer Lansky, Khrushchev and Kennedy bringing the world to the brink of nuclear war over missile installations, the disaster at the Bay of Pigs, the charisma of Che, and endless embargoes. The last year of the millennium marked the centennial of Hemingway's birth and the fortieth anniversary of Fidel's Revolution.

How had the once beautiful colonial city of Havana weathered the revolution? If you went to Cuba today, what would you find? What would you do? Sooner or later the veil of mystery would lift. This was the magic moment before it opened up to Americans, and McDonalds arrived. Then it would be gone forever. But now, Cuba before franchises: a time capsule containing a century of revolution and upheaval. And rum, and salsa, and beautiful women in colors from vanilla to licorice. Forbidden fruit.

I was tired of charging up the same old hills, following the same predictable paths. My business experience had begun to atrophy into dull routine; I felt my horizons diminished. After 40 years of work a question nagged constantly: what next ? Instead of being dead at 50, which was likely if we had been born in 1900, many of us now have an extra third of life and we have not been trained in how to use it. Why shouldn't the rest of us, the non-academics, take sabbaticals of our own to invent the third and final act in the show?

It was time to explore a hill covered with palm trees instead of sugar maples. Now that the Hemingway haunts had been turned into tourist attractions, I would ferret out the new hangouts and dives, the places devoted to rumba, mambo and salsa. I would find Hemingway, and Pilar, and maybe in doing so I would exorcise that old ghost. I paced off the distance from Burlington, Vermont to Havana with an atlas and a pair of navigation dividers: about 1,600 miles as the crow flies, many more miles on a boat following the waterways.

That evening, friends came out to the boat and I explained the rough beginnings of my plan. A woman raised a question that took the search in yet another direction, "Who will go with you? You can't go alone."

Divorced, living alone, with age 50 vanished in life's rear-view mirror, it was a question with no immediate answer. I probably could do it alone, but it wouldn't be nearly as much fun without someone to share it with. My kids, now busy building their own lives—two out of three married and providing me with beautiful grandchildren—might make some passages with me. There were a few friends who could get free, but not for the entire trip. "I'll have to find someone, but this kind of thing isn't for everyone."

"It should be a woman," she declared.

"She would have to be very unusual."

"Obviously, she has to like to sail. She has to like adventure."

"It would help if she spoke fluent Spanish."

I knew some words, but had trouble stringing them together into sentences.

Her French companion added, "Of course, she has to like older men because she will be much younger than you."

So Pilar took on yet another persona: an elusive Latina crew member who loved to navigate, varnish, cook Caribbean dishes, stand the lonely watch at the helm just before dawn, and negotiate in the market-place. Over time, friends warmed to this game of inventing a Pilar to be found and won and brought on board. They became involved in the search and contributed to creating a fantasy character.

Pilar sings softly to herself in Spanish while cooking and allows no one else in the galley. She loves leaving one port behind and, even more, loves arriving in new and unfamiliar ports, the mindset of the cruising sailor. Pilar has a mysterious secret in her past, and I will never know what it is. She is a certified scuba diver and navigates intuitively, like a Polynesian. Some day she will abruptly vanish, leaving me heartbroken. Pilar represented the new; an adventure. She was not necessarily even a person. Pilar was life reinvented. It could be done, this sail to Cuba.

1 | Southbound to Margaritaville

It was time to leave Vermont behind and push off for Cuba. The signs of an approaching winter were all around.

Down at Lake Champlain Yacht Club we were now finishing our Wednesday night races in the dark. Hard to miss that clue that the days were getting shorter.

The streets of Burlington, Vermont, were suddenly jammed with expensive sports utility vehicles piloted by returning university students who wore their baseball caps backward and were learning life's essential lesson: how to live off the land in a college town with nothing but a Swiss Army knife and a Visa card backed up by Dad. Where I live, near the university, at 2 a.m. we began hearing the primal calls of young males, full of mojo and draft beer, screaming their way back up the hill from closed saloons, clear harbingers of the autumnal equinox.

A cold front from up above Georgian Bay had already sent a surprise snowstorm rattling through the Green Mountains, dusting the sugar maples with grainy snow while they were only vaguely considering slipping out of their summer green wardrobe and into the brilliant golds and reds of autumn. Leaf peepers would soon arrive from all over the world.

At the next full moon a killing frost could be expected to answer the silent prayers of vegetable gardeners becoming weary of canning tomatoes, freezing pesto and composting mammoth zucchinis. They would rise early in the morning, survey limp tomato stalks and flattened squash plants and think the treasonous words they would never utter to their neighbors: Thank God I can finally plow it under.

And, in the most reliable of all indicators, my boat was getting heavier as my checking account balance simultaneously got lighter. Jibs had been re-cut and roller furling installed, the soft main had been replaced with a new and battened main with lazy jacks for easy dousing, running rigging had been replaced, standing rigging inspected with a magnifying glass and caressed with a nylon stocking to reveal fractured stands, and a new stove replaced the old pressurized alcohol stove. The Sears 12-volt batteries in the bank reserved for accessories had been replaced with two six-volt Trojan golf cart batteries hooked in series to make one massive 12-volt power reservoir. The bottom had been scraped to bare fiberglass, sealed with two-part epoxy and covered with a tropical bottom paint so heavy with cuprous oxide that with a gallon in each hand I could barely waddle out of the marine supply store. No barnacle would dream of sticking to the bottom of my boat.

DREAM WEAVER, a 22-year-old Endeavour 32 sloop, was as ready as she would ever be. So was I, having passed through three distinct phases that had spanned more than two years: a relentless malaise or boredom that could only be cured by drastic change, deciding what that change would be, and planning and implementing the details. For the last three weeks, phase four had been kicking in regularly at 3:30 a.m., when the suppressed inner voice of reason shouted me out of a sound sleep by asking: "What have you done, you picklehead? You could die out there!"

A raw, 15-knot breeze laced with occasional showers whipped around the four of us as we carted boxes and bags of provisions and gear down the dock to DREAM WEAVER. Our loading crew included Bob Platt, his wife

Thea, Dale Sutherland, and myself. It was September 10, but November was in the air. A cold front was supposed to deliver 35-mph winds and drive out a rainy low that had delayed our start for a day. Our gear bags contained swimming suits, wool caps, thick fleece jackets and long underwear, the basic stuff for almost any Vermont weekend.

Bob, who owned the boat moored next to mine at Lake Champlain Yacht Club, would be the only other sailor on board, at least for a while. We had never really sailed together before, but had developed a sort of neighborly friendship. He was an experienced sailor, frequent racer with Thea as crew, and had recently sold his business. Thea described him as a "neatnik," which on a small boat is a virtue of the first magnitude. He came down into the cabin as I jammed provisions and clothing into storage bins. I was more concerned about getting things secure against the rough weather than organizing the boat. His eyes came to rest on a six-pack of Spam, and for the first time I saw a flicker of doubt.

"For emergencies only," I lied, not wanting to scare him off. I happen to like Spam, America's pâté.

"Whew, you had me worried there for a minute."

"No, that's for Cuba. We'll have to organize this stuff later. I have no idea where anything is in here." I climbed out onto the dock. "Is that it? Everything's on board?"

"Nothing left in the cars," Dale said, a note of false cheerfulness in her voice. She was being a good sport. In her yellow foul-weather gear, her cheeks red from the chill, she was beautiful, but wistful. "I wish I was coming along."

"You will be, on the next leg." I was going to miss her. When this voyage was first conceived our bumpy, ten-year relationship was on hold. But things had definitely changed for the better.

There was nervous laughter, a few photos for the record, hugs and kisses and an appearance by a crew member, Ralph DesLauriers, whose business pressures had forced a last-minute cancellation of his plans to sail with us. He brought a bottle of Goslings rum and best wishes.

At the finger dock next to us Shel Reilly was alone on his Mason 43 SEA SHELL, also making preparations to head south in a week or so. SEA SHELL, and CIRCE, a Krogan 38, with Chris Stevenson, his wife and crew on board, would soon be heading toward Norfolk, Virginia to take part in the Caribbean 1500 starting November 1. This was a cruising race, still at the edge of the hurricane season, from East Coast ports to Bermuda and on to the British Virgin Islands, about 1,500 miles. I hoped I would see the two crews along the way, since they would probably travel a little faster than DREAM WEAVER. We had been comparing notes on our schemes and dreams.

"Time to go," I said but I was thinking, "let's not drag this out."

The lines that held us in place were cast off. I put one foot on the dock that represented everything I had known until now, and the other on the deck of the sailboat that represented the unknown. I hoped and also feared that, by the time I saw this place again, my life would have changed forever. I committed my weight to the boat and pushed.

Nine miles west of Havana is a red sea buoy that marks the approach through the reefs to Marina Hemingway. It is at Latitude 23 degrees 05.4 North, Longitude 082 degrees 30.6 West. Months ago I had measured the distance from northern Vermont to Cuba quickly with an atlas and a pair of navigation dividers. It was

1,600 miles as the crow flies, and a lot farther as the waterways meander. When I got a little handheld Garmin Global Positioning Satellite unit I entered the sea buoy's coordinates and in a second or two I was told that the distance was 1,566 nautical miles, and I could reach the buoy by sailing a course of 218 degrees.

Unfortunately, most of the East Coast was in the way. DREAM WEAVER would probably average four knots per hour. It would be a long trip. Not only long, but risky. The U.S. Treasury Department can get very grumpy with people who sail off to Cuba in violation of the embargo. If you hit them on a bad day and they learn you have spent money in Cuba they can fine you a couple of hundred thousand dollars and seize your boat.

Skeptics thought I was off on a daffy quest, but it was important to me. Some people memorize baseball statistics and make pilgrimages to halls of fame honoring sports icons. Not me. Not only am I unable to watch sports played with balls for more than about 17 seconds, I have a panic attack if, seated and trapped in the barber's chair, the man with the sharp implements in his hands opens with, "Hey, what about those Red Sox?" I would rather talk plasma physics, which I don't know anything about either, but at least we would be even.

Sure, I wanted to see Cuba before it opened up to Americans and we swiftly turned it into just another homogenized, pasteurized, sanitized, franchised real estate development. But there was more to it than that. I was going to track down my high school hero, Ernest Hemingway.

In those days I knew I was going to be just like swashbuckling Hemingway, hanging out with bullfighters, safari hunters and movie stars, traveling around the world to write about exotic places. But I turned out to be just another ordinary guy. I never got over it. One thing I had learned during a career in journalism was that there was no substitute for actually going to the scene of the crime. Things always were different from second-hand reports. So I would go to Hemingway's haunts and see for myself, and if I was very lucky when it was all over I would have shaken off his ghost, which still came around to hint that I hadn't tried hard enough or simply didn't measure up. I had no idea how that could happen. Others might be sailing off for adventure, but I was on a mission. It simply had to be done, and done now.

Even in Vermont, many people are surprised that a boat can be sailed from Lake Champlain to the ocean, but two options are available. The northern route heads toward Montreal and then out the St. Lawrence River, but most cruisers head south to the lake's pointed end, where it becomes much more like a river and feeds through the Champlain Canal into the Hudson River. The canal was completed in 1823 to provide a route for commerce between the forests of the Champlain Valley and the manufacturing centers south to New York City. A few cruisers go each autumn, easy to spot because they have taken their masts down to clear the low bridges over the canal, and they carry them over the deck in temporary wooden supports resting on the bow and stern rails, or in taller, X-shaped supports. DREAM WEAVER took this southern route, although I had chosen to sail down the lake to the northernmost lock before stepping the mast at Lock 12 Marina in Whitehall, New York.

Bob and I settled into a comfortable routine, assisted by Otto, the Autohelm 3000. Over the next few days we made our way through a dozen locks on the Champlain Canal and into the Hudson River at Troy, New York, where we were joined by young Ed DesLauriers, Ralph's son. I was learning as I was going. In the Hudson River, Bob and I had pulled out our new Global Positioning Satellite units and learned how to use them before we had to do the overnight passage from buoy to buoy off New Jersey. We continued on down the Hudson through New York Harbor to Atlantic Highlands, New Jersey. Next was a 23-hour offshore passage down the New Jersey Coast, with Atlantic City glowing through the night on the western horizon like a setting sun frozen in place. We rested at Cape May, New Jersey and then headed up Delaware Bay for a day and into the Chesapeake and Delaware

DREAM WEAVER going south under sail. Photo courtesy of Sue Stephenson.

Canal. At the end of our two-week trip we anchored out in the Sassafras River at the top of Chesapeake Bay near Baltimore. A bagpiper on a small sailboat piped the sun down on the last day of this leg of the trip.

The next day we stored the boat at Fairview Marine on Rock Creek and caught an Amtrak train back to Vermont. I had six weeks of work to complete before resuming the voyage at the end of the first week in November.

I returned to the Chesapeake in November with a dark cloud of foreboding hanging overhead, an angst I could not shake as the Amtrak train clicked off the miles and hours to the station at Baltimore International Airport, where I was to meet Dale's plane.

Just one day before I left I learned that CIRCE had run into Hurricane Mitch while participating in the Caribbean 1500, and had been abandoned. The other boat, SEA SHELL, was also in the Caribbean 1500 and could not have been far away. I knew everyone on that boat, but had no word about them. The crew of the abandoned boat had been picked up by a German freighter bound for Hamburg, and all were well. But the skipper and I had talked frequently about our cruising dreams, and his experience drove home just how fragile life at sea can be. The notion that some day I might have to face that kind of circumstance sat on my heart like a cold rock. I would not be going very far offshore—except for the Gulf Stream crossing to Cuba—but I was going alone for much of the voyage and it was inevitable that I would be getting in over my head, taking the tests before getting the lessons. It did not take long.

The trees were bare by the time Dale and I left Vermont early in November, but the Chesapeake was still wearing the muted tones of autumn: straw-colored marsh grasses, russet browns of late season oaks, a few bright maples, but not the explosive colors of autumn in Vermont. Dawn came on thin light, purple and grey and peach, with watermen working their crab lines and sending the sound of small diesels across the water. The geese were usually awake before us, exchanging morning greetings along the shore.

We were about three weeks late to be cruising south on the Chesapeake. Morning temperatures were in the mid thirties or low forties, and condensation hung overhead until it mustered droplets that plopped onto forehead or ear. After two deep breaths I would jump from beneath the quilt, turn on the boat heater, turn off the masthead anchor light, and dive back under the quilt. In less than 10 minutes the cabin was warming and there would be another dash to dress and put on the coffee water. The sailing uniform was the same as a skiing uniform: polyester long johns, turtleneck, fleece, windbreaker, blue jeans, foul-weather pants, parka, gloves with silk liners. The decks were soaked with dew. Dale smiled through it all, and in the evening curled up in fleece from head to toe in the starboard bunk and devoured a series of books.

The days and anchorages clicked past. In Annapolis we rode the dinghy from an anchorage in Spa Creek to McGarvey's Saloon, where we sat in our foul-weather gear until it stopped steaming and then peeled down to eat. En route through Knapps Narrows to Oxford, Maryland, I learned it is a mistake to mount the GPS on top of the Autohelm control unit: the electronic interference makes both units crazy and we completely missed the Trent River. We sat out a day of bad weather in Oxford, a charming town from the 1940s that was closing

9

down for the season. We found the free pump out station in Solomons and picked our way into Dividing Creek at dusk. When you sail the Chesapeake in November the anchorages are empty, the days are short, the boatyards are crowded with boats being hauled, but the ice lasts a long time. Suddenly we were running late for Dale's plane; she had to get back to work.

It would be wonderful to say I never make mistakes, but the best I can say is that I have survived them so far. On November 14 a low was forecast for late in the day, and we had a long haul into the York River to find a marina before dark . . . longer than I realized. By early morning the mackerel clouds announced the low, and it was moving in fast. The wind started building out of the southwest, and by the time we reached the light at Wolf Trap it was 15 to 17 dead on the nose and visibility was shrinking. We missed the channel marker for the York River. Light rain began falling and the light failed as the afternoon wore on. We could see no land, but I realized we were in the shipping channels when huge ships loomed at us out of the mist.

"Is that going to miss us?" Dale asked quietly as a freighter appeared to port, headed right for us.

"We're going to pass ahead of it," I said more confidently than I felt, knowing it was traveling at three times our speed. By 3:30 I grimly realized there was no way we would be in the York River before dark, which was just an hour away. I tried to get fixes with the GPS on the marks, but there would not be time to get back on our old course before dark. While I was doing my macho thing with the GPS, Dale said, "I think I see a point of land over there. Let's go for it. Can you tell what it is?"

I knew where we were, the land had to be Point Comfort. There was a lighthouse, the entrance to Mobjack Bay. I studied the charts. Some distance beyond it was a marked channel up the East River, and there appeared to be anchorages right off the channel. That was good because I wanted to find a spot just off the channel and not poke around in the rain in the dark. We began motorsailing for the point as fast as we could under full main and genoa, still heeled over to starboard in a breeze that had dropped a bit and was about 12 knots.

The Endeavour 32 has a peculiar design flaw and it was now on my mind. The fuel tank is a flat, 30-gallon pan squeezed between the cockpit sole and the hull. The engine fuel intake is mounted off-center on the port side. When the tank starts to empty—after eight to 10 hours of motoring—and the boat is heeled to starboard in lumpy conditions, the intake can be exposed causing the diesel to gulp air and quit, not to be restarted until the fuel line is bled. I could now see the lighthouse and knew there were navigation aids on the point. We would not make the point on this tack, and I should probably turn off the engine and not restart it until we got onto a starboard tack or were flat in the water. At that moment the diesel coughed, quit, restarted briefly, then quit for good.

We were boiling toward the point and the lighthouse; the engine would have to wait. I could see one navigation aid and the lighthouse just ahead, but could not see the second one and thought it was behind the lighthouse. I glanced around the windward side of the jib, and there it was, off to port. We were about to run up on the shoals off the point. I looked down into the water and it was milky blue with turbulent sand.

"Tacking now," I shouted and spun the helm, waiting for the crunch as the hull swung through the vertical, expecting to be plastered on a lee shore without an engine and in the dark. We went onto starboard tack, miraculously without bumping, although not very gracefully.

"Look," Dale exclaimed. I thought, now what? Three dolphins had appeared right next to the low side, cavorting and blowing as if nothing in the world was amiss. I hoped that if they had enough water to swim out of here, I had enough water to sail out.

We held our course just long enough to safely clear the navigation aid on the point, then tacked back into Mobjack Bay. In the distance the flashing red light of a navigation aid was visible in the gloom. Crab trap floats and fish sticks now appeared here and there in the water. Dale steered for the light while I studied the chart and tried to figure out which of two possible marks it was. We sailed over and identified it, and now, with the binoculars, I could see a green light which must mark the beginning of the channel leading up the river, but it was far in the distance. The wind was gradually dying and soon we would be drifting. I went below to try to revive the diesel.

Bleeding the air from the fuel line of a diesel engine is not rocket science, but the task is more demanding when you are pitching around in the dark, tools flying into the bilge, with visibility provided by a small flashlight gripped in your mouth. You simply open a screw in the fuel system, crank the engine until the diesel fuel runs clear and there are no air bubbles, then quickly close the screw. The problems usually surface when you run the battery dead or crank it so much that the exhaust system fills with water—normally the water is pushed out by exhaust gases—and the water runs back through the manifold and floods the engine. In that case, you are basically shafted for a while. I was lucky. The previous owner of DREAM WEAVER, a mechanic, had cut the fuel line and installed a squeeze bulb like those used on the fuel tanks of outboard motors. I opened the screw, pumped the bulb until diesel fuel ran out all over the place, then closed it. If the engine balked and stuttered as it turned over, a few more squeezes of the bulb usually pushed enough fuel through to get it going. It worked this time. Soon we were motoring toward the East River channel lights and, if not jubilantly happy, we were at least relieved. I did not think Dale knew how close we were to being shipwrecked at the lighthouse, and I was not going to bring it up. We dropped the anchor off the channel in seven feet of water and I poured enormous drinks for both of us.

"You were wonderful," I said, and I really meant it. "That was very difficult and scary."

"I think we did a pretty good job."

"Leave it to a woman to come up with a reasonable solution like heading for the only land in sight while the man screws around with his GPS."

She laughed. "There was just one moment, when I couldn't see the green flashing light, and you kept saying it was right there. I just couldn't see it."

The morning came up clear blue and peaceful, with dry leaves softly rattling in the gentlest of breezes in the yard of a home on the shore, and a crab trap float tapping softly on the bow. We had to figure out how to get Dale from Mobjack to Newport News for a flight that had already been pushed back twice. One directory said there was a marina here, and a phone call roused a sleepy man. "Jesus, Captain, it's Sunday morning. I'll be along in an hour or so." He thought he might have some fuel and thought maybe, possibly, a friend might be coming down who could give Dale a ride in to New-port News. It all sounded a little too casual, but I hoisted anchor and followed his directions into a narrow channel, then into a small boat basin with one catama-ran tied to the pilings. I docked against a retaining wall and we started looking around for a marina. Certainly not here. A big old brick house on the point overlooked Mobjack Bay, but offered no sign of life. The sound of a small congregation singing hymns drifted toward us from a tidy white clapboard church that could have been in Vermont.

We followed the only road and it led to a new, ram-bling home on a point overlooking the water. A broad lawn ended at a front porch where several people were having coffee and watching us with a mixture of cu-riosity and suspicion. A couple about our age was sur-rounded by a scattering of young people who fitted so comfortably they must have been the grown children.

"Good morning," I said, "we're trying to find a ma-rina that's supposed to be somewhere around here, but I think we're basically lost."

Paul and Sue Rosen had every reason in the world to send us back down the road, but they didn't: their kids were visiting, there was a new engagement to celebrate and wedding plans to construct. But they listened to our story, made phone calls, shook their heads about the ex-istence of a marina, allowed as how there was no rental car anywhere around that would provide a lift to the airport, and then looked at each other.

"Can you drive a stick shift?" Paul asked.

"Sure, why?"

"We're going to lunch with the kids, but I have this pickup truck . . ." Paul glanced at Sue and she nodded encouragement. "I'll lend it to you so you can take Dale to the airport."

I was stunned, but I was also desperate. "I really didn't expect that. I'll make a deal with you. Over there, tied to the dock, is a 32-foot sailboat. The keys are in the ignition. If you lend me your truck and I don't come back, it's yours."

Paul laughed. "I've been thinking about getting a sailboat." He checked us out on the truck and we followed them to their turnoff for lunch, waved goodbye, and rolled on to Newport News.

The Newport News airport is big, new, glassy, and in need of a lot more traffic. I did not want to say goodbye, but that is what was left, now. We agreed it would be fun to get together wherever the boat happened to be at New Year, and then she was gone.

Mobjack was quiet, peaceful, with a few neighbors visiting each other on a Sunday afternoon. I filled the gas tank on the truck, but the Rosens were not yet home when I parked it in the driveway. I walked back to DREAM WEAVER. Leaving money would have been something of an insult. The night before I left Vermont for Baltimore, a friend had wrapped up three bottles of Absolut and sent them along for emergencies. I wrapped one up in a piece of yellow legal paper with a note and left it in the truck.

I motored DREAM WEAVER away from the collapsing dock, wondering where I would find fuel. I anchored off an abandoned building and dock. I would be alone now for the very first time. I launched the dinghy and searched the river for a marina or provisions, and found only Zimmerman's Boat Yard. Tomorrow I would try to buy a few jerry cans of diesel fuel. I returned to the boat to watch the sun go down and reflect on what I had learned.

Several lessons were clear. First, be very sure just how far you have to go before you start. I had been switching between charts of different scales and misjudged the distance. I had learned in New York City that commercial harbors are huge by the standards I was familiar with, and there is at least one "harbor hour" of added time required just to make it around in the harbor. Second, the later the hour, the greater these distances become. I had learned that I could make it into a strange harbor in the dark by reading the channel lights, and that was valuable. Now that I was alone, I realized that as a singlehander the situation of the day before would have been much more difficult. And I learned that if you want to run a harmonious boat, don't shout at people. As darkness settled onto Mobjack Bay and the East River, I began to understand loneliness, and why solo sailors go a little daffy after a while. I could almost imagine Dale curled up in the corner of the port bunk, reading her book as usual. She had left an aura behind.

Bob Platt and wife Thea had headed south for the Carolinas in their camper in November, and two days after I left Dale they turned up at a little public dock just through the first lock at Deep Creek, Virginia, on the Great Dismal Swamp Intracoastal Waterway (ICW) route. I couldn't believe they had found me.

"The bridge and lock tenders make a note of who has passed through," Bob explained, "so all we had to do was narrow it down."

Thea joined me for a day of bumping over mysterious things in the narrow canal, where the tannins in the water from the roots of the cypress trees have turned the waterway the color of coffee left on the stove too long. Thea had talked with boaters who had seen a bear in the trees along this stretch, a landscape painted in the earthy hues of autumn, but all we saw were snags, fallen trees, and the remnants of canal construction that dated back to the days of George Washington, an early investor in the canal venture.

Now in the shallow "ditch" of the ICW, a mechanical problem became evident. My depth sounder was no longer reading any depths under eight feet. It was old, and over the summer I had sent the gauge back for some new electronics. It seemed fine in Lake Champlain, but that was a different kind of sailing. There we would get nervous if we were in less than 15 feet of water. On the ICW I would be going for days without seeing much more than eight feet, and often a lot less. Most of the time the depth gauge was showing not numbers, but double dashed lines. The nautical term for this is "seeing the double dashes of doom," since it is often followed by the sensation that the shoreline is no longer moving past and the boat is tilting at an odd angle. It is called running aground.

At the Virginia/North Carolina state line, Bob picked up Thea at the North Carolina Visitors Center, which serves tired drivers on the highway and provides free overnight dock space out back on the ICW. They promised to catch up with me down the line and headed off in the RV. There was only one other boat at the dock, a 34-footer with a wind generator and a solid fiberglass dodger, WHIM OF ARNE. The skipper was a handsome Brit in his 60s with a gray beard and shock of grey hair, and the woman was a distinguished-looking diminutive bundle of energy. I had chatted with them briefly as I was running aground back at the Deep Creek lock. It was getting dark and I was closing up the boat when the woman called over. "I'm baking an apple pie, I'll send a piece over." The man had pedaled seven miles on his bicycle to find ice cream to go with it, and it was worth every mile.

Their names were Gordon and Enid, and they were from Manchester, New Hampshire. Gordon met Enid through a classified ad in a sailing magazine. Enid wanted to write a story about people she had met through classified ads in sailing magazines, and as she described these characters it clearly would be a dandy tale. They had two cats on board, neither of which was allowed outside because they had not acclimated to the boat and were likely to wander off.

Late that evening I spotted a movement on the dock. It was the Siamese cat from WHIM and it had somehow slipped away. I knocked on WHIM's hull to alert them and soon after capturing the cat in the shrubbery we were making plans to rendezvous the next night at Elizabeth City.

Later, I was returning from the visitors center with jugs of water when a ghost ship appeared out of the darkness. It had a tall, pointed stem like a Viking ship and in the dark the skipper's winter hat with ear flaps looked exactly like a horned helmet. I grabbed a bow line from a crewman as they crashed into the dock. The skipper jumped ashore. "Isn't it great," the young Viking exclaimed, "another successful landing. What a great life. I love it."

The young skipper of WINDBLOWN was from Cleveland. The boat was steel, and designed by an orthodontist. It was unusual, indestructible and painfully slow. The centerboard was a slab of iron that could be cranked up and down in a metal trunk, but the fit was so loose the arrangement clanged hellishly when the board was down, so usually it was up and the boat tipped precariously from side to side. I noted in my log, "WINDBLOWN looks like a nautical disaster waiting to happen, but it has made it this far from the Great Lakes." The skipper loved his quirky craft and had managed to terrify all his relatives by dragooning them as crew for various legs of his voyage. He was working through the last remaining relative, a cousin, who looked somewhat dazed and said his nautical experience until now had been limited to driving a tractor over rolling midwestern fields. Perhaps that is why the bow line I caught from him was, in fact, the jib sheet. It was clear the cousin ached to get back to the farm as soon as he could escape.

DREAM WEAVER, WHIM OF ARNE and WINDBLOWN were the last three boats to pass through the Dismal Swamp ICW for the season. Low water caused the canal to be closed just behind us. We traveled on together, with WINDBLOWN trailing so far behind it usually came in after dark after we hailed it on the radio. The next night it crashed to a stop against the wall of the free public slips at Elizabeth City, North Carolina, and the lads went off to find a replacement for the one bolt that held the drive train together. Gordon, Enid and I had dinner with Bob and Thea in the RV in the parking lot, and the following day Bob jumped aboard for the sail across the Albemarle Sound. We said our goodbyes at a marina at the bridge over the Little Alligator River, where Thea met us with their RV. It was like saying goodbye to a brother.

I continued to learn. I learned to detour around places where the banks of the waterway show steep fresh sand, because in those places powerboat wakes have broken down the banks and sandbars form. I bumped over a few.

I learned that where a current was running it was a good idea to look back at the markers from time to time to be sure I wasn't being swept out of the channel. I learned to be very careful where the permanent day markers are supplemented with small floating buoys, particularly around inlets from the sea, because it means the bottom is moving around constantly.

WHIM and DREAM WEAVER strayed off the channel and ran aground briefly north of Beaufort, North Carolina, while supposedly being led to deep water by a Sea//Tow boat. It was the day before Thanksgiving, so we decided to pause in our sprint south and stop at Beaufort for Thanksgiving dinner.

"I want a nice Thanksgiving dinner," Enid had directed, "and this year I don't want to cook it myself." WHIM and DREAM WEAVER pulled up to the public pier across from the post office and asked a lean, bearded sailor in his late fifties if anything would be open for dinner on Thanksgiving.

"Oh sure, mate. There's a pot luck dinner for sailors at the Back Alley Pub. They'll do the turkey and trimmings, you just have to bring a side dish of some kind." His name was Robert Daniel and, with partner Sue Stephenson, he was off a 28-foot catamaran, TIGER LILY.

Sue was a teacher in a high school in the San Francisco area, teaching an advanced placement course in statistics via the Internet, a cell phone and a notebook computer. Robert was a New Zealander who had literally grown up in a boatyard and went to sea in his early 20s, adventuring through the Pacific. Gordon and Robert connected instantly. Gordon, a retired aeronautical engineer, had bought a bare hull, built the boat and sailed it to the U.S. Robert and Sue had bought an open catamaran on the East Coast and Robert had built a small cabin on it just a little bigger than a two-man tent. For the next weeks our trails crossed and re-crossed as we followed the waterway south. WINDBLOWN left us in the Cape Fear River. The cousin was making a run for his life back to solid ground.

Weeks rolled by, anchor up at first light, bundled up against the dew-soaked cockpit and chill morning air, motoring or motorsailing all day, dashing below with the boat on Autohelm to pee or rustle up lunch, anchoring at dusk, finally rendezvousing over drinks or dinner to map out the next night's destination. At first this schedule of beginning each day not quite certain where we would spend each night provoked apprehension. Then it became routine. Finally, it was difficult to spend more than two days anywhere without becoming anxious to move on. On the last day of November we entered South Carolina. As December unfolded the docks along the waterway began to sport Christmas decorations.

Ralph DesLauriers, our canceled crew member on the first leg, finally joined me in beautiful, beguiling Charleston, South Carolina, for a week of southbound cruising. Destiny had slated us for another nautical lesson.

He pleaded with me not to leave Charleston. After a day of touring the city we had encountered two lovely women at the Roof Top Terrace at the Vendue Inn, a location that provided a panoramic view east over the converging Cooper and Ashley Rivers, Fort Sumter and Charleston Harbor. We had gone back to the boat at the municipal marina for drinks, then on to Jones Island for dinner, and finally for a walk along the beach in the dark. When they dropped us back at the boat it was clear they wanted to go sailing the next day.

"Please, please stay one more day," Ralph begged

shamelessly Sunday morning, but I was determined to push on and stick with Gordon and Enid. A lingering morning fog pushed our start back and we were only an hour out of Charleston on the ICW when the fog settled back in and we had to drop the anchor with several other boats at the edge of the channel and wait for it to lift. Ralph was below working on the galley table with a South Carolina highway map and our charts, trying to find a place where the highway and ICW met, a place that would provide an anchorage and where we could pick up our friends in the dinghy. I suggested finding a boat launch area for fishermen. Ralph worked with feverish determination, moving back and forth between map and chart like a general planning the invasion of Normandy. Finally he found a spot near a bridge south of Yonge Island, and I agreed it looked like the perfect rendezvous.

The fog lifted and we continued south, alternating stretches at the helm, picking our way between red and green navigation aides through the low-lying countryside.

"I can't see the next mark," said Ralph, who was at the helm.

"Sometimes there are no marks, if there is a long stretch of deep water." I was occupied with the logbook, not paying attention.

"Okay."

DREAM WEAVER glided through the familiar time/space disorientation of running aground, causing me to snap to full attention. "Quick, into reverse."

We weren't moving. The channel had dog-legged off to the right around a curve, and we were nowhere near it. We were pointed at some grassy mounds in the channel. The tide was falling now and the boat began to lean. A 34-foot trawler came up behind us and I thought he was coming to give us a tow. He ground to a clunking halt 30 yards behind us. It was a few minutes after 2 p.m.

"We're aground," I said stupidly to the skipper of the trawler.

"I was on a range," he called back. He had seen red marks ahead, lined them up, and thought he was on the course through the channel. The marks were not a range, they were just peeking out from behind the tall grass of the mounds.

The tide was running out quickly, and books stored on shelves behind the bunks began to tumble to the cabin sole as the boat leaned farther. Soon the water was only a foot below the rail and we were having trouble moving around.

"How far will it lean over before water starts coming in through the vents?" Ralph asked.

"I don't know. Let's start plugging them." There were three clamshell vents outside the cockpit coaming, just one on the starboard side. I jammed plastic bags into it without much conviction they would stop rising water from flooding the interior if it came to that. The boat had never been on its side in the water before; this was a new experience. I went below, sliding and crashing, and found water under the bunks and a few inches of water in the low corner of the forward V-berth. It could be coming from one of three places: the holding tank for the toilet, the swamp outside the boat or our own fresh water tank. I dipped my finger into it and smelled it. Vague odor of chlorine. It was from our fresh water supply.

I heard a call for DREAM WEAVER on Channel 68, which I monitored while traveling with Gordon and Enid. They were hard aground two miles ahead.

The water was dropping fast. The tidal range was about six and a half feet. I took the Danforth anchor out to the stern in the dinghy, but there was no way we were going to kedge off at this point. We would have to wait for high tide, which was around 11 p.m. The boat leaned, the water crept up to within four inches of the toerail, things crashed, the dinghy's outboard was scraping the bottom. I returned to the boat to find it almost impossible to move around with DREAM WEAVER tipped on her ear.

"I ripped out the transmission on one of my engines," the trawler skipper yelled over. He was outside his boat, walking around in the mud in rubber boots. We could see tree stumps among the mud. "I've called TowBoat US. I've got full coverage. I'll need to get pulled back to Charleston."

His wife radioed over and asked for our address. She had taken our picture, and would send it. I took his picture, just to get even.

"God, what if we're on top of a stump? We could fall way over," Ralph said. We were surrounded by mud. The boat was resting comfortably on its side, and we were completely high and dry, a foot above water level. The track our keel had made into the mud looked like a giant slug had passed through. The sun was sinking, and with the fading light the no-see-ums swarmed up to gnaw on our ankles. "Davy, Davy, I begged you not to leave Charleston. We'd be making cocktails right now with those two beauties on board."

"You're right. One more word and I'm going to kill you."

"First I was worried about the boat, then I was worried about you. Now I'm just thinking what might have been."

24

"Would you prefer death by flare gun or knife?"

Later, in the dark, waiting for the tide, we had a wonderful conversation with the tow boat captain and his wife, the second of two tow boats to come down the 20 miles from Charleston. The trawler was already under tow, headed back to Charleston. We discussed how boats with fin keels sometimes sink straight down into the mud and come to rest on their bottoms more or less upright. "And they wonder why I can't pull 'em out with four feet of keel straight down in the mud."

His wife listened to our rambling conversation from the darkness of the cabin, her cigarette glow the only sign she was there.

It was after midnight when the tow boat finally had us settled in a wide spot off the channel. The bill was $640. I was insured for $350. I didn't want to hear anything more about how I should have stayed in Charleston. The lessons were clear: pay attention to the charts every moment, and never tempt the wrath of Aphrodite, patron goddess of sailors on shore leave. When we told Gordon and Enid our story, she said, "We loved Charleston. You should have said something, we'd have happily stayed another night." Ralph's eyes rolled back into his head.

He ran out of time and left DREAM WEAVER at Kingsley Plantation north of Jacksonville, Florida, after a rough sail off the Georgia coast. He said he was going to visit someone in Florida. I suspected he was headed back to Charleston.

A few days later, coming out of an unmarked anchorage south of New Smyrna Beach, Florida, I cut a corner too short and plowed into a sandbank, once again at high tide. Gordon quickly anchored and jumped into the dinghy with 200 feet of one-inch line, one end attached to the stern of WHIM, the other clasped in his teeth. He rowed against the strong current with Enid shouting "Gordon, be careful" and I wondered if he had good teeth and a good heart. He certainly had a big one. He ran the line back to WHIM, but was unable to tow me off. I ran the Danforth out as a kedge, put the rode through a snatch block on the bow and led it back to the starboard primary winch and cranked. But I was sentenced to spent another 24 hours at various angles of heel. At sunset I tried unsuccessfully to kedge and motor off at high tide. I settled down to watch the dolphins socialize in the silver sunset water and wait for the next high tide at daybreak. The motor was smoking in protest and the shaft of the anchor was bent into a soft "U" when I finally broke free at dawn. Gordon had poked a stick into the mud bottom near where he was tied up, watched the water rise on the stick, and on a handheld radio coached me on exactly when it was high tide.

A first Christmas on a boat can be lonely, depressing, deadly. Mine was wonderful. WHIM and DREAM WEAVER picked up moorings at Vero Beach Municipal Marina. I would stay here and visit friends Don and Gael Steffens. WHIM headed off the next day to cut through the Okeechobee Waterway to Cape Coral on Florida's west coast to spend the holidays with friends there. Don dressed me up in his shirts, ties and blazer and their friends in Vero Beach welcomed the curious sea orphan to spiffy cocktail parties and family Christmas dinners.

On Christmas Eve the Vero Community Church was a sea of poinsettias and candles. When the 50-voice choir began *Oh Come All Ye Faithful* I was swept back to the little Lutheran church in Neenah, Wisconsin where my father was pastor and that hymn was the processional that we little kids in parochial school sang to open the Christmas Eve service. During the program some of us had to march up to the altar carrying cards, each one of which had one letter of Christmas spelled out in glue and glitter, and recite the meaning of our letter: C is for the Christ child, A is for the Angels. . . . My mother sat near the front of the church, smiling peacefully. My father in his black robe sat on an ancient chair near the sacristy door, watching proudly. Afterward, under a huge balsam tree, we picked up paper bags containing hard candy, nuts, an orange and an apple. The old German church, the parents, many of the friends are gone now. The chorus in Vero sung the hymn magnificently and the worshipers chimed in with gusto, except for me. The memories had constricted my voice. I was so happy to be here tonight with my pals and their friends I knew it was time to leave. Lutheran logic.

I sailed to Stuart, anchored out in Manatee Pocket, and rented a car. Dale appeared on the concourse at Miami Airport at 11:30 p.m. on New Year's Eve. I tried to sneak a kiss on the Florida Turnpike at midnight without becoming a holiday statistic and scared us both. Life on shore is dangerous. We had a balmy New Year's Day to enjoy at the beach, then turned in the car and headed into the Okeechobee Waterway just in time for a norther to roll in with a thunderstorm that sounded like a train rushing through. It was almost a replay of the Chesapeake. We again froze in 30-degree temperatures and stiff north winds that stalled us for two days at the lock at the east end of Lake Okeechobee. When the lock opened to the lake it was like a stage curtain being drawn open on a tempest. Whitecaps rolled across our view through the gate. We clipped into safety harnesses and flew across the shallow lake with the rail buried. Gradually the warm weather returned as we motored through orange groves along the waterway, looking for alligators but seeing only water birds and white Brahman cattle. White ash drifted past the boat from burning sugar cane fields in the distance. Dale left from Fort Myers Beach and I sank into a lonely funk until the cellular phone rang one night. It was Bob Platt.

Thea was going on a cruise that didn't appeal to Bob, so he joined me in Fort Myers Beach for a week of warm weather sailing: a run from Fort Myers Beach to Seven Mile Bridge and Boot Key Harbor at Marathon in the Florida Keys. He would leave me there and I would try to round up crew to make the passage to Cuba. It was late January. Vermont, where we had started this odyssey together in September, was having a winter of the worst kind: little snow but deep cold—30 degrees below zero early in the month—punctuated by days of thaws. Bad skiing, poor sledding. In Fort Myers Beach, I was eating oranges fresh off the tree and splashing in the Gulf of Mexico.

The west coast of Florida offers a strange variety of cruising experiences. Fort Myers Beach had been sand and beach bars and easy shopping, with a convenient trolley running along the beach and over the bridge to a shopping plaza complete with a marine supply store. I could dinghy over and buy a shower at the Palm City Marina or groceries at the Tops market on the beach.

Naples was almost too rich and too perfect to be comfortable for cruisers. The first night we anchored out among million dollar homes, were kept awake by a barking dog that deserved to attract the attention of an alligator, and in the morning cruised up to the city marina to explore the town and provision. The little grocery store within walking distance of the city docks sold designer food; duck and bottled French lemonade were not on our provisioning list. A cruiser told me he had called a cab and a Lincoln Town Car showed up. After being trapped in Naples by fog for two days, we headed south past Marco Island, giving a wide 10-mile berth to Cape Romano and its surrounding shallows, and finally heading in at Indian Key Pass for an overnight anchorage at Russell Pass, a spot just off the channel up the Barron River to Everglades City.

This area of the southwest coast of Florida is called Ten Thousand Islands, part of a million and a half acres of Everglades National Park that starts just south of Marco Island and stretches to Florida Bay. Mangrove forest to the left of us, mangrove forest to the right of us, behind us, ahead of us. Through the mangroves run rivers and channels that hide manatee, tarpon, snook, snakes and smugglers. The place names reflect the charm of the area: Shark River, Lostman River, Sandfly Island, Alligator Point, Snake Key.

We motored up the channel, turned left toward Russell Pass just before a Flashing Green Mark number 7, and picked out a spot to anchor. Then suddenly we were aground again. Damn, damn, damn. I looked over the side. The current was rushing past from the starboard quarter, pushing us farther aground. The water churned under the hull like we were sitting in a kettle of boiling coarse sand. I tried reverse: the best solution is to get out the way you get in. No deal. DREAM WEAVER was stuck on a sandbar that had built up where a creek flowed out of the mangroves. We were a half hour from high tide, and possibly we would be lifted off.

"I'll take the dinghy out and see if I can find some deeper water," I said to Bob. I probed with an oar and found our bow was only a few yards from where the bar ended and deeper water began. I took the anchor out in the dinghy and set it to see if we could kedge off when the tide was highest. There were two other boats anchored out across Russell Pass: a sailboat whose skipper couldn't come in to help without going aground himself, and a power cruiser named THE CAPTAIN AND THE KID, which had dispatched an inflatable dinghy in our direction.

The skipper of THE CAPTAIN AND THE KID was a pleasant man who had a big powerboat but the mentality of a sailor. He and his attractive wife liked to anchor out for days at a time, feeling no urgent need to plug into shore power every night to watch a 24-inch color television and cook with a microwave. They had a golden retriever on board, which the skipper had to take for a walk in the dinghy, looking for a patch of beach somewhere among the mangroves.

"We went exploring yesterday," he said. "I won't do that again so soon. After a couple of bends through the mangroves we were lost for two hours. Some fishermen finally led us out. Everything out here looks the same."

It was almost high tide, and we weren't budging.

"Let's take a line to the top of the mast," Bob suggested, "and maybe you can tip us enough by pulling with the dinghy to get us off." We attached a long line to the main halyard. The skipper of THE CAPTAIN AND THE KID secured it to the stern of the dinghy and headed for the far shore. With some noisy maneuvering we popped free beyond the sandbar, but almost ran over our kedge anchor line. We said our thanks to our rescuer and found a spot to anchor on the deeper north side of Russell Pass just in time for the cocktail hour.

I sleep like the dead on a boat except on windy nights at anchor. At around 3 a.m. I was jolted awake by a noisy reunion. Two boats—one small, one larger from the sound of them—rendezvoused in the dark. There were loud voices, shouting, some laughter. Then they took off in different directions. Nobody was fishing for tarpon or snook at this hour. There was some other kind of business going on out here, conveniently close to the open Gulf of Mexico and to the maze of mangrove forests. But they certainly were noisy about it. I had been advised on a trip years ago down Hawk Channel not to go flashing spotlights at boats that meet in the mangroves in the dark. I went back to sleep, and could tell from the sound of Bob's breathing he had not been roused.

In the morning the weather forecast was for two days of 15 to 20+ knot winds directly on the nose, heavy going in the shallow water along this shore. We read the cruising guides and decided that rather than hang out we would motor up the channel to Everglades City. Seven feet of water was promised up the channel, with a couple of warnings about shoaling at certain day marks.

Everglades City is definitely no Naples. "This is not what I expected," I commented to Bob as we rounded a bend in the channel and had our first look. We had been motoring through the vast mangrove forest on a well-marked channel that leads up the Barron River. We had passed touring kayaks and nature tour boats full of people looking hopefully into the water for a manatee, but we saw no sign of civilization on shore except for some kind of radio tower that rose out of the trees ahead of us. I expected a ranger station, a few mobile homes, and a dilapidated waterfront Rod and Gun Club.

Instead we were passing a tidy row of pastel bunga-lows, each with a dock and fishing boat out front. A red BMW roadster was parked at one of the bungalows. A row of neatly-painted white pilings curved off to the right and identified the 1,000-foot face dock of the Rod and Gun Club, where we docked cautiously in the swift river current. The big pale grey building sported bright yellow awnings and rambled off out of sight behind palms and palmettos.

It had the look of a 1940s country club, the kind of place where you would find a character like Burl Ives sitting on the front porch in a wicker chair, fanning himself and sipping bourbon. As it turns out, he probably had done just that since he had stayed there in 1945 with Gypsy Rose Lee to film *Winds Across the Everglades*. Except for the microwave tower and fancy new cars around the club, the whole city was a time warp back into the Forties.

Everglades City is a tiny community three and a half miles from the dead end of Route 29. It has about 600 residents, most of whom are tucked out of sight in a development southeast of downtown.

It feels like a movie set, and in fact it has been one several times, for Sean Connery's *Just Cause* and Disney's *Gone Fishin'* with Danny Glover and Joe Pesci. It also had the right feel for Miami Vice crews and Burt Reynolds and Sally Field in *Cannonball Run*.

And like a movie set, it is not exactly what it appears to be. The tidy pastel bungalows, the classic City Hall, the vintage street lamps, the old green Chevy at the restaurant, the paneling and wooden shutters of the Rod and Gun Club's trophy room all carry you back to the Forties or Fifties. In the evening a singer strums a guitar and sings (no tunes newer than early Simon and Garfunkel) to a dinner crowd. The diners pay in cash, the club doesn't do credit cards. Guests here have included four U.S. presidents—Nixon being the most recent—and, in 1942, Ernest Hemingway. At last, I was getting into Hemingway country.

The working waterfront, a short walk up river, is piled with crab traps and lined with fishing boats and a few small shops that sell right-off-the boat seafood. Pelicans float near the fish cleaning stations, waiting for pelican welfare. Timeless.

But where cities usually have a park with a fountain, Everglades City has the huge microwave tower. Nearby, well-maintained tennis courts attract players in snappy tennis togs, arriving in expensive sports utility vehicles and playing under the lights in the cool of the evening. The noise of ball and racket can be heard from the dock until 10 p.m.

Along Route 29, two convenience stores, the Circle K and BP gas station, actually have ATMs. The handsome pastel green building that says "Everglades National Bank" on the front side, is in fact a bed and breakfast, which is painted on the side, right above the antique Ford.

During the day, kayaks follow park trails through the vast mangrove forests and tour boats leave the ranger center on a regular schedule. Fishermen weave through the mangroves in search of tarpon and snook.

But at night. . . . "When you're anchored out," said the National Park Service ranger, "it's a good idea not to pay too much attention to what goes on after dark." I had asked her why the rangers carried sidearms—no gators, too salty—and mentioned the noisy rendezvous during the previous night. "They aren't interested in you. After all, what are you going to do? You know, where money is involved there are always some people who can't resist. You know about the raid?"

Everglades City has a little secret that time is slowly

erasing. In 1983, 200 local state and federal law enforcement officers sealed off Route 29 and conducted one of the largest drug smuggling raids in its history. Around 70 percent of the adult male population of Everglades City was arrested, some 200 people in all.

Agents seized 14 boats, two airplanes, an arsenal of weapons and 500,000 pounds of marijuana. One local fishing guide and hero was applauded when he posted his multi-million dollar bail with travelers checks. The raid came about because the local sheriff kept chasing and losing smugglers in the mangrove maze. Fishing community by day . . . but at night, who knows?

We cleaned and greased winches, provisioned, did laundry at the Right Choice Supermarket and Laundry. "I wish we had more tourists in July," the woman at the supermarket cash register drawled. "It would give the mosquitoes somebody else to eat for a while."

We loaded some beer into the dinghy and explored the river beyond the city until we were warned away because of the airboats speeding around giving thrill rides to tourists. They sometimes crash into things and each other. Bob said he might come back some day with his RV and find a spot at the park next to the river. "This is a very strange place, but I kind of like it."

The weather promised to improve so we motored back down to Russell Pass and anchored out to get an early start in the morning. As I paid my dollar-a-foot Rod and Gun Club dock bill, I asked the affable young man behind the desk, "Everglades City is a great place to visit. Have I missed anything? What's its best kept secret?"

He raised an eyebrow and smiled. "Oh, I guess just about everything's been found out by now."

It was a fast beam reach down the uninhabited coast

to Little Shark River. The national park boundary is marked by posts set out in the water offshore. Inside the posts, crabbing is not allowed. But I was cautious about the water depth. Even a half mile outside the boundary we were in just seven feet to 11 feet of water, and running a slalom course around crab trap floats. There are millions of crab traps down the west coast to the Keys, and we were traveling at the height of snow crab season, which runs from mid-October to mid-May. Crabbers harvest only one short, thick leg and claw of the stone crab and toss the critter back in to grow another.

The markers for the channel up Little Shark River were tough to spot against the mangroves, but once inside we found a community of cruisers anchored out. Little Shark River is memorable, not for its fishing, which is good, or its primitive beauty, which is there, but for its mosquitoes. We plugged engine compartment ventilators, the deck fitting for the anchor rode, every possible crack and crevice we could think of, but still they found their way in. These mosquitoes of Little Shark River do not wait for dusk; they attack in broad daylight and do not relent. I suspect it is from mosquitoes, not fish, that the area gets its name. They are flying little sharks. We turned in early so we could head to the Keys at first light.

"Man, we are moving. We'll be there in plenty of time," Bob said. East Cape, the southern tip of Florida, was behind us. Somewhere ahead was the Seven Mile Bridge and the Florida Keys. A spicy 12- to 18-knot breeze from the east-northeast brought clear, cool weather and had us flying on a beam reach. We were headed for Boot Key Harbor at Marathon, but had a fallback plan for anchoring out behind a deserted key if we lost the wind. But by 2:45 we were under the Seven

Mile Bridge despite a little confusion over contradictions between the charts and the markers. The approach had been re-buoyed, and even the green light at John Sawyer Bank that we had programmed into our GPS as our first mark approaching the Keys was now a white light on what looked like bird roost.

The wind that had worked so well for us on our run down nearly stopped us in our tracks as we turned east into it, fired up the diesel, and headed for the channel and bridge at the west end of Boot Key Harbor. We crept toward the channel at just over one knot. For a thousand miles I had been frustrated by my slow pace motoring. Everything passed me, and there was no way to analyze and correct the situation short of hauling the boat. In Fort Myers I had installed a tachometer, which required removing and adding a connecting wire to the alternator. I had made a dozen phone calls, all providing conflicting information on propeller pitch. But the basic questions remained the same: what's the current pitch (I didn't know) and what rpms can you run at? Between the depth sounder and the propeller problems, the boat had to be hauled for repairs.

Signs of damage left over from Hurricane George greeted us inside the channel. At Faro Blanco Marina, houseboats—two-story wood frame houses built on floats—had been knocked down; one had been re-floated and stood intact with water marks above the first floor windows. Battered wooden motorboats and catamarans remained dangling from the mangroves, high and dry. In the anchorage area, boats were partially submerged on a shoal in the middle of the north side, and floats marked other wrecks just below the surface. We had two anchors down by 5 p.m., and Bob packed up. I took him ashore in the dinghy, and he headed by bus for Miami and his flight back to Vermont. I was sorry to see him go. We were getting good at this life.

Driving through Marathon on U.S. 1 a traveler sees nothing but a strip development of shopping malls, supermarkets, a Home Depot, restaurants, liquor stores, marinas and fishing and diving supply stores. An entirely different world exists to the south of the highway, in Boot Key Harbor and beyond to Hawk Channel and the Atlantic. The long, protected harbor is screened from the commercial development along the highway by a wall of mangroves. The opposite shore is another wall of mangroves along the west end, then Sister Creek—a channel to the ocean with a controlling depth of about four feet—and a bank of condominiums and residences reaching east to Sombrero Marina. Here the channel runs along the shore next to the condos.

Sombrero Marina, and particularly Dockside Bar, is the hub of cruising activity for the harbor. Dockside is an open-air tiki bar with live music every evening—100 ways to sing Jimmy Buffett tunes—and a revolving collection of local characters, liveaboards, transient cruisers and a few tourists looking for local color at a sailors' hangout. Sunday night is particularly lively; for cruisers, every night is a weekend. A small grill serves up good sandwiches. The same familiar faces are either tending bar or sitting on the other side of it. For $15 a week the Dockside provides dinghy docking privileges in two slips: one for inflatables and another for hard dinghies. This allows sailors to dock, pick up mail and overnight courier deliveries—all the mail is jammed into bins at one end of the bar—buy a shower for $1.50, and do the laundry at washers and dryers in a little shed. Two banks of pay telephones are available, and one of the phones that happens to be facing south in the pounding hot sun has been wired with an RJ-11 jack, so sailors can plug in their notebook computers. They sit on a length of sawed-off log, plugged in, with their spouses holding a blanket or beach towel over their heads so they can read the computer screens. At the far end of the building is a cluster of phones in the shade of a palm tree, where people come and go with their calling cards; the tidy folks from up north calling their brokers and families, and the weatherbeaten locals trying to find the cheapest possible boat parts or a quick job to re-plenish the kitty. Usually a business card from the local taxi company is wedged into the phone some-where: "Cheapo Taxi 743-7420 We Deliver". Around front by the tiki bar is the bulletin board, offering boating gear for sale, crew notices, and, yep, one boat headed for Cuba looking for someone to buddy-boat across the Gulf Stream . . . David and Jim on *Surprise*, fans of the Patrick O'Brian novels, no doubt, from the name of the boat.

I ordered a Rolling Rock, and elbowed up to the bar next to a bulky grey-haired sailor with an American flag bandana tied over his head pirate-fashion, an aging Easy Rider. He was joking with the bartender and was no stranger here. A sign on the post next to him said: "Save the Keys—Blow the Bridges". The conversation around the bar drifted between fishing, boats, weather, sudden accidental death, women who were bitches and the damned government intruding in our daily lives. One particularly loud voice was saying, "Jesus, spare me from those people from the Northeast." I wondered if I had been spotted, but looked so seedy in my Spam T-shirt I was sure I blended in very nicely. The women behind the bar could hold their own in these discus-sions. In fact, the marina owner was a woman. For many of these folks the marina or harbor is home; Dockside the community center. Dockside is a genuine place where good stories loosely based on the truth are appreciated, but pretensions are not.

With Bob's departure I was alone again with that anxious feeling that I had crawled out on a very long limb. But not for long. Almost immediately, at the dinghy dock, I ran into Sue Stephenson and Robert Daniel from TIGER LILY.

"Come over for dinner tonight," Sue said. "You'll be our first dinner guest. I only have three plates."

They were making final plans to cross to the Bahamas and were looking for a larger dinghy with a motor. Robert was sketching plans to build one. I returned to DREAM WEAVER in the dark, feeling much less lonely. The next morning I discovered WHIM OF ARNE anchored behind me. We had a reunion dinner on DREAM WEAVER, and a few days later WHIM hauled anchor, bound for the Bahamas.

I had a few tasks ahead of me: find a crew member for Cuba, follow up on a request I had sent to the U.S. Treasury Department for a license to go to Cuba legally as a freelance writer, pick up paperwork from the Coast Guard for departing for Cuba, and make arrangements to haul the boat to solve depth sounder and propeller problems before heading for Cuba. The days spun into nearly three weeks. I was sliding into the Keys frame of mind as I became a resident of Boot Key Harbor. I could see how sailors got stuck here.

Boot Key Harbor is protected all around, has a good holding bottom and little current; boats swing with the wind, not with a current. Supermarkets, drug stores, and a post office are within easy walking distance of Dockside. A 10-minute ride in a dinghy out Sister Creek toward Hawk Channel is Sombrero Beach, a sandy ocean front park with a convenient cove off the creek to haul dinghies.

I had heard radio chatter in the morning among the liveaboards, arranging who would drive kids to school and sorting out work plans. Many of the people anchored out worked in the service industries. I ran into the clerk at West Marine at Dockside getting into her dinghy, and the young man with a red beard anchored next to me went off every morning at 7:30 to work as a carpenter. A couple on a large, tidy boat on the other side were constantly cleaning and polishing. He went off to work, she would row out in the dinghy and inspect her floating nest from a distance, as if visualizing landscaping.

Changes are in the wind in Marathon and the Keys. After years of studying pollution problems, communities like Marathon and Key West are taking over management of their jurisdictional waters and installing mooring systems and pump out stations. Hundreds of boats in Boot Key Harbor pump overboard despite its designation as a no-discharge zone, and there is little natural tidal flushing. Boats are not the only problem; the condominiums and homes around the harbor are built on cesspits. Around Dockside there were murmured conversations about what was happening at Pat and Kelly's Marina across the harbor, so one day I motored over in the dinghy and tied up at a floating dinghy dock. Pat and Kelly's was the haven for the liveaboard community and had acquired a legendary reputation for a salty ambiance involving a couple of parrots, a raccoon, dogs and independent liveaboards who had little time for established governments.

The western Keys are the home of the secessionist

Conch Republic, a political state of mind that is only partly tongue in cheek. In the Keys, the native born are called conchs, a term that can be traced back to the way birth announcements were made in the days before radio and newspapers. When a new baby was born, the vital information was written on a conch shell and posted out front where all could see the news: a new conch had been born.

Next to the face docks, in a warehouse building, a parrot sat on his roost calmly watching the demise of Pat and Kelly's. A smudged woman in a tank-top dragged a dinghy anchor out of a back room and dropped it on a little mountain of used anchors. Other piles of boating gear and smelly black radiator hose and fittings removed from toilets created the topography on a concrete floor. At the far end were a few pieces of crumbling furniture that looked like they had spent 10 years in the basement of a fraternity house. "Most of this crap should go directly to the dump," the woman said. "What do you need?"

"Pat or Kelly here?"

"Not right now."

"What's going on?"

"Cleaning out. County's taking over." She vanished back into the store room, and I left. When I returned five days later everything was gone, including the woman, the parrot and Pat and Kelly, who, with the raccoon and parrots, were living on board somewhere in the harbor.

A new harbormaster and a man from the Marathon development corporation explained. After a long study, Boot Key Harbor would become a managed mooring field—at least partly—operating from the former Pat and Kelly's, now renamed the Florida Keys Marina. The property had been owned by the county and leased by Pat and Kelly, but now the county was investing in a pump out station and other improvements.

A newly-arrived boater came past with his toilet kit heading for the bathroom and returned a few minutes later. "That place is filthy. There's a man, a woman and a dog taking a shower in there."

"The powerwashers are coming this afternoon," said the new harbormaster, heading for the showers to create order.

A grizzled man in a T-shirt and jeans was taking this all in from the big doorway overlooking the docks. With his red headband and beard he looked remarkably like Willie Nelson.

"What do you think of the changes?" I asked.

"Good riddance."

"Why?"

He just shook his head.

"You live here?"

"I'm anchored out. That's my 24-footer out there." He pointed to a small sailboat anchored off shore. "I'm a single parent. I have a son and daughter. They go to school here."

"Yeah? How old?"

"My son's 16, a good kid, a man among men. My daughter's 14, she's . . ." He got stuck there, not quite ready to say she was a woman among women. I wondered what life would be like for a 14-year-old girl on a 24-foot boat with her father and older brother.

"Will this affect you, the changes here?"

"They say it won't. I'll wait and see. I've been thinking about pulling up anchor and sailing off to the Bahamas. There are too many rules and regulations here now. What are you writing this down for?"

"I do a little writing for sailing magazines; I'm writing about the changes here."

"You ought to write about my life, I could tell you some stories. You wouldn't believe the things that have happened to me."

"Why don't you write them?"

"Got no time." Funny, time appeared to be the one thing he had in abundance.

There was a buzz in the harbor that hinted the county was trying to drive out the liveaboards by making it expensive, and a few entrepreneurs were concerned about government-subsidized competition.

The new management spoke of the big picture. "The liveaboards are part of the community, their needs are taken seriously. We studied this for 12 years and came to the conclusion that this harbor needs some tender loving care, and not just because of the boaters. We need a sewage treatment plant for all these buildings, too, as well as a managed harbor. We have a protected harbor, air service, boat repair services, boat stores, supermarkets and restaurants all within walking distance. We're getting ready. We expect a lot more cruisers through here when Cuba opens up."

When Cuba opens up. I sat on a piece of sawed-off log at the Dockside phone booth for hours, dialing up potential crew members and checking my voice mail for good news. As a carry-over from my home office days, I had brought with me a steno pad to use faithfully for recording phone numbers and notes on conversations. It saved an enormous amount of frustration, for all the numbers, notes on conversations and dates were all in one place. Lines were being drawn through a growing list of potential crew names.

I received good news from the offices of the two United States senators from Vermont, Jim Jeffords and Pat Leahy. I had copied them on my Treasury Department application for a license to go to Cuba, and although I did so only as a courtesy because I used them for references in the application, both took up my cause. I had sent the application from Vero Beach between Christmas and New Year, and after being buried in the backlog of holiday requests from Cubans anxious to get home for the holidays, mine was working its way to the top of the pile. It was the second week in February, and I had been in the harbor about 12 days. Applications took four to six weeks, so my job was to sit and wait it out.

After months of dawn to dusk travel, the waiting at Marathon should have been a relief. It was agony. During the day I wrote, went to the beach with Robert and Susan, or took unnecessary walks into town to buy provisions. I began to draw $100 a day out of the ATM at Publix to provide cash for Cuba, since U.S. travelers checks and credit cards are no good there because of the embargo. At night I poured through Hemingway's books, listing in my small notebook the places I wanted to visit in Key West and Cuba.

We were all changing in this cruising life, forced into a reality that consisted of wind, weather, boat, navigation aids and the quest for ice, showers and a laundry. I had been warned of it by my friends Don and Gael Steffens, who had gone out for years at a time, and they were right. It meant leaving behind all the shore values by which I was measured and judged: in the Keys the work ethic was being replaced by the sloth ethic. I was worried that I was achieving Keys consciousness: It took me all day to tighten two screws and buy a six-pack.

We sought diversions. Robert and Sue rented a car to visit the Miami Boat Show, and before turning it back in we drove down to Key West to explore. One evening we went to a slide show on Cuba in Marathon's little theater, put together by Marathon photographer Larry Benvenuti. Chatting with him during the intermission, I met three West Coast sailors in their thirties bound for Cuba on a 34-footer named WIND LINE. Jake, the owner-skipper worked on a tugboat that brought supplies to Indian communities in Alaska. Kevin worked in film and video production in the San Francisco area. Will, who was nicknamed Kodiak, was a salmon fisherman in Alaska. We compared notes. They planned to sail ahead to Key West in a few days, hang out in America's southernmost party town, then head for Marina Hemingway near Havana. They sailed past on their way to Key West and shouted, "See you in Cuba."

Later that day, Sue, Robert and I sat in the shade of a stubby palm tree on Sombrero Beach and solved the riddles of life. "We'll go over to the Bahamas," Robert explained, "and maybe put the boat up for sale before we go. Then the plan is to find a place somewhere near the water here in Florida where I can build and launch a bigger cat."

"I'll go back and teach for a year while Robert builds the boat, then I can take early retirement and off we'll go again," Sue said. "What about you?"

"The only thing on my mind right now is getting to Cuba. If I stay around the Keys much longer I'm going to start retreating back into the mangroves like some of these liveaboards, moving back down the evolutionary scale. This sitting around endlessly makes me crazy."

"Well, mate, just remember that nobody cares about that except you," Robert said. "You have options; you just have to see what they are and recognize them for what they are. You don't have to do things the same way forever. Your condo is rented, you could just keep going."

Robert was firm in his belief that men were put on earth primarily to sail to endless horizons. Of course, Robert also firmly believed that the round flattened-down patterns in hay fields in the English countryside were left there by alien spacecraft. Marathon must be some kind of test, I concluded. I would make the trip to Cuba alone if necessary, but turning back was out of the question. Hemingway would not have turned back. This time I would not give up easily.

2 | *The St. Tropez of the Poor*

I stood at the foot of the bed that Ernest Hemingway had shared with Pauline Pfeiffer, listening with the other tourists as the guide explained the history of the room's furniture. One piece, a thick, dark Spanish birthing chair, looked like an instrument of torture.

The guide pointed to an abstract ceramic of a cat. "Pauline found this in a box in the basement and asked Hemingway about it. It turned out to be a gift from Picasso." An unusual find in an unusual place. Homes don't have basements here. Just four blocks up Olivia Street in Key West Cemetery the dead are "buried" in vaults above ground because of the high water table and tough coral rock.

Hemingway's study, Key West.
The Key West years were his most productive.
Here he wrote *Snows of Kilimanjaro, Farewell to Arms, To Have and Have Not.*

I went through the French doors onto the second story porch. Once a catwalk had gone across a small courtyard from here to the second floor study of the carriage house, where Hemingway wrote surrounded by books, trophy heads and other African memorabilia collected on a 1933 safari. The safari was the basis for much of the writing that went on in this workshop. It is tidy now; then it was usually a mess. A black Royal typewriter with a sheet of paper cranked into position stands on a round table, as if waiting for Hemingway to walk in, sit down at the cigar-makers' chair he favored, and struggle to write one true sentence after another.

Here in Key West, young Hemingway was prolific, turning out all or parts of most of his best work: *The Snows of Kilimanjaro, A Farewell to Arms, To Have and Have Not, Death in the Afternoon, Green Hills of Africa, The Short Happy Life of Francis Macomber, Winner Take Nothing, The Fifth Column,* his only play; a script for a documentary film *The Spanish Earth* and possibly some early work on *For Whom the Bell Tolls.*

Below the workshop is a gift and poster shop opening onto the swimming pool Pauline had constructed for more than twice the cost of the house and property. In the courtyard below the bedroom stands a peculiar fountain: a large bronze-colored clay Spanish olive jar towers above a basin that was once a urinal in Sloppy Joe's bar. Hemingway claimed he had pissed so much money through the urinal he had a right to own it.

The group had moved on and I was alone in the bedroom with a yellow cat named Archibald MacLeish, curled up asleep in the center of the bed. Hemingway knew poet MacLeish from Paris and he was a frequent visitor to Key West, but the friendship almost sunk in 1936 when the two went out fishing and drinking on

PILAR, began to argue about writing, and Hemingway stranded him on a key off Boca Grande to be devoured by bugs. Pauline made Hemingway go back and get him.

I felt no sense of Hemingway in this room and hurried on to catch up with the tour. They were in a front room where the books are behind chicken wire and the walls are adorned with photos of Hemingway and his four wives: Hadley Richardson, the Paris years; Pauline Pfeiffer, the Key West years; Martha Gellhorn, the Cuba years, part one; Mary Welsh, the Cuba years, part two.

All these women had created nests for Ernest, only to learn he was not a nesting bird, at least not with the same mate. If his life had not been running out, the 60-year-old Hemingway would probably have left Mary to go off with young Adriana Ivancich, who had not made it into this photo gallery as a wife but was Papa's last great infatuation.

This house at 907 Whitehead Street was the nest Pauline had created. It is built of the blocks of coral excavated for the basement, painted off-white, with tall windows flanked by lemon-lime green shutters. Porches supported by iron grillwork run almost entirely around the second floor, giving it a Spanish Colonial look, and both the house and carriage house out back are engulfed in jungle gardens. As Hemingway's fame grew and tourists invaded, Hemingway had the property walled in with brick. It is a beautiful, airy house, designed by its original owner—a Connecticut Yankee who made much of his money building Confederate ships—to repulse hurricanes, and it has done its job, although the banyan tree that Pauline planted in 1931 as a centerpiece of the southwest garden was taken by Hurricane George on September 25, 1998. The little

Hemingway's house on Whitehead Street, Key West.
It is now a museum.

tree had grown to dominate the garden, which now looked naked with its new plantings, the palm trees propped up with two by fours. A white cat with a black tail and black patches at the ears sat in the garden and surveyed the tourists with regal indifference. The six-toed cats which Hemingway claims to have created as a new breed are part of the Key West legend. About 50 of them roam around the grounds now, but the Heming-ways had only two cats, a few peacocks and pet raccoons in a cage in Key West. The cats overran the Cuba house.

The tour guide was wrapping up the Hemingway life chronology. "He died in 1961 in Ketchum Idaho . . . you know, Sun Valley . . . of a self-inflicted gunshot. He was 61 years old."

My age. A little chill went down my back as the co-incidence struck home. By the time he was 61 Heming-way was rich, had created a legend, become delusional, lost his ability to write, and feared life as it was more than death. Toward the end, Hemingway had told his friend John Dos Passos, who had first steered Hemingway to Key West decades before, that he feared he would never make love again, never fight again, never write again. He had slid down from the pinnacle. He had wrangled life on his own terms, but now he was all for death.

He had left Cuba in 1960, expecting to return despite the fact that Castro's Revolution had become stridently anti-American. He rose early the morning of July 2, 1961, at the house in Ketchum, slipped into his robe, found keys to the locked gun cabinet, removed the double-barreled Boss shotgun he preferred for pigeon shooting and went to the small entry hall where he liked to work. Hemingway pressed the twin barrels against his forehead just above the eyebrows and tripped both triggers. Mary found him dead, 19 days before his sixty-second birthday. Ernest had even rehearsed this act in Cuba, for friends. His father had taken the same route out of the world, via Cavalry pistol.

At my age, the man who had told us that courage was grace under pressure was only months away from checking out of a world that had come to overwhelm him. Ultimately, it is our own closely guarded image of ourselves that betrays us and does us in.

At 61, I had no desire to die or even be thoroughly terrified. I fully expected to make love again, and devoutly hoped it would be some time quite soon. As for writing, that would go on for a while, if only yarns for sailing magazines, if we got to Cuba and back in one piece.

Ironically, Archibald MacLeish had the last word. *Life* magazine asked him to write a memoir in a special section of the magazine published on July 14, 1961 after Hemingway's death. It was far short of a glowing eulogy and speculated about what the critics would say about Hemingway now. Maybe MacLeish was remembering the mosquitoes and no-see-ums from the time Hemingway beached him:

"Writers with us are supposed to be watchers: 'God's spies' as John Keats put it once. They are supposed to spend themselves observing the world, watching history and mankind and themselves—particularly themselves: their unsaid thoughts, their secret deeds and dreads. Hemingway was not a watcher: he was an actor in his life. He took part."

MacLeish told of how Hemingway could not resist becoming engaged in dangerous blood sports—war, big game hunting, boxing, fishing the Gulf Stream. MacLeish added, "Danger is not the least revealing of the mirrors into which we look." Those words stuck in my mind.

Hemingway arrived in Key West in April of 1928 from Paris at the age of 29 with his new and pregnant wife Pauline Pfeiffer. His first wife, Hadley, and a young son Jack were left behind in Paris. He was enjoying a growing reputation as a writer resulting largely from the success of *The Sun Also Rises*. He had his work cut out for him; he was writing *A Farewell to Arms*.

The young Hemingways had no immediate plan to settle in Key West. They had come to pick up a yellow Model A Ford roadster, a gift from Pauline's rich Uncle Gus, then travel to Pauline's home town, Piggot, Arkansas, and on to Kansas City, Missouri, to have the baby. But the car had not arrived and the embarrassed Ford dealers at the Trevor and Morris Company offered the couple an apartment over the showroom at 314

Simonton Street. Hemingway settled in to finish *A Farewell to Arms*. Pauline went on ahead and by the time son Patrick was born in June, Hemingway had joined her.

But first, Hemingway began to assemble the "Key West Mob." Like a little boy organizing clubs, Hemingway had a pattern of surrounding himself with tight groups of pals who enjoyed literature, war, fishing, hunting, bullfights, carousing or drinking—not necessarily in that order depending upon the circumstances. The groups were given names that suggested tough-guy camaraderie. The Key West Mob included four local charter fishing boat skippers, among them Joe Russell and Bra Sanders; Charles Thompson, whose family was the most affluent in Key West; Earl Adams, bureau chief for the *Miami Herald*, and a machine shop owner, J.B. Sullivan, called "Sully."

In May, this local mob was supplemented by other friends, whom Hemingway summoned by letter claiming that Key West was "the St. Tropez of the poor." They were John Dos Passos; artists Waldo Pierce and Henry Strater, both acquaintances from the Paris days; Bill Smith, a boyhood friend from Michigan, and Archibald MacLeish.

The mob was allowed to swim in the deserted Navy Yard after Thompson pulled a few strings. They took a fishing trip out to the Marquesas Keys and Dry Tortugas. Pierce painted an oil of the mob killing a shark and did a pen and ink portrait of Hemingway that ran in a 1929 *Saturday Review of Literature* with a glowing review of *A Farewell to Arms*. His portrait of Hemingway fishing in a blue and white striped shirt—a 1929 shirt—made the cover of *Time* in 1937. They cruised the restaurants and dives. Prohibition didn't mean much in Key West.

Skippers like Joe Russell made sure there was plenty of rum from Cuba. Key West was depressed, off the beaten track, full of sailors and speakeasies. Many of the Hemingway and Key West Mob hangouts of the early years are gone now or altered beyond all recognition: Delmonico's restaurant at 218 Duval Street, where the Cuban fare included green turtle steaks; Ramon's; the Cuban Cafe at 1111 Duval Street; Raul's Club on East Roosevelt Boulevard, which had a first class dance floor, live music, a view of the Atlantic and a tank full of grouper that were trained to eat out of the owner's hand; and Pena's Garden of Roses, a beer garden in the Old Town where double martinis were 25 cents.

Hemingway would work in the carriage house in the morning, then, if not going fishing, hike the eight blocks northwest to the old Sloppy Joe's—now Captain Tony's—a cool, dark cave offering sanctuary from the bright sun and a study of Key West characters. Key West has had its ups and downs, but some constants remain over the years: smuggling, stunt drinking, a celebration of seaminess; all good stuff for a writer. In *To Have and Have Not*, Sloppy Joe's is called "Freddy's," a place where smuggling deals were cooked and Depression-era vets on work crews building roads and bridges in the Keys pounded the snot out of each other as a form of male bonding. The bar's owner, Joe Russell, became Hemingway's mentor in fishing the Gulf Stream and adventuring in Havana. He survives in literature as Harry Morgan, the ruthless protagonist of *To Have and Have Not*. Many of the smugglers, drinkers and fishermen, even his lawyer in Key West surfaced in that book, not one of Papa's best. It was cobbled together from short stories, but is his only novel set in the United States and one that captures the outlaw Key West/Havana connection. His alternate work location for these stories was the Ambos Mundos hotel in Havana.

Hemingway's reputation and successes grew in Key West. He found an outlet for his love of boxing just a few blocks from the house at the Key West Arena, where Depression-era conchs could have a cheap night out watching mostly black boxers mix it up, sometimes with Hemingway as the referee or a sparring partner. Once in a while the residents got to see Hemingway perform himself. He punched out poet Wallace Stevens in a brawl at a 1929 party at a little house he and Pauline had rented at 1100 South Street before they bought their home.

I found the old boxing arena at the corner of Thomas and Petronia Streets in Bahamas Village, Key West's black neighborhood. Now painted white with blue shutters and red trim, the arena has a new life as the Blue Heaven restaurant. The Blue Heaven is an off-the-beaten-track favorite of Key West insiders, especially for breakfast at the outside tables. Live chickens are likely to be underfoot, and coincidentally chicken is on the evening dinner menu. Free roaming chickens are protected as wild birds by an old ordinance that not everyone loves when the roosters begin crowing at the break of day, or at the moon or a streetlight. The wild chickens are descendants of roosters brought by Cuban immigrants for cock fighting, which went on into the 1950s.

I set a course back to Duval Street. Whitehead and Duval Street parallel each other one block apart, with the Hemingway house between them at Olivia Street. It is about eight blocks to the end of Duval and Mallory Square, where thousands turn out most nights to watch the sun go down—assisted by the bagpipers—to drink, to watch the big charter sailboats parade past loaded with tourists, to watch the street buskers perform, to be there just because it is the place to be at sundown. Some nights Navy Seals with smoke bombs lashed to their ankles spiral on parachutes above the crowd, landing on the far side of the Marriott.

Duval Street is devoted to drinking establishments and T-shirt shops. A few shop owners have been convicted of adding a zero to the credit card slip of distracted tourists buying a $20 T-shirt, providing a poignant memory when a $200 bill appears. Rascals still abound in Key West. Drinking here is a competitive, participatory sport. At least half the police reports in *The Citizen* have something to do with drugs or alcohol:

—The local whose dinghy was found overturned off Key West. Friends had seen him the night before, drinking. The Coast Guard launched a $5,000 search only to find the man had indeed fallen out of his dinghy, but had climbed aboard someone else's boat and passed out in the cockpit.

—The man who got beat up after breaking into an apartment, watching television and falling asleep in a stranger's bed.

—The Miami chicken cook arrested with crack cocaine in the battery compartment of his pager.

—The California man arrested on South Street, masturbating with his right hand while rubbing chocolate ice cream on his face and chest with his left hand.

Key West is not ashamed; T-shirts declare: "Rehab Is for Quitters".

I walked passed a young man sitting on a box reading George Orwell's *1984* out loud expecting contributions to be placed in his hat, and a college-age woman sitting on the curb, head in hands, her face the grey-green color of someone enduring a near terminal hangover. The tears on her cheeks suggested regrets about last night that went beyond a hangover and fell into the category of "Oh, my God, what have I done," and not remembering too clearly what happened. It was spring break in Key West.

Sloppy Joe's on Duval Street is, like so much of the Hemingway legend, tangled in revisionist history. The original Sloppy Joe's is not even in Key West, it is in Havana, but the current one packs them in. I stood outside a window on Greene Street watching a singer/guitarist named Pat Dailey get the crowd churned up with songs of the drinking and screwing life. His signature tune had him lamenting his job as a singer in a tourist-town bar, contemplating leaving, but deciding after the seventeenth beer "to stay right here." The place was jammed with young people. Across the room I could see a collection of black and white photos that I recognized, even at this distance, as the standard Hemingway photos. Beyond them, through an open door guarded by a bouncer the size of a Buick, was the Hemingway memorabilia gift shop. The task of this young man with no neck was to see that no one slipped into the bar ($5 cover charge) from the Hemingway memorabilia shop.

I went into the shop and for $8.50 bought a green commuter mug with a likeness of Hemingway and "Sloppy Joe's Key West" printed on it. I had been looking for a new commuter mug because the one from Bruegger's Bagel Bakery in Burlington that had traveled 2000 miles as my designated coffee, orange juice, vodka and tonic and otherwise all purpose mug was making strange hissing and cracking sounds when I dumped in the hot morning coffee. On DREAM WEAVER each crew member has a commuter mug used for everything, and is responsible for keeping it somewhat clean, a rule that prevents having to clean up a sink full of dirty cups and glasses every day. Might as well be Hemingway's licensed image and likeness, even though Hemingway never looked anything like this when he lived in Key West. The licensed image of Papa in the bulky turtleneck and beard is from a photo by Yousef Karsh taken in Cuba in 1957.

This highly-merchandised Sloppy Joe's is a Johnny-come-lately in the Hemingway saga. The real Sloppy Joe's from 1933 to 1937, most of Hemingway's Key West years is, in fact, Captain Tony's at 428 Greene Street, just down the street. Before 1933, Russell had owned a speakeasy on Front Street. Russell moved Sloppy Joe's to the current location on Duval Street in May 1937, when the rent went up a dollar a week for the Greene Street property. He enlisted the aid of every drunk in town to pull off the move in one night to dodge the terms of his lease. If I had to bet, I'd say that's the night Hemingway got the urinal. Hemingway said he was a silent partner in Sloppy Joe's and the real money was made out back at illegal gambling, because the only expense was buying police protection. By 1937, Hemingway was running back and forth to Spain to cover the Spanish Civil War, and less than two years later he was gone for good.

Hemingway, especially when the mob gathered, often began the day at The Electric Kitchen at 830 Fleming Street, where owner and cook Rhoda "Rutabaga" Baker would whip up breakfast for less than 45 cents each. It is not that far from Sloppy Joe's; in Key West nothing is very far. The Electric Kitchen is now a proudly gay Flaming Maggie's Books, Art and Gallery. I sat outside in a white wicker chair, drinking coffee, watching young lovelies in bikini tops and cut-off shorts hum past on in-line skates, hoping vaguely that they were straight and not gay, although it really wasn't going to make any difference to me personally. I had shoes in my closet older than those skaters. They couldn't remember Oliver North; I was remembering Hemingway.

Joe Russell, frequently traveling back and forth to Havana on his fishing and smuggling boat ANITA, introduced his new pal Hemingway to Gulf Stream fishing, and in 1932 to the carnal joys of Havana. Hemingway was hooked just as thoroughly as any fish. Two years later, passing through New York on the way back from a safari, Hemingway made a deal with Arnold Gingrich, founding editor of *Esquire*, to write monthly articles on manly sports like hunting and fishing. With his $3,000 advance check, Hemingway put a down payment on his most-prized possession, the fishing boat PILAR, which would cost $7,500 f.o.b. Miami. PILAR was a code name for Pauline when they were having an affair in Paris, and the name of the guerilla fighter in *For Whom The Bell Tolls*, which was written after Hemingway left both Pauline and Key West. A Hemingway daughter would have been named Pilar, Pauline told a crewman on the boat.

Hemingway was a happy man. Not only could he fish the Stream, he now could roam back and forth over to Cuba without relying on Sloppy Joe Russell or anyone else. With the end of prohibition in December 1933, Sloppy Joe was too busy legally selling beer to sailors in his Greene Street saloon to make the Cuba run. When Hemingway went to Cuba for good, PILAR went, too.

The Hemingways had a growing circle of friends in the 1930s, including Grant and Jane Mason who lived in Havana, but frequently came to visit. Papa and Jane raced around the Keys in her sports car, playing a form of "chicken" about who would be first to say "slow down." Pauline was worrying about her marriage. It had been under stress since the very difficult birth of the second son, Gregory, in 1931. There would be no more children, but Ernest, the biggest, neediest child of all, was no longer the center of Pauline's attention. And Jane Mason was beautiful and beguiling.

It was time for me to scout Key West as a place to bring DREAM WEAVER, going to or coming from Cuba. Key West is not quite as cruiser-friendly as Marathon. The favorite anchorage is off the northwest side of town between Mallory Square and Christmas Tree Island, but the bottom is sandy and provides unpredictable holding. The first time I saw it a strong norther was blowing and the boats at anchor were pitching on multiple anchors, exposed to wind and waves from the north. A huge schooner, aground and on its side, defined the northern end of the anchorage. It was not a place where I wanted to spend any time. Key West, like other communities in the Keys, is concerned about pollution from boats and is attempting to manage its anchorages by installing permanent moorings on the north side of the island between Fleming Key and Sigsbee Park at the site of a former seaplane base.

Key West Bight, the former working waterfront, has several marinas and after years of being a political white elephant it has been reborn as Key West Historic Seaport with new restaurants and stores appealing to the tourist trade. It is expensive for cruisers like me. In Hemingway's days, much of it was owned by Charles Thompson's family, Papa's close fishing and safari friend. The family holdings included the Turtle Kraals, still a restaurant, and a fleet of 125 fishing boats, plus some turtle boats, Thompson's Docks which became Land's End Marina, a canning company, marine supply store and several other businesses. Green turtles were hunted almost to extinction in the Keys and many were butchered on docks in the bight as late as the 1960s, coming and going as source of revenue just like so many other promising enterprises: sponges, shrimp, rum running, cigar making, hauling Cuban refugees. Only tourism has had staying power, and it is for tourists that green turtles were reintroduced in the turtle kraals with no risk of winding up as steaks or soup.

The Schooner Bar, which one long-time resident told me was "the best heterosexual bar in Key West," is on the east end of the bight near a low, white, unmarked building that is supposed to be Jimmy Buffett's recording studio.

I explored with a sailor's priorities. Although there is no major supermarket within walking distance of the bight, there are two very good grocery stores nearby that approach supermarket status and are more interesting than the Publix out in the mall: Fausto's Food Palace on Fleming where Bahamas Street intersects, and the Waterfront Market, just beyond the Schooner Bar and easy to spot because the side wall is painted with a huge undersea mural. Across the parking lot is a West Marine store, and across Caroline Street is Pepe's, a funky restaurant serving all three meals. Here I actually found some locals, and although it sounds like it serves Cuban food, it doesn't. Around the corner on Simonton is an organic food store. In the other direction, at 301 Simonton, is a federal office building made of cut coral blocks and housing U.S. Customs. I would have to deal with them sooner or later.

Across the street, at 314 Simonton, is the old Trevor and Morris Ford Dealership, the first Hemingway residence in Key West. If you know its history, you can see the shape of an auto dealership behind the balconies and flower boxes. I walked over.

"I didn't know there was any Hemingway connection until people started coming in here and telling me about it," said the current owner. She and her family operate a gift shop called the Pelican Poop Shoppe, where you can buy fudge shaped like excrement and other curiosities that will start or stop a conversation. She maintains a Hemingway room in the northwest corner, where the shabby apartment was located over the showroom. The huge interior space that was once the auto workshop is now an atrium with a beautiful garden, fountain and pool named for Hemingway. It is open to the public for a small fee. The owners' private home surrounds the garden.

A generation of Americans has forgotten how close the U.S.-Cuba connection was fifty years ago. Two ferries—one of them a car ferry—ran back and forth to Havana from docks at the north end of the bight. Shortly after the Cuban revolution, the abandoned sheds on the north bight were used by the CIA to store small arms and ammunition in preparation for the Bay of Pigs invasion of Cuba. With the redevelopment of the bight as a historic district a new ferry company arrived on the scene. Buquebus moved in to provide a high speed service to Fort Myers, a trip 50 miles longer than a run to Havana. The Keys have one eye on Cuba, getting ready. One expert on the Keys thinks two things will happen when relations become normal, whatever normal means in the peculiar tension between the two countries. First, the Keys will be flooded with fleeing Cubans, and second, many tourists won't stop and spend money in Key West when they can keep going and discover exotic Cuba.

Evening was settling in as I headed back up Duval Street and detoured into Captain Tony's for a draft beer to consider my situation. I had been stuck in Boot Key Harbor for three weeks waiting for word from the Treasury Department on my license to Cuba and calling around for a crew. There are times, a sailor learns, when it is prudent to wait things out. The Treasury clearance should come in the next batch of forwarded mail. Then what?

I ordered another beer. Sloppy Joe's—Captain Tony's—is still a cool dark cave, now with thousands of business cards pinned to the ceiling along with a few bras and panties. Captain Tony doesn't own it any more, but in a corner you can buy a T-shirt bearing his likeness and philosophy:

"All you need in life is a tremendous sex drive and a great ego—brains don't mean shit." Captain Tony ran for mayor of Key West, but with that philosophy he should have set his sights for Washington.

Perhaps he was also speaking of Hemingway, because it was in this bar in December 1936, that Hemingway spotted a pretty blonde in a simple black sundress perched on a bar stool in the company of a young man and an older woman. Both Hemingway and the blonde, Martha Gellhorn, returned the next day and struck up a relationship. Skinner, the bartender that day, called it beauty meeting the beast. It would end Hemingway's marriage to Pauline and his days in Key West. It started that evening, when he blew off a dinner with Pauline and Charles and Lorine Thompson. Everybody found out where he was because Charles went to

Sloppy Joe's to find him. He was with a blonde, Charles reported, and would meet them later at Pena's.

Martha Gellhorn was not only attractive; at 28 she had two books to her credit, had worked as a journalist in France for *United Press* and as a correspondent for the *St. Louis Post Dispatch*. Her father was a prominent St. Louis physician, her mother a graduate of Bryn Mawr who worked devotedly on social issues, including women's suffrage. Marty Gellhorn was as bright and tough-minded as she was attractive, and had left Bryn Mawr before graduation to pursue journalism and fiction writing. With few rewards and substantial risk, she was happy living a minimalist life "seeing and writing." Eleanor Roosevelt became an advocate for Marty's second book, *The Trouble I've Seen*. Reviewers compared her prose to Hemingway's. She was traveling with her younger brother and mother; her father had recently died. Ironically, her brother picked Key West for a December trip—the first Christmas without Dr. Gellhorn—because he had never heard of it. Her mother decided to go into Sloppy Joe's because it had such a peculiar name. But given the fact that Marty knew of and admired Hemingway, it is hard to imagine she was just tagging along. In Martha Gellhorn, Hemingway, then 37, would meet his match. Brother and mother left Key West, but Martha stayed on into January 1937, gradually becoming a friend of Pauline's. For the second time, Hemingway brought a future lover home to his wife, as if looking for approval, and they became friends. When Marty left, she corresponded with Pauline. Over time, the one thing the Hemingway women could agree on was that when Hemingway drank he was one mean son of a bitch.

It was not by accident that early in 1937 Hemingway and Martha Gellhorn wound up together in Spain as correspondents covering the Spanish Civil War: he for the North American Newspaper Alliance and she as a freelancer with credentials as a "special correspondent" for *Colliers* magazine. For a young woman she witnessed plenty, often at great personal risk, and wrote powerfully about it. She connected with Hemingway at the end of March 1937 in a Madrid that had been under siege for five months. The front was only 1,200 yards away, there was little food, and during one of the bombardments she watched a woman and a child running across a square, then saw the child killed by shrapnel.

Hemingway tried to take charge of her in a way she found heavy handed, but she tagged along with him and the experienced war correspondents to learn the ropes and learn Spanish. Her first story for *Colliers* magazine, *Only the Shells Whine*, put her name on the masthead as a legitimate war correspondent. Marty and Papa made a foray in an armored car that was hit four times by gunfire and Hemingway instructed her on the sounds of different kinds of gunfire, and when to fall flat on the ground.

Years later she wrote, "I think it was the only time in his life when he was not the most important thing there was. He really cared about the Republic and he cared about that war. I believe I never would've gotten hooked otherwise." Hemingway was in the war zone for two months, then returned to New York in April to work on the film *The Spanish Earth*. Both were back in Madrid by early September, and two thirds of Spain was controlled by Franco's fascists. She viewed the front, watched the soldiers bury their dead, lived out of a truck, and on weekends they played in Madrid.

For the next two years, both Hemingway and Marty were on separate schedules dictated by their work, back and forth to Spain, New York, and Washington, arranging rendezvous when they could. Pauline knew the marriage was unraveling, but could not rescue it.

He returned to Key West just before Christmas to find Pauline had left for New York for the holidays. He spent a week packing up personal possessions, and on December 24 he loaded up the Buick convertible and left for Havana on the car ferry.

In the closing days of 1938 Uncle Gus and his wife arrived, and shortly afterward Grace Hemingway, Ernest's mother, showed up. All showed concern about the disintegrating marriage. Hemingway put up a good front during the visits, but on February 15, 1939, he pushed off for Havana on PILAR. Hemingway was only 39 when he left Key West and Pauline for good.

He had deposited boxes full of stuff cleaned out of the house in the back room at Sloppy Joe's on Duval, a fact he mentioned to his friend A.E. Hotchner and Mary when they rendezvoused at the Key West house in July 1955. Pauline had died in 1951; Hemingway was sipping vodka with breakfast and had come back to deal with property issues. In Pauline's will the house was left 60 percent to sons Patrick and Gregory and 40 percent to Hemingway, although the house was purchased by Uncle Gus. The house was full of painful memories. Hemingway had not recovered from two plane crashes during an African safari in 1953-1954, was in constant pain, drinking heavily, and a lymph gland under his arm was swelling. He told Mary and Hotchner, "If this balloons up, we clear out of here fast. I'd rather eat monkey manure than die in Key West."

The January after Hemingway's death, Mary and a friend came to Sloppy Joe's, borrowed bartenders' aprons, and worked for a month sorting through thousands of papers mixed in with the skeletons of mice, rats and cockroaches that had nibbled at the family letters and drafts of early Hemingway short stories and *A Farewell to Arms*. A half-dozen boxes of significant papers were salvaged and eventually went to the fifth floor of the John F. Kennedy Library near Boston, where Hemingway's papers and many photographs are collected. That April, Mary sat next to John F. Kennedy at a Sunday White House dinner for Nobel Prize winners, and scolded him about U.S. policy toward Cuba. He did not want to hear it. The failed Bay of Pigs invasion was having its first anniversary. Kennedy would be assassinated by a man who had connections to both Russia and Cuba.

I resumed my trek up Duval. On a previous trip to Key West I'd found, in the 700 block, a T-shirt shop called Last Flight Out. A clipping on the wall shows a young Clay Greager, owner of the shop, sitting in the open door of a helicopter in camouflage fatigues and staring at the jungle below. He was a helicopter scout in the First Air Cavalry, and had been shot down and surrounded by Vietcong, who were closing in on their position. He had been plucked, just barely, out of the jungles of Vietnam by a rescue helicopter and photographed by a combat photographer. He was staring at the jungle with what the caption described as "a 10,000 mile stare."

Greager designs, prints and sells stuff that focuses not on his own experience, but on the notion that for every person there is an opportunity to catch a "last flight out" of their routines to take a new path they have always dreamed of following, but did not have the courage to pursue. They sit forever in the waiting room, never catching the flight. He publishes little pamphlets full of bad poetry on that theme, and a Last Flight Out state of mind checklist. I picked one up and had it on the boat. One item on the checklist says "Don't open any door you don't intend to go through."

On my first visit I browsed around; nice graphics, interesting notion, but I didn't buy anything on that trip. I wished I had talked to Greager but he wasn't there. Now as I passed by in the dark I could see a man in his fifties seated at the far end, behind the counter, so I wandered in.

"Are you Greager?"

"I am."

I introduced myself. "Interesting store. Interesting idea. Who are your customers?"

He smiled and shook his head. "I think everyone has a germ of this in them. Caught in their own traps. People, strangers, come in here and tell me things they wouldn't tell a priest. A guy from New Jersey was in here the other day with his T-shirt on and tells me how he's almost ready now. But he's afraid to wear the T-shirt in New Jersey, he comes down here every year and wears it, and buys a new one. He's revving his engines. Maybe some day . . . There are a lot of desperate people in this world."

"Is Last Flight Out about that Vietnam clipping over there?"

He thought a moment. "Let's just say that when I came to Key West in the seventies I wasn't searching for the meaning of life any more." He wanted to get away from the subject, so he laughed. "Part of the meaning of life is not freezing your ass off up north for half the year. Where you from?"

"I'm off a boat, heading for Cuba."

Greager showed me an old photo of the building across the street. It had been the offices of Aero Marine, the line that flew seaplanes into Havana in the early 1920s, carrying not only passengers, but homing pigeons to be released in case anything went wrong and the plane was going down. Nobody wants to go down in the Gulf Stream. The airline failed and was bought by what would become Pan American.

"When are you going?"

That was the question, wasn't it. I had opened the door, and I had not come this far to turn back. Not this time. "Right after the next batch of mail catches up. A couple more days." With crew or without.

Two days later I phoned John Dupee, an experienced bluewater sailor in Vermont, a man I knew from the yacht club. He had a weird sense of humor that matched mine. I had avoided calling him because I suspected he might have had enough of sailing for a while. He had been on SEA SHELL, caught in the hurricane. I was wrong. He would be down in a few days. He could make the trip one way, but he would have to fly out of Cuba to Puerto Rico to meet his wife on a vacation that had been a long time in the planning. Late that afternoon, the bundle of mail at my general delivery address at the Marathon Post Office contained the Treasury letter clearing me to Cuba.

3 | *Key West to Havana*

The passage to Cuba, which only days before had been tantalizingly out of reach, was now falling into place. A burst of preparation followed: make the 40-mile run to Stock Island, have the boat hauled to solve the propeller and depth sounder problems, collect John, complete Coast Guard forms, provision, launch, go. And as a bonus, a surprise telephone message on my voice mail provided me with a friend to crew on the run down to Key West.

I was making calls at the pay phones in that pounding sun behind the Dockside Bar at 10 a.m. when the battered blue El Cheapo cab deposited Phil Moizeka and his duffle on the asphalt.

He saluted. "Seaman Moizeka reporting, Captain." He and his wife, Nancy, were from Burlington and good friends. The bottles of emergency Absolut had come from them.

"Good to see you, pal."

We walked around front to the tiki bar. "So this is the cruising life. You look good. It agrees with you."

"This is the bar, this is the water, and here are the dinghies that take us from the boats to the bar. That's cruising in the Keys. But I've been here too long, almost a month."

"What's the plan?"

"The plan is to leave about noon and make it a two-day trip to Key West. We could do it in a day, it's about 40 miles, but we're getting a late start and I'm interested in stopping at a park called Bahia Honda. There is a catamaran, TIGER LILY, that will be going down with us, although they'll breeze past us. Sue was married to a military guy at one time, so she has military privileges and can stay at the marina at the Boca Chica Naval Air Station. The guy's name is Robert; he's from New Zealand and has been on boats all his life. He built a little cabin on an open catamaran; it's about the size of a tent. We'll go into a yard at Stock Island and haul the boat. We'll find somebody who can tell me why the propeller doesn't propel, and replace the transducer on the depth sounder so I don't have to keep judging the depth by hitting the bottom with the keel."

We settled Phil's gear onto the boat and began the messy task of hauling up three anchors that had been burying for weeks. The bottom of Boot Key Harbor is a grey-white paste that looks like wallboard mud mixed with sand, crushed sea shells, live crustaceans and dissolved toilet paper. A milky white cloud drifts from chain and rode as they are tightened to a vertical position, and soon a stubborn paste builds up on deck and sailors. The tail end of a norther was blowing itself out, so the Danforth set to the southwest came up first and easily from behind the boat. The new Claw, set to the north, came up reluctantly after we drew the rode up tight vertically, cleated it off, and then both walked to the stern to let the boat's buoyancy do the heavy lifting for us. As a secondary anchor, it had to be hauled, cleaned and stowed in the lazarette while we swung onto the CQR, which lived on the bow as the primary anchor.

TIGER LILY sailed by as we were finishing up.

"How are you coming?" Robert called.

"We'll be off in about five minutes."

"Then I'll head out now, we're going out Sister Creek. See you out there."

I didn't trust the depths in Sister Creek—four feet at low water was reported—or my depth sounder, so I headed west out the channel under the draw bridge and set a course southwest, angling away from the Seven Mile Bridge. Bahia Honda is only about 12 miles west of Marathon, and with a breeze building from eight to 17 knots we sailed at hull speed, still enjoying some protection from the waves because of the Keys to our north.

It was sweet to be on the move again, traveling in the right direction at hull speed on a sunny day, with a good friend, fresh ice, clean laundry, a good weather forecast and an anchorage never before seen in easy reach before nightfall. I was back in the real world, the world of weather and the boat working cleanly, and moving through a green sea. Entering the real world forever spoils one, I would learn, for re-entering the other one that is so contrived, so wrapped into important-sounding trivia.

"I can't tell you how glad I am to be out of Marathon. It felt like I was going to be stuck there forever, but now it has all dropped into place." A movement in the water caught my eye. "Over there, dolphins." Phil grabbed his camera and moved forward as five dolphins joined us to play in our bow wave. He stretched out on the bow for a long time.

He came smiling back into the cockpit. "I could almost touch them. There was a pair that just stayed right there on the wave. It was amazing."

"They always make me feel good. Even when I'm aground they make me feel good. Some day I think we will learn that they are gods, and we will have to answer to them for what we do to the sea. I hope they keep their sense of humor then, the one that makes them play with us now. If you take the helm for a while I'll put together sandwiches and beer, and then I'll ask you how you like the cruising life so far."

Phil had talked often about getting a boat, but although his wife loved kayaks, she felt claustrophobic on sailboats and I knew his plan was doomed. "Nancy thought I should come on this trip and get it out of my system."

We burst into laughter.

A distant sail had been approaching us from astern, and I suspected it was TIGER LILY. The catamaran closed with us quickly and passed to starboard as we took snapshots of each other. It is hard to get a picture of your boat under way, because you are always on it.

The water changes between Marathon and Bahia Honda. Near Bahia Honda it loses its flat, murky look and changes to vivid colors that can be read more easily. The tropical water colors have inspired a set of rules for sailors: If it's brown, you're aground. If it's white, you might. If it's blue, sail on through. If it's green, keep it clean. In protected waters, and most of the Keys are protected, if a boater damages a reef or sea grass by anchoring or running aground he or she is facing serious fines and assessments. A licensed captain teaching navigation to a student hit a reef off Marathon and was fined $10,000.

Sea grasses—turtle grass, manatee grass, red and green algaes—are also protected and tearing them up with anchors or by running aground makes the boater liable for the costs of sending someone out to investigate how much damage was done, repairs, and then the fines. It is like ripping the surface of a pool table with your cue; expensive beyond the extent of the damage. A 44-footer ran aground off Pigeon Key several years ago near the Seven Mile Bridge and was fined $49,867 to cover survey and repair costs for ripping up a patch of grass about the size of the boat. Fines in the $25,000 range are more common, but many of them are litigated to lower numbers, not counting legal fees.

Government organizations, primarily the National Oceanic and Atmospheric Administration and private volunteer groups like Reef Relief, work to both protect the reefs and keep them accessible. Blue and white mooring balls are set up over selected reefs from northeast of Key Largo along Hawk Channel to an area west of Key West. Boaters can pick these up instead of anchoring and then snorkel or dive the reefs. Usually these sanctuary preservation areas are outlined by yellow floats, with the mooring balls inside the perimeter. Commercial snorkel and dive boat tour operators use this system, but it is available to anyone who knows about it and keeps an eye on the charts for shallow areas. One of the most popular buoyed dive sites was a few miles ahead of us, Looe Key, a 5.3 mile area south of Newfound Harbor.

Our anchorage choices for the night were Bahia Honda or Newfound Harbor a few miles beyond. Bahia Honda was more exposed to the north wind blowing into the anchorage through the newest of two bridges on Overseas Highway as it meanders down the Keys, but I had lobbied for Bahia Honda because I had read there were sea turtles in these waters, good snorkeling, and it was a pretty place with the potential for a hike out onto the old bridge or on nature trails. A span of the old bridge along the south side of the key has been removed so sailboats can get in and anchor off Bahia Honda Park, which has a sandy beach and small marina.

Approaching from the east it is necessary to hook around a shallow island off the key and follow the dark blue water through the bridge cut into the anchorage. TIGER LILY already had her anchor down and, like the two other boats in the anchorage, was bouncing around in the sloppy waves coming in under the bridge. I set two anchors against the chop and north wind. There would be no walks on the beach or bridge this time around, it was too rough to row the dinghies against the wind and waves.

A few minutes before sunset the radio came to life. I was monitoring Channel 68, which had become our habit when traveling together. It was Robert on the catamaran. "Sue wants to know if you have seen the turtles yet."

"They're everywhere, aren't they?" All I could see was waves rolling toward us.

He laughed. "Talk to you in the morning, mate." I would hear about these turtles again, I knew.

The wind continued into the night, tossing us around in our bunks.

The next day DREAM WEAVER and TIGER LILY had the same destination, the Boca Chica Channel. It cuts north off Hawk Channel between Boca Chica Key and Stock Island. Key West and Stock Island are adjacent, separated by narrow Cow Key Channel. TIGER LILY would follow the Boca Chica Channel to the Naval Air Station marina, and DREAM WEAVER would at some point bear off to port on a secondary channel that led to Peninsular Marine on Stock Island.

Out of Bahia Honda we set a course for Nine Foot Shoal and then for a lighted green can "1" that marked Boca Chica Channel. It is easy to overshoot the channel and head into another channel toward the big building with Oceanside Marine painted on its arched roof. We picked our way up the Boca Chica Channel with the dark green water turning to a light green through which

I could see bottom features, and I didn't like it. A bare post stood where the secondary channel entrance should begin. Usually a bare post without a green square or red triangle means that the water has shoaled and the post has been abandoned as a navigation aid. Instead, it could now be a hazard. I raised Bobby Minj at Peninsular Marine on the radio, and told him what I was seeing.

"You're okay," he said. "The hurricane took the green marker off the first post and the second one is upside down." I could see it. In silhouette it looked like a triangle because it was not completely upside down, it had a pointed top. "Keep on coming and turn to port before the power lines when you see our sign. Give me a call when you get closer."

Stock Island is a working maritime island. Here are men who know about diesel engines and propeller pitch and marine electronics and how to paint their identifying marks on crab trap floats by stringing them on a line, holding the brush steady, and spinning the foam. After the shrimpers left Key West Bight, Stock Island became their home base. The economy of the lower Keys shifts and changes like the shoals at an inlet. For a time Stock Island became a safe haven for the cocaine mother ships and a port for the working boats that shuffled Cubans from Mariel during the boatlift. One travel guide to the Keys says that even the cops don't like to go into the trailer parks on Stock Island after dark.

But Phil and I liked Stock Island. I had called ahead to have DREAM WEAVER hauled out at 2 p.m. We arrived at the face dock near the Travelift bay at 1:50 and by 2:05 the boat was hanging in slings having the bottom power washed. An hour later it was blocked up on the hard and arrangements had been made to pull the propeller first thing tomorrow morning. These folks didn't fool around, and their prices were right, especially compared to Key West. Along most of the East Coast we could find dockage for about $1 per foot per night, with prices declining gradually as the boat moved further south. But in Key West, where every bar and bath house boasts its position as the most southerly in the continental U.S., the fees started at $1.75 per foot per night and went up from there. Everything in Key West is expensive.

Phil wandered through the boatyard, fascinated by the characters and their ventures. A plywood PT boat was being restored down the line from us. The guy on the boat next to us was living on board and went off to work in his Honda every morning. A plywood work table behind the stern showed that he was rebuilding the interior. A young woman whose boat sunk off Fleming Key in the hurricane five months before was excited about getting launched and back to living on board. She had painted her boat purple and it looked like an Easter egg. Our favorites were two grizzled characters who were ostensibly rebuilding a boat that stood across the dusty lane off our port quarter. They lived in a tiny shed wedged between the bows of two boats, and at about eight each morning they started vigorously with their day's chores of sanding and sawing. By ten they were in lawn chairs, drinking beer and watching a television set at the door of the shed, their work done for the day. When an attractive woman walked by their heads turned to follow her like baby owls watching a rabbit; they instinctively knew they should do something, they just didn't know what.

"They're going to be here forever at that rate," Phil said.

"Or until they run out of money. Then the yard will auction off whatever it can for the outstanding yard bill."

"Ever wonder if you'd wind up like that?"

"I worried about it some in Marathon. Now I don't think it would be so bad, just a different reality."

For a thousand miles I had been asking for expert opinions about why the boat wouldn't go any faster, entering the mysterious world of propeller pitch: part science and part voodoo. I had gathered a ton of opinion and misinformation, ranging from the diesel salesman's assurance that the engine was too small and should be replaced with a larger one, to the propeller manufacturer's fax-back conclusion that the 16 x 12 propeller had too much pitch and should be re-pitched or replaced with a three-blade prop. The 16 x 12 designation meant that the prop was 16 inches long—the diameter—and that in one complete revolution the angle of the blades would—theoretically—propel the boat 12 inches forward. I hoped the hardworking, no-nonsense tradesmen of Stock Island could provide a consistent answer.

The next morning, precisely at the promised hour, Jeffrey, one of the yard's repair people, came over and pulled the propeller off the shaft with a homemade pulling tool, checked the cutless bearing—the rubber section similar to a piece of hose that steadies the propeller shaft in a strut molded into the bottom of the boat—and declared it sound, and told me the secret of how to put the prop back on when that time came.

"If you don't do it right, you'll shear off the key and the shaft will spin, but not the prop. We see it all the time," Jeff explained. The shaft and the hole in the prop both are grooved, and a slug of metal called the key fits into the grooves. The key locks the two pieces together, preventing the prop from slipping on the spinning shaft, which is slightly tapered to allow the prop to slide into position.

"Get yourself a punch. First clean off the shaft and then slide the prop all the way up the shaft until it's good and tight, but do this without the key in place. Scribe a mark on the shaft at the forward side of the prop to mark the spot. Then put the key in and slide the prop on. Now here's the trick. With the punch or something pointed, make sure the key is riding somewhere in the middle of the prop, not jammed up against the end of the groove on the shaft. Then put on the nuts and tighten them up until the prop is at the mark you scribed. That will make sure there's no slop, no play that can snap off the key."

Prop in hand, we headed for the Island Propeller Shop but came across Boater's Choice, a Yanmar diesel dealer and repair shop directly across from the yard. I told the man in a blue shirt my problem.

"I can't get any more than about 5 knots out of it and then the governor throttles it back down. Hull speed should be about 7.25 knots. I'm on my way to the prop shop now. This fax-back service from the manufacturer says I should go to 16 x 11."

"Does the engine lug down or stall when you hold it at 2600 rpm?"

"No. I can go higher than that, but it smokes a lot."

"Then you don't have enough pitch. You want more, not less. Let me check." He made a phone call and gave someone information from my fax-back form. "Here's what you need: re-pitch to 16 x 13, you could probably go a little higher, and you need a clamp like this to put on your throttle cable so you can run it faster. With this engine you get maximum horsepower at 2,600 rpm. You should be able to run it at about 2,300 with no trouble. Yanmars like to run at higher rpms. We see this all the time, people can't get the power out of engine."

The clip cost $17. I'd never heard it mentioned before in all the conversations I'd had with experts. I bought the clip and we marched on to see a man named Tom Graham at the Island Propeller Shop. Props of all shapes and sizes hung from the walls and the modest garage was set up as a machine shop. I repeated the story. He asked questions similar to the Yanmar dealer's, then punched numbers into a little calculator.

"You should be 16 by 13, maybe a little more."

"I just had this same conversation with the Yanmar dealer to see what he thought."

"What did he say?"

"Same thing."

Tom chuckled, his expert opinion verified. "I don't know about the smoking at higher rpm's though." He made a call, then turned back to me. "When you run at those higher rpms it doesn't mean the engine is wearing out, it's for other reasons. You should be okay. Can you leave the prop for a couple of days? I have to send it to Miami to be re-pitched because my equipment is for one-inch shafts and this one is seven-eights."

"Sure."

Phil had been wandering around the shop and inquired about photos of a prop set up in a sort of tunnel, and the prop wasn't completely in the water. It was one of Tom's inventions. "Some people interested in marketing it are coming down. Who knows, maybe some day I'll make a buck. Boating is one of the most expensive things you can get into, except maybe for airplanes, but it sure doesn't filter down to this end of the business."

We headed back to the boat as the morning sun began to show its strength. Phil, who loves to tinker with technology, liked these gritty, outspoken Stock

Island characters whose heads were crammed with years of useful, tried and true experience. "These guys are amazing; they've seen everything."

"Makes me feel better. This was the first time two people in a row agreed on what needed to be done."

On the way back we reconnoitered for sailors' essentials: the local Maloney Avenue bus stop for transport to downtown Key West; beer from the beverage store across from the bus stop, noting that it sells big blocks of ice; fuel for the alcohol stove at S & V Hardware, a small, shed-like building crammed with boat and hardware items at bargain prices; a quart of Trinidad bottom paint at Standard Marine just down the street, also at less-than-boatyard prices. Stock Island is an oasis of no-nonsense boating competence next to one of the wackiest communities in America. We learned it also has two good, inexpensive restaurants: Chico's Cantina on Route 1 near the turnoff to MacDonald Avenue, and the Fisherman's Platter.

Next we tackled the depth sounder's transducer, which was mounted through the hull in a shaped wooden block bedded with adhesive. We couldn't make it budge with the hand tools on board, so once again Jeffrey came back and cut and banged until the old unit was in pieces, but removed. A woodworker came by, picked up the remnants of the shaped wood block, which was shattered, and came back later with a new one for Jeffrey to install.

On the second day, the new transducer was bedded into place and Nancy arrived with part-time Key West residents Frank and Sylvia Kelly for a walking tour and dinner in Old Key West. "I'll show you one of the best restaurant deals in Key West," Frank promised. A short block northeast of Sloppy Joe's, on Greene Street, a tall sign advertises auto body repair and painting. A smaller sign attached to the same post simply says Thai Cuisine. Frank was right.

Nancy and Phil drove me to Key West Airport to pick up John Dupee. We went on to the Coast Guard station to file a form I had picked up in Marathon, "Acknowledgment of Security Zone and Permit to Depart During a National Emergency." The national emergency is our embargo of Cuba. The form is faxed to Coast Guard headquarters in Miami with copies of passport photos of everyone on board. The Coast Guard people in Marathon asked no questions and didn't blink an eye when I requested the form needed to go to Cuba. They simply want to know who and what is moving around out there in the Straits of Florida. The Straits are also watched electronically by *Fat Albert*, a tethered blimp that flies, weather permitting, above Boca Chica. At Key West, the Coast Guard officer was particularly interested in the Treasury Department license to go to Cuba. I left him copies of the paperwork and the fax number at Peninsular Marine.

Three hours later, Phil and Nancy were headed back to Boca Raton, and John and I were touching up the boat's bottom paint. Tracey, a young woman from the office at Peninsular, arrived with the Coast Guard form, all signed and approved.

"We're good to go, assuming the prop gets back on time. I'll make arrangements to get launched. We don't have a Customs sticker, but I have 48 hours to get that after I get back, and I'll just check in at Key West."

"That was fast," said John.

"Yes, I had figured 16 hours minimum. I guess it's just Treasury that busts your chops on Cuba."

"Just don't try to bring any Cubans back."

Cuba took that seriously, asking for life imprisonment for two Florida residents who had been caught with a half dozen Cubans on board when their boat swamped off Mariel. Cubans were being landed up and down the Keys and in south Florida by smugglers who charge from $1,000 up to $8,000 a head to bring them across in mother ships, then drop them in small boats not far from shore. Given the $10 monthly average income in Cuba, the money usually came from relatives outside of Cuba. If the Cubans reach American soil under their own power they are allowed in under the Cuban Adjustment Act, but if they are picked up at sea, they are sent back to Cuba. Newspapers in the Keys carry accounts of Cubans landing almost weekly, and the smuggling trend was on the rise, the latest growth industry in the Keys' shady history of smuggling. A few Cubans were still trying to make it by raft, despite the risk of being shot, rammed and sunk, or imprisoned for up to eight years by their countrymen . . . not to mention the risk of drowning, death by dehydration, or being picked off by sharks. Little Elián Gonzalez' story had been just one of thousands.

Brothers to the Rescue, *Hermanos al Rescate*, based in Miami, is most famous for having two of its little Cessnas shot down by Cuban jet fighters early in 1996 while flying to Cuba to toss out leaflets. Four people were killed. There have since been claims that CIA operatives were involved in the leaflet mission, and that the flights were being monitored by several U.S. government agencies . . . even though the planes had ostensibly been cleared to go to the Bahamas. The incident triggered passage of the Helms-Burton Act, introduced in 1995, which tightened the U.S. embargo, tried to forbid other nations from trading with Cuba, and shifted fundamental control of foreign policy on Cuba from the President to the Congress.

Brothers to the Rescue was started in 1991 as a sort of Civil Air Patrol of the Florida Straits, with volunteers flying search missions for rafters trying to make it from Cuba, then alerting the Coast Guard. The group claims success in the thousands. In some cases, the Brothers are tipped off by relatives that rafters are on their way. The organization was formed following the death of a 15-year-old rafter. Gregorio Perez Ricardo died of dehydration shortly after being picked out of the water by the Coast Guard, despite attempts to revive him. The Coast Guard estimates that for every Cuban rescued, one is lost at sea.

The rafters, called *balseros*, began to flee Cuba after the Soviet Union collapsed in 1989 and Cuba entered its "Special Period." With $6 billion worth of Soviet aid gone and Panama—a source of Cuban trade—in turmoil with the arrest of General Noriega, basics vanished. People went hungry.

This was almost a decade after the Mariel boatlift in 1980, when Castro finessed the Carter administration's "open arms, open heart" policy by releasing 120,000 Cubans, many of them criminals, dissidents, or mentally ill, to be taken to the U.S. The Key West shrimp fleet, numbering in the hundreds and harbored in the bight during the 1970s, turned to transporting Cubans for up to $2,000 a head, dropping them at a dock at Truman Annex for processing and resettlement in Homestead and Miami. When the administration realized what was going on and called a halt, the shrimpers ignored it. Their boats were impounded and at one time 80 percent of the shrimp fleet was tagged and seized. The impoundment was ruled illegal so the shrimpers picked up their boats and went back to work. But shrimping had become highly competitive and the shrimp were getting harder to find. The remnants of the shrimp fleet moved over to Stock Island.

In 1994, rumors circulated in Cuba that a flotilla of boats was en route from Florida and another major exodus was to be permitted. Crowds gathered on the Malecón, Havana's broad ocean drive overlooking Florida Straits, and clashed with the police. Two were killed. Castro declared that, if the U.S. would not live up to past agreements on legal immigration, he would not stop the Cubans from leaving. He lifted the requirement for exit permits, and thousands fled on dangerously flimsy rafts. In the next three weeks more than 20,000 Cuban rafters were rescued at sea and transported to the U.S. Naval Base at Guantánamo Bay, a U.S. enclave on Cuban soil secured in perpetual lease after the Spanish American War. By September, another 12,000 had been picked up. The U.S. and Cuba negotiated an immigration policy that allowed Cubans to stay if they reached U.S. soil, but provided that Cuba would take back those intercepted at sea. Cuba, however, began refusing to take them back. Those were busy times for Brothers to the Rescue, but things had slowed down by the time the leaflet flights began. Fidel's "let 'em leave" policy was also a thing of the past.

"I've thought about what I might do if we come across a raft full of Cubans getting smacked around out there in the Gulf Stream."

John raised an eyebrow. "And?"

"Save any lives at risk and get on the radio to the Coast Guard."

"My son is in the Coast Guard," John said. "He used to say that if they didn't like Castro, why didn't they just have a revolution and get rid of him. Then he was on a boat that picked up some rafters. There was a 13-year-old girl on board, and he said when he saw the terror in her eyes he changed his mind about the Cubans."

"The idea of having my boat full of terrified, desperate people and being caught between two governments sounds like a nightmare. When we get to thirty miles or so out there we won't be in radio range, unless somebody is on patrol. It's not a perfect plan."

I checked the radio forecast and it was good. We would leave tomorrow. I went to the office to make arrangements to be launched.

"You'll come back and tell me how it is, won't you?" asked Tracey as I paid my boatyard bill the next morning.

"I will if I come back this way."

"We really want to go to Cuba. So come back and tell us. I'll take you diving."

Tracey was a certified scuba diver and a nurturer. She told me how she had rescued a five-foot nurse shark that had been hooked by a fisherman, who left eight feet of line on when he cut it loose, only to have it tangle in coral and trap the shark. Tracy had cut the line at the shark's mouth to set it free. "You know, it was just a nurse shark, but I was scared." Tracy had also offered to let me use her motor scooter to run my propeller to the prop shop.

"Are you headed for Cuba?" asked a man who had been browsing the marine supplies. I nodded. "Marina Hemingway?"

"Yes."

"I have a friend there at the marina, a nice kid who worked on our boat when we were there. I have some things I'd like to get to him, medicine, a few things. He has a sick kid. Would you take it? I'll show you what it is, it's nothing illegal."

"Bring it over. The boat is right behind the building, DREAM WEAVER. But they're going to launch us in about a half an hour, so we'll be over in the launch bay."

It was 10:30 on the last Saturday in February, and the marina closed at noon on Saturdays. I had asked for a spot on the face dock to tie up for a while so we could make sure everything was tight. We had temporarily removed the knotmeter to make working room to replace the transducer. Both, of course, are plugged into large holes below the waterline—large enough to allow 80 gallons of water or more per minute to pour into the hull if they fail. I wanted to make sure they were tight, and I wanted to be sure we had done the right thing to the propeller. I did not want to head across the Gulf Stream without knowing if I had a working engine and prop combination. I had been uneasy about the Gulf Stream crossing from the very beginning of this trip. It can be a very rough, very wet ride that takes a toll on equipment and crew.

Harry Morgan, the doomed smuggler, had said it in Hemingway's *To Have and Have Not*: "Brother, don't let anybody tell you there isn't plenty of water between Havana and Key West. I was just on the edge of it."

As I paid the bill another boat, ROSINANTE, radioed in also looking for space at the crowded dock. It was resolved by having DREAM WEAVER stay in the launch bay, since I would be the last boat launched for the weekend, and ROSINANTE would head for the face dock.

Things were moving quickly now. We calculated that we were about 110 miles from Marina Hemingway if we did not head straight down, but instead put in some miles to the west toward the Marquesas Keys, so that we would not be cutting diagonally into the flow of the Stream, but instead cut it at right angles. Depending upon what we ran into, the sail would last 20 to 24 hours if we averaged five knots. We wanted to arrive in daylight, with plenty of elbow room in case something went wrong. The approach to Marina Hemingway is marked by a sea buoy hard to spot against the shoreline and lights. The bottom rises swiftly on the approach, from thousands of feet to less than 100. We then had to pass between two lighted posts that sat on a gap in a reef just a short distance beyond the sea buoy. Not much room for error. John and I poured over the charts, plotted a course, and set a departure time for 2 p.m. While I was inside, he programmed the buoys and markers on our course into his Global Satellite Positioning unit. My GPS had been carrying coordinates for the Marina Hemingway sea buoy in its memory for the past six months.

I re-checked the weather forecast. We had a perfect weather window for crossing to Cuba. A weak cold front had passed through, bringing us a few chilly nights, but now we were at the point where the winds had diminished from the north and northeast and the prevailing easterlies were again taking over. The forecast was for southeast winds around 10 miles an hour building to 10 to 15 and then clocking to the southwest before another weak cold front came through, which would send the winds back into the north. North winds collide with the northeasterly flowing Gulf Stream, creating rough conditions. Some sailors describe the waves as "square" or "elephants", the kind that give you a pounding. But by the time the weather shifted, we would be in Cuba.

"We'll go," I said to John, "it's the same."

We cleaned the boat, tanked up on fresh water, and walked down Maloney Street to the convenience store for a few last-minute provisions and basic gift items for the Cubans. Mark, the carpenter who wanted us to bring something to his friend in Cuba, picked us up after doing his shopping and drove us back to the marina with a 25-pound block of ice from the convenience store stashed in our soft California cooler.

We sat in DREAM WEAVER's cockpit and went through the items we were carrying for him. He had left them unwrapped in a box that also contained wrapping paper with an address on it. Aspirin, a tube of neosporin, cough and cold medicine, tampons, soap, shampoo, a baseball hat that said Peninsular Marine on it.

"His son has some kind of allergies, can't sleep at night. And the Cubans love anything with an American logo on it. His name is Johnnie. Just ask around the marina, everybody knows him. He's a great kid, speaks perfect English. Give him our best, from me and my wife." He gave me his business card; he was a cabinet-maker from Key West.

The skipper of ROSINANTE had picked up on the conversation.

"You're going to love Cuba, man. We'll be there in a few days ourselves, me and Charlie. My name's Tomás." Introductions. Charlie was crew. "My first time there was in '96, I think; that's when I had my first Cuban wife." Tomás was about 40, weathered, happy.

"You got married in Cuba?"

He laughed. "No, man, it's not like that kind of wife. They're just with you, you know, while you're there. You meet the family, you take them dancing, you take them to dinner—they eat like a horse—they live on the boat with you. You are the ticket to all the things they can't get. You are *The Man*. You take care of them, they take care of you."

I was skeptical. "Where do you find them?"

"Different places. The *jineteras*, the prostitutes, will walk right down the dock at the marina. You'll hear a knock on the hull. Want to party? Like me? Like my friend? Then there are just normal girls you meet out dancing, or on the street. The *jineteras* also hang around the discos and the beaches east of Havana. *Jinetera* is the feminine version of the Spanish word for jockey. Makes quite an image, doesn't it? The Cubans have a sense of humor. The other ones are just regular girls. You go meet their family, take a few presents. How's your Spanish?"

"Pretty weak."

"Too bad. Work on it. The Cubans are great, man, friendly, generous. If they have something, they'll share it with you. They expect you to do the same, so don't be surprised if they ask for something and just take off with it. But they love life, they love to dance, they love their families, very strong families. If you have good Spanish you can practically be one of the family."

"Then how would they let a daughter go off to live with an American?"

"You must show that you will treat her well, with respect. Not like the Italians. The Italians have a reputation for being bastards with the women, abusing them. But, you know, their daughter having *something* is better than their daughter having *nothing*."

"It's the American dollar, then."

"Well, that's part of it, but not all. They like Americans. Everybody in Cuba seems to have a relative in the U.S. who is doing well. It's the dream. Like Mark says, they like American stuff, anything with an American logo on it. They don't expect you to marry their daughter and take her out of Cuba. They might wish for that, but they don't expect it. It's understood that you will leave, but believe me you will hate to leave. Cuban women are something. Cubans are great. They're smart, they're educated, they're funny . . . and most of them have nothing. The government sucks, but Cubans are great. Work on your Spanish. I have to get to work on my boat."

He started for his boat and then turned around. "You guys aren't married, are you?"

I looked at John and chuckled. It was Key West, after all. "Not to each other."

Tomás went back to his boat. The solar panels, the wind generator, the jerry cans, and the cluttered but organized anchors and lines on deck pegged him as a serious cruiser or liveaboard. The boat was registered in Key West.

We checked the through-hull fittings for leaks and backed out of the launch bay.

"It backs, good sign." I said, easing it into forward gear. "It goes forward."

We kept going forward out of the marina, past Key West, and another five hours across the shipping channels toward the Marquesas Keys.

"So far," said John after we passed the shipping channels, "this is pretty much as advertised." The sun shone, the breeze held at about 10 knots. Small, unpopulated Keys passed by to starboard.

As Key West fell behind us I had the nagging realization that John would leave in Cuba and no one had agreed to crew on the return trip. John had said that another yacht club member was interested, and I made a call to Fritz Horton just as we sailed out of cell phone range. He did sound interested.

We headed for the light at Cosgrove Shoal, dodging

crab trap floats. "Is this the first ocean trip you've made since Mitch?"

"Yes." John had been on board SEA SHELL on the Caribbean 1500, running first into a big storm and then Hurricane Mitch after receiving a weather forecast that said there were no significant weather events in the area.

"How do you feel about it?"

"I think you could go out a hundred times and not have something like that happen again."

"Did you ever doubt that you were going to make it through?"

He thought for a moment. "I've never seen anything like it. Seventy foot waves. At one point the fish were jumping out of the water on the leeward side and they were blown over on their backs before they hit the water. I've been out when it's rough and my wife will ask me if we're going to be all right, and I always say: sure, no problem. On that trip, though, I would have said: I'll have to get back to you on that one. Bob Lyman was great. He was singing these crazy little songs. We had an experienced crew. It was eighteen hours of hell." One of the other members of that crew had popped a hernia during the storm, but was healing up and was headed back to Antigua to help bring SEA SHELL north.

The last hint of land, the fading white shape of a cruise ship docked at Key West, had fallen below the horizon an hour ago. The navigation aid at Cosgrove Shoal was a quarter mile ahead of us and we were racing into the setting sun to round it with enough remaining light to dodge the crab trap floats that appeared every few yards, waiting patiently to snag themselves on a careless sailor's propeller. The idea of going over the side in these three-foot waves in the dark with a saw-toothed knife to get a tangled line off the propeller was not at all appealing. Once past the light we would turn almost due south into the Gulf Stream and the depth immediately plunged to hundreds, then thousands of feet. The next approach to land was the narrow passage through the reef, then a marina landing. We needed the engine.

John turned to me with a grin. "You know, of course, when you sail a small boat into the Gulf Stream you immediately go to the bottom of the food chain."

"Thanks for reminding me. Anything else?"

John lit a cigar. "The Stream is blue, a deep blue like you've never seen. It is like sailing across an inkwell." It was dark by the time we turned south into the Gulf Stream, so I would have to wait and see about the inkwell blue. Now, with the wind abeam instead of behind, it felt breezier and bumpier, but we had no problem carrying a full main and genoa.

"Let's do two hours on, two off. I'll take the next two. Get some rest." An ivory moon, not quite full, provided comforting light. We had no navigation aids to watch for; we just had to keep our bearing of 189 degrees into the Stream and check the horizon all around from time to time for shipping. I assumed that any shipping would be going north, riding the Stream. These could be busy waters, full of pleasure cruise ships. The silhouette of a large ship came up on the horizon over the port quarter and I studied its lights, finally realizing that the red port light was, unlike in sailboats, near the stern and it would pass behind us. I settled into a comfortable corner of the cockpit and smiled. It was a beautiful sail, even if the occasional wave sent a splash of spray into my face.

On my second watch, starting at midnight, the wind piped up to 15 plus, the waves built to about five feet and books began flying around the cabin. I furled the genoa a few turns, but so far it had not been as rough as I expected. At the end of my watches I plotted our course on the chart that was spread out over the dining table, held down by shock cord. We were doing fine.

It was ten minutes before four in the morning, time to relieve John at the helm. This would be the day. Only 30 more miles of Gulf Stream separated us from Cuba. I could see the gray outlines of the portholes in the moonlight, but nothing else. I stretched out in the V-berth and listened carefully. Living on a boat is like living inside a musical instrument and you quickly learn to pick out discordant sounds. When the wind blows at 11 knots, the yacht club burgee flaps at a frequency that sets off a rattling sound where the halyard is attached to a shackle at the toe rail. At 16 knots the main halyard starts a metallic thumping against the mast and the rigging sets the wind to whining. At sea, there is a small creaking in the wooden panels over the berth as the hull flexes through the waves. Waves slapped and pounded next to my head; less than half of an inch of fiberglass separated us. The sounds told me the wind was between 12 and 15 knots, the waves three to four feet. It was settling down a little, and now the flapping of the jib hinted that the wind was clocking from southeast to south. If forecasts were correct the wind would keep clocking on to the southwest, then to the west and finally to north. We wanted to be safely in before the norther arrived.

As I worked my way back through the cabin to relieve John, my hand brushed across the chart of the Florida Straits and came away wet. Spray had found its way in through the overhead hatch, so I closed it. At least the spray we took in the face in the cockpit from time to time was warm, not like New England sailing.

"Pretty quiet out here," John said. "There are some lights off to the east, but they don't seem to be moving; at least they're not closing with us. There's a cruise boat over there looking like a Christmas tree, but they'll pass behind us. It seems to me that from the time you first see shipping until the time you hit it, or miss it, you have about an hour to figure out what to do. It's all yours."

It was chilly and I put on the foul-weather jacket I had brought. Our speed had dropped to about four and a half knots.

The moon was now heading for the western horizon and had changed color from ivory to butter. Less than two hours later it looked dusty in the sea mist on the horizon, became the color of a marigold and dropped into the sea, a moonset to remember. It was a clear night, with the Southern Cross above the mast to starboard, but soon the stars began to fade and the first hints of gray, then peach and indigo defined the eastern horizon.

As the morning blossomed our speed continued to drop and we began motorsailing, engaged the Auto-helm, and had breakfast. Finally the wind came around, blew lightly over the bow, and I took in the sails. Our newly pitched propeller was doing nicely, holding us above five knots into the breeze. Now in Cuban waters, I went forward to raise the yellow quarantine flag and the Cuban courtesy flag, being careful that the single point on the star pointed upward, and we were not flying it upside down, a declaration of war. A huge ship, its square profile looking more like a skyscraper than a ship, headed in our direction from the portside, but would pass behind us. Another appeared in the morning mist to starboard, then another and another. They were not ships, I realized, it was the skyline of Havana.

Two hours later we spotted the tower on top of the Old Man and the Sea hotel, flanked by a water tower shaped like a flying saucer. The hotel is at the east end of Marina Hemingway. I went forward with the binoculars and John set a GPS course toward the sea buoy, which finally appeared against a strip of light-colored beach west of a line of condominiums. We left the buoy to port, spotted the two navigation aids marking the pass through the reef, and began to pull out dock lines and fenders.

"Well, I wonder what happens now." I said.

"Did you tell Fidel we were coming?"

"He said he had a surprise for us."

Suddenly a high-speed powerboat roared toward us out of the marina entrance. We strained to see its markings, or to spot fatigue uniforms and automatic weapons, but its bow was riding too high to see much of anything. It was coming closer, but not slowing. The boat roared past and we could see it was pulling four water skiers. They laughed and waved and pointed at our American flag.

A small guard house was on the wall to port. As we pulled near, the man in the military uniform waved us on, and gestured that we were to make a hard left at the end of the channel. Another sailboat and a catamaran were tied to the wall near an open pavilion, where people in various uniforms came and went. We found an open spot and docked.

I went below to set out a plate of Chips Ahoy cookies. We had put beer and Coca-Cola on ice, planning to make this as pleasant as possible. I dug out the paperwork I had prepared in advance at the suggestion of Nigel Calder's *Cruising Guide to Cuba*: a list of people on board and their position, details on the boat's size, registration, construction and engine, along with similar information on the dinghy.

First on board was Dr. Umberto, who had good English, and wore a white doctor's smock. This was the health inspection. When he had settled down with his paperwork, we offered him a Coke and cookies.

"I am diabetic," he said, "and cannot have the sweets. I can, however, have vodka, rum or scotch." John was shaking with silent laughter as I broke out the last bottle of Absolut that had come down from Vermont.

The doctor filled out the paperwork and told us how things were. Once it was good to be a doctor in Cuba, but now they can only diagnose but have no medicines to treat the ailments. He made $20 a month. It was too bad about the embargo, but he did not blame the American people. "In my heart, I like the North Americans best," he said, lamenting that the governments could not get along. He asked if we were bringing gifts of medicine for Cubans. A few, we said. Next time bring much more, he advised, particularly the medicinal ointments. He looked into our toilet and cautioned about letting mosquitoes breed there, then asked if we had a holding tank, completed his paperwork, and had another drink. He was liking Americans more by the minute. Eventually he left.

A parade of officials began, most of them asking the same questions, writing on forms interleaved with carbon paper. The answers were covered on the sheet I had prepared. The agriculture people were interested in our garbage, and any fresh meats and vegetables we brought in. They accepted Cokes, and asked if it was all right if they didn't drink them now, but brought them home to their kids.

The Ministry of the Interior official was interested

Clearing Cuban Customs. These customs officials were polite and friendly as they asked their questions and conducted a brief search of DREAM WEAVER.

in filling out forms, and inquired politely as to whether or not we wanted our passports stamped. The Cubans understand that a Cuban passport stamp can complicate the life of a visitor who plans to leave no evidence that he has been on the island, screening the visit behind passages to or from Canada, Mexico or the Bahamas. We said no to the passport stamp, and he merely stamped an innocuous number. Next, three gregarious Customs officials conducted a quick search of the boat, asking if we were bringing any gifts for Cubans. I hesitated a moment and said "Yes, we have medicines from someone for a friend here, and we have soaps and shampoos to give to people. They are in the hanging locker."

An official glanced in the direction of the hanging locker. "Anything else?"

"No, that's it." He never checked.

They inventoried equipment like VHF radios, tele-

vision sets, stereos and radios, bicycles, GPS units . . .
anything likely to be brought in for sale or trade.

Finally two stern-faced members of the *Guardia
Frontera*, the Coast Guard, boarded. "Do you have any
guns on board?" asked the larger one with the thick
moustache. From what I had read, the *Guardia Frontera*
was the group responsible for the security of the bor-
ders, and they were not to be taken lightly.

"Only a flare gun, for emergencies." I pointed to the
orange canister full of flares and the plastic pistol. He
shook his head, he was not interested. After the paperwork was done he asked again whether we had guns
aboard, and hit us up for an unrecorded audio cassette.

As they climbed out of the cabin he turned and
asked one last time, "No guns on board?" I shook my
head.

Each boarding party had left us with a form or two.
We had been at it for more than two hours. "I think
we're done."

Right on cue, the doctor came aboard to direct our
ride over to the dock space we had been assigned. "You
will get your visas when you register at the marina
office."

The marina issues visas, not the government? Then
it dawned on me that the marina is the government. In
Cuba, everything is run by the government.

Marina Hemingway's entrance from the sea button-
hooks around to the check-in point, then turns back toward the sea and opens into four long, narrow channels
that run parallel to the sea. The channels have been
blasted out of the coral, and at the far end have culverts
connecting them to the sea to allow the water to circulate.

We docked DREAM WEAVER near a string of bright
yellow condos that showed no signs of life. A big cruiser

Marina Hemingway. Four long, narrow channels hold hundreds of boats. The marina has a hotel, several restaurants, a large swimming pool, condominiums, shops, and 24-hour security guards.

out of Halifax, Nova Scotia was tied up ahead of us. A stone's throw away a sparkling blue swimming pool beckoned me to go in and shed the sweat and salt spray. We had left Stock Island 25 hours ago and were gliding along on adrenaline and euphoria at having crossed the Gulf Stream, reached the forbidden island, and found it friendly. Behind us, swooshing down the canal was a scull propelled by two attractive brown young women in tank tops. They smiled, not missing a stroke, as we waved at them. Maybe only Fidel wore fatigues.

"Rum and cigar expedition?" I suggested.

"Definitely," John agreed.

A road runs the length of each channel. Between Channels 2, 3 and 4, the Cubans have developed the Garden of Eden hotel, restaurants and condominiums. Channel 1 has remained undeveloped except for the far western end, where Papa's disco and tennis courts are located next to the showers, laundry and rest rooms just a few steps away from the marina offices and a commissary. A fuel dock is between Channels 2 and 3.

The eastern end is more developed. A guarded gate faces Avenida 5, the highway into Havana, and along the road at the end of the channels are three restaurants, a post office and telephone center, the marina's yacht club, Club Nautico, and a complex that includes a small supermarket, a cigar store, a shop selling apparel, sports equipment and appliances, a T-shirt shop, a music shop and finally, at the sea, The Old Man and the Sea hotel.

Marina Hemingway is a guarded gate resort community.

4 | *Marina Hemingway*

John and I explored our way to the marina office to check in and pick up our visas for $15 each, paid a visit to the shops at the end of the canal, and returned with some four-year-old Havana Club rum, a bottle of Cuban whiskey, mixers, snacks and a few *Romeo y Julieta* cigars. We made drinks and headed for the pool and our first encounter with cigar hustlers.

A lithe, mocha-colored young woman dangling her legs in the pool eyed my plastic Sloppy Joe's-Key West commuter mug and said something to her chubby young companion. When I climbed out of the pool he approached.

"You like cigars? I can get you a good price on Cohibas. My brother works in the factory." Although not everyone prefers them, Cohibas are supposed to be the Mercedes of Cuban cigars.

"I don't smoke them, but maybe my friend would be interested."

John was suspicious but curious. The young man led us to his car where he produced an authentic-looking Cohiba box full of cigars in Cohiba labels. He offered them for $125, but came down to $100 after a modest amount of quibbling.

John said, "If you let me take one tonight and I like it, I'll talk to you tomorrow." The lad wanted a sale now, but reluctantly agreed to let John have a trial cigar, and they set up a meeting for the same place at 9:30 the next day.

John tried the cigar that night, and although it did a first class job of keeping mosquitoes out of the boat, it was no Cohiba. Lighting it once again, he commented, "I'm getting a hernia sucking on this thing to keep it lit."

John Dupee smoking a Cuban cigar.

Security guards patrol the docks 24 hours to prevent thefts, keep an eye on things, and particularly to keep Cubans off foreign boats, with exceptions that exist in some unwritten code. After dark one of the young guards—a Tom Cruise look-alike—stopped in to meet the new boat on the block and we invited him on board for a chat and a glass of rum. He was a fountain of local knowledge.

Best local beers: Cristal and Buccaneer dark.

Best rum: seven year old Havana Club, although there was some old Havana Club that was so good Cubans can't afford it: Havana Club Gran Reserva, 15-year-old and $80 a bottle: four months salary for the diabetic doctor.

Cuban pay: He said he made $30 a month—more than a doctor?

Cigar hustlers: Black market boxes and wrappers, bad bootleg cigars from Mexico and Jamaica or the sweepings of Cuban cigar factories.

Best place to buy cigars: Old Havana, on Mercaderes Street between Obispo and Obrapia, the House of Cigars. You could be sure of what you were getting; the prices were fair. It was a little museum devoted to cigar lore.

Best way to get to the House of Cigars: My cousin, who has a car, but I will need $10 so he can buy gas. I can have him pick you up outside the gate, down the block, tomorrow at ten.

Cuban women: Fantastic, but no longer allowed on boats in the marina. There was a hint that a way around that might be found.

The guard was joined by his boss. The boss liked to talk about Cuban women and make suggestive hand patterns in his lap, putting together his thumbs and then touching his fingertips together. Apparently it was not a conflict of job responsibilities to get drunk with Americans on their boats. Finally they staggered off down the dock.

We crawled into our bunks and crashed into sleep, exhausted and rum mellow . . . for about 20 minutes. Then the cigar smoke cleared out and mosquitoes poured in through the open hatches and companionway, driving us under the sheets to spend the rest of the night slapping and cursing.

The next morning we had breakfast at the Boise cafeteria by the pool—named for a favorite Hemingway cat. The marina's businesses are named after vague Hemingway connections: The Garden of Eden hotel, after a posthumously published novel, the Masai restaurant after the safari books, and some I couldn't connect.

The cigar hustlers did not show up at 9:30. We walked to the gate and down the block for the 10 a.m. ride to the cigar store. The car never showed up. We never saw the guard or his boss again, and certainly would never see the $10 again. We were getting valuable lessons in Cuban dealings: don't give money in advance, and if it's beyond an hour from now, don't count on it.

By late morning, after checking flights schedules with the concierge at The Old Man and the Sea hotel, John had packed up and headed to the airport for the vacation in Puerto Rico. His flight would take him to Costa Rica and Venezuela before Puerto Rico. I was disappointed he would not have more time to explore Havana with me and did not get to the House of Cigars.

I returned to the boat, which again felt empty, turned on the portable radio and briefly picked up a station in the Keys, but it faded away. I dialed around and found several Spanish language stations but no one was speaking at the one-word-a-minute pace that I could comprehend. A squealing electronic stutter at the high end of the dial was, I assumed, Radio Martí, the Washington-conceived and Cuba-jammed broadcast that was supposed to be propagandizing Cuba except nobody could receive it. I tuned the VHF radio to Channel 72, the marina's hailing channel, while I cleaned up. A distant voice crackled out of the radio: "Marina Hemingway, Marina Hemingway, this is the sailing vessel WIND LINE."

"This is Marina Hemingway."

"We're about six miles out. We'll be coming into the marina."

"Thank you, we'll be expecting you."

"Thank you, WIND LINE out."

So the lads from Marathon had made it after all. I wondered where they had gone in between. Almost four hours later there was a lot of shouting when they saw me waving to them from the dock. They pulled into a slot on the dock two boats ahead of me. Soon after, ROSINANTE showed up and tied up ahead of WIND LINE. The *pepes* were gathering. In Mexico, we may still be *gringos*, but in Cuba foreigners are *pepes*.

Rubén, Prince of Darkness

Rubén, the marina electrician, came around to hook up my shore power the next morning. Rubén is a pleasant, smiling, handsome man with an ancient voltmeter and a screwdriver. In his white uniform shirt with gold piping he looked more like the purser on the *Love Boat* than an electrician, and perhaps that should have been a warning. The face docks along Channel 2 have utility kiosks that house electrical and water hookups, but the marina was designed for big boats so all the power is 220 volts. The principal role in life of the marina electrician is to step this down to 110 volts by hooking a wire into one side of the marina's 220 sockets, poking it into your shore power cord, hooking up a ground and wrapping the whole thing up in a wad of plastic bag and electrical tape. To my surprise, he actually did turn the power off before attempting this maneuver.

In some yet-to-be completed sections of the marina a large black electrical cable stretches down the dock and is tapped in much the same way. Boat boys go into the water in diving gear to clean boat bottoms, but why they aren't electrocuted is a mystery. In fact, the Marina Hemingway wiring system figures prominently into a mysterious death in Martin Cruz Smith's novel *Havana Bay*, featuring the same Russian detective who was the protagonist in *Gorky Park*.

Rubén finished his work, left, and my battery charger promptly fried. It was an old automotive battery charger that had not been called on to do very much in the dozen years I had owned the boat, but its sudden death made me curious so I probed the incoming power with a multi-meter a couple of times over the next few days and found it to be a fairly constant 137 volts, dropping from time to time to 134 volts. The powerboaters plugged in with no apparent problems, but the experienced sailors were suspicious of the whole thing, from polarity to grounding to frequency, which is 60Hz in Cuba.

Tomás and Charlie were walking with me to the post office when we found the concrete lid off one of the concrete foxholes that provide access to the marina's electrical system. It was full of water, beer cans and a jumble of big cables wrapped up with black plastic tape. Tomás peered into the hole. "Scary, isn't it. I'm never plugging in here. Let the windcharger and solar handle it."

Cheap Rum, Expensive Onions

Cuba is no bargain. Restaurant and hotel prices are comparable to those in a large U.S. city. With U.S. dollars, anything is possible. To my surprise, the Marina Hemingway supermarket between Channels 1 and 2 is well stocked. Meat, juices and milk are available, with cold cuts and cheeses usually originating in Canada and the juices in Argentina or Cuba. One surprise was the lack of fresh vegetables. An onion costs $1 when available, and produce like onions and peppers are sold in plastic-wrapped six-packs, looking exhausted. Heads of cabbage wrapped in plastic go boldly on forever, but little else is available and soon I would have killed for broccoli. The answer was to find a farmers' market; the obstacles were transportation and the language. The best bet was to make a deal with a driver for an hour or two and go to one of the two nearby supermarkets and a farmers' market. The driver was willing to buy for me in pesos instead of dollars, a huge saving.

The marina also has a friendly ship chandlery that delivers everything from ice to French and Italian wines within a few minutes of a call on Channel 77. Liquors are not taxed, so a bottle of seven-year-old Havana Club rum was $6.60, Cutty Sark $8.60 and Stolichnaya vodka $7.90. A case of Cristal beer is $12. A can of sliced pineapple is $6.80. The chandlery also carries meats and cheeses. A price list is included with the marina information package, usually provided by Isadora, the public relations person, who speaks English and will send and receive faxes for boaters.

The Lobster Man

The characters who inhabit the marina soon become familiar faces, and they are quite a collection. The purveyor of lobster tails is a slim but muscular 50-year-old man named Carlos who works on the boats and is one of the most resourceful and honest of the dock denizens. He pedals down the dock with his tools in a wire basket on the handlebars of his bicycle, circa 1953. He will clean your boat, redo the varnish and perform other tasks, but he is also a sort of Cuban back-to-the land survivalist. He has chickens, rabbits and a garden at his home near Santa Fe, and takes orders for excellent lobster tails for about $2 each. He swims out into the reefs with a snare on the end of a rod, spots the lobsters' antennae sticking out from under a ledge or rock, and snares them. On our first transaction he reluctantly brought just one, but it was not much trouble for him because the three guys on WIND LINE had ordered two each. The next time I ordered two, but a half hour later he was back with three and I was expected to buy them all because that was how many he had to sell that day, so I did.

He speaks little English, but one morning he stopped to talk. With some difficulty I understood he wanted to borrow a small brush for a boat-cleaning project. I showed him what I had—explained my best boat brush had gone overboard—and he selected a small wire brush from the galley. I assumed that would be the last I saw of it; if you have, you give, it is expected. I left the boat for a few hours and returned to find my brush and a replacement for the one that had gone overboard.

Carlos seemed to be a man who had things under control, but he did have one little problem that he told to the crew from WIND LINE when they went to his house for dinner one night. He had a much younger wife who was very demanding, and he was thinking about getting rid of her and finding an older one who would be a better companion and demand less attention. Even in Cuba, high maintenance people have problems in relationships. His other little problem is that shellfish are protected, and only the government is supposed to deal in them.

Don't Leave Home Without It

Paper and toilet paper are in short supply, and the wise traveler out and about in Cuba will carry a supply of toilet paper in a plastic sandwich bag. This does not only apply to the back country. Jo-Ann Ramsey of Mahone Bay, Nova Scotia, was crewing on the big boat ahead of me, and we were bouncing along in the VW bus returning to the marina from Havana, where she and the daughter of the boat's owner had been to see *Carmen* at the National Theater. Earlier in their visit they had been to the famous floor show at the Tropicana; big hats, little costumes.

"How was it?"

"Expensive. It cost about $65 for the show and one drink, and when I went to the bathroom they tried to charge me $1 for the toilet paper. But the show was good."

The marina also has a 24-hour medical aid station and pharmacy in the hotel complex, and they responded quickly on the one occasion when I saw them in action. An elderly French tourist collapsed near the pool. I ran over to alert Chéla, the hostess for poolside entertainment, pointed out the cluster of people who had gathered around the woman, then ran to DREAM WEAVER for the first aid kit and a cold wet towel. The woman on the ground had been done in by the heat, and had cut herself falling. The medical folks had already taken her into their care by the time I returned, and she was gone. Cuba is world famous for its advanced orthopedic medicine, and people come from everywhere for complicated joint surgery. For most Cubans, however, it is tough to get a bottle of aspirin.

"In Cuba, this is new."

The Cubans have a good news/bad news joke: "The good news is we have excellent health care, education and sports teams. The bad news is we have no breakfast, lunch or dinner."

Cuba would be a wonderful place to send the disaffected, Gothic youngsters who mope around on the streets of comfortable middle class communities, the next best thing to having them drafted. Cubans have to hustle every day to survive.

Nowhere is Cuban ingenuity more challenged than in the maintenance of motor vehicles, many of them American cars brought in before the revolution. Some new Mercedes and Mitsubishis cruise the streets, along with rattling Russian Ladas, but there is a huge fleet of old Ford Fairlanes, slab-sided 1957 Chevrolets, even vehicles like the first one I recall in our family, a 1940 Plymouth making its war-year rounds on ration stamps. These American cars run now on hybrid parts, many of them Russian, and when it comes to keeping the vehicles moving the Cubans excel.

Kodiak's little folding boat bicycle with 20-inch wheels had blown out a tube and tire on one of his extended solo ramblings into Havana. He had searched all day for a replacement, but inner tubes and tires are precious commodities in Cuba and only boat people have bikes with undersized tires. He was trying to patch it with some gasket material I had found in my clutter box, but it would not hold.

"You know, I just remembered something," I said. "Paul on that big Irwin has a bike on board. Maybe he has spares."

Kodiak left and returned a few minutes later with a new tire and a new tube, a fact which immediately attracted the attention of one of the boat boys, who strolled over, and a security guard named Hermes, a pleasant young man who loved music and played the guitar.

"What are you going to do with the old inner tube?" Hermes asked.

"It's shot," said Kodiak, holding up the tube and poking his finger into a hole the size of a nickel.

"Can I have it?" Hermes asked.

"Sure, I guess so."

Hermes carefully inspected the tube. "In Cuba, this is new."

The boat boy nodded, smiled and lifted the tube out of Hermes hand, sending a flash of nervous surprise across his face. "Let me show you." He found a pair of scissors among the tools on the ground and cut the tube in two places, eliminating the blown out spot. He folded one end back about two inches to reveal the inner surface. "You put cement here where it's folded back, and here on the other side." He slipped the cut end into the folded back end and then pushed the fold out so that the inside and outside cemented patches met. "It's about two inches shorter now, but that doesn't matter. On my motorcycle I have tractor inner tubes cut up and put together this way. They will never blow out."

Hermes looked relieved when the boat boy handed back the inner tube. I wondered how a boat boy could snatch something away from a security guard with such impunity. By what secret rationale were some people given free access to everything in the marina, while others could not get in through the front gate?

A Different Dream

A young Cuban in T-shirt and shorts pulled his bicycle to a halt on the concrete next to DREAM WEAVER as I was cleaning up the breakfast dishes.

"Good morning. You must have just come in, I haven't seen you here before."

He was a pleasant, smiling, handsome lad who reminded me of one of my son's best friends. His English was good. His name was Cristóbal.

"I came in two days ago."

He studied my teak coamings, which were badly in need of refinishing.

"I could varnish your teak for you." He sized up the teak trim. "About two days. Strip it all down, re-varnish."

"I use Cetol."

He nodded. "Three coats. Do you have Cetol with you?"

"Yes. How much would it cost?"

"A hundred and fifty dollars."

I would do somebody else's teak for a hundred and fifty dollars.

"No, I'll wait until I get back to the States."

He negotiated some, but could see it was not going to work.

"Have you been to Cuba before?"

"No."

"How do you like it?"

We talked of Havana and the conversation got around to Hemingway and El Floridita restaurant. Students in Cuba have read Hemingway's works as part of their curriculum, so everyone knows Hemingway.

"My grandfather was a bartender at El Floridita. We have pictures. He told me of serving Hemingway his daiquiris. He came in a Chrysler convertible late in the morning, had a few daiquiris, and then he would be back late in the afternoon for more. His record was 12 daiquiris."

I brought out my Hemingway books with pictures of El Floridita in the old days. We spread them out on the concrete and on hands and knees we looked for his grandfather's picture but did not find him.

"Would you like to see the pictures from my grandfather?"

"Yes, very much."

"I will bring them if he lets me. When he worked there, El Floridita was much more profitable, it made a lot of money." A dark expression like a cloud passed across his face. "Since the revolution we have a different dream."

At the time of the revolution, the United States had more money invested in Cuba—sugar, mining, utilities, banking, manufacturing—than in any other Latin American country except Venezuela. The U.S. received two thirds of Cuba's exports and provided three quarters of its imports. But with the revolution, relations were shaky from the start, in part because of U.S. support for Batista—which in fact ended before the revolution when the U.S. saw Cuba sliding into chaos. The U.S. ambassador intervened and asked Batista to resign in favor of a new government, in part to deny Castro's rise to leadership by providing a moderate government that would defuse the revolution. Batista was promised safe haven in the United States. He refused.

On January 8, 1959, a triumphant, 32-year-old Fidel Castro arrived in Havana a week after Batista fled. By June, Che Guevara had been in touch with the Soviet Union and gradually relations blossomed. Beginning in July 1960, U.S. property in Cuba was expropriated. First the farms and industries were seized, by September the banks were confiscated, and in October wholesale and retail establishments followed. In October, the Castro government began expropriating Cuban businesses, too, including all the sugar mills, banks, large industries and major wholesale and retail enterprises. Management was turned over to faithful revolutionaries, no matter how incompetent they might be as business people. Full employment was achieved by giving nearly everybody a government job. Productivity plummeted.

Many of Castro's comrades-in-arms in the revolution were stunned by the new communist agenda and left, some of them forming a government in exile in the United States. Of 21 Cuban ministers appointed immediately after the revolution, 16 of them had bailed out or been driven out by mid-1960. Military leaders followed suit. Russian Prime Minister Nikita Khrushchev said that Soviet missiles were prepared to defend Cuba. President Eisenhower instructed the CIA to begin training exiled Cubans for an invasion, and training camps for Brigade 2506—a brigade of Cuban exiles—were set up in Guatemala and Nicaragua.

Between 1960 and 1962, some 200,000 people fled Cuba. Most were the economic and social elite, the businesspeople and managers. By the time the reforms had run their course in 1968, every taxi, restaurant, bar, and hot dog stand was run by the government. Now, about one million Cubans have fled. Castro has skillfully exported many of his dissenters.

The economic policies that emerged from the revolution were heavily influenced by Che Guevara, who held the title of Minister of Industries. He believed that money was an evil motivator, that supply and demand were not sound foundations for a socialist regime and a planned economy was the answer. The economy plunged, and even Castro was not immune from strikes and dissension. He called a 400,000-person strike "absenteeism" and set up organizations to spy on and ferret out dissenters.

One of these was the Committee for the Defense of the Revolution, a network of citizen snoops in nearly every city block and hamlet watching their neighbors, monitoring the comings and goings of strangers. Everybody knows it, but I was warned by one Cuban, "The ones to watch out for now are the Young Communists, the UJC. They are becoming the true believers." The *Unión de Jovenes Comunistas* is the youth affiliate of the communist party. Their meeting places in Havana appeared to be newly painted and spruced up, and we could see them from time to time being mentored by Ministry of Interior officers, teenage spooks in training.

Yes, Cristóbal, it is a different dream now.

Rebecca on the Run

Five boats flying the American flag were lined up in a row, only one of them legally in Cuba. One was a red cruising trimaran named DOS DIABLOS. The skipper was an easy-going man in his seventies sporting a white moustache. His wife, perhaps a decade younger, was his only crew. It was common knowledge along the dock that the skipper was actively seeking a third crew member to make a run back across the Gulf Stream, first to the Dry Tortugas, then to Florida. Rebecca appeared as if in answer to a sailor's prayer.

Rebecca was a pretty, pleasant English woman of an age that suggests it is time to settle down if there are to be children in the future, and she was clearly in a quandary. Her mouth wrinkled into a peculiar "W" when she was distressed, and her mouth was quite wrinkly as we parked our bodies in the plastic lounge chairs at the pool. She had just moved onto DOS DIABLOS from her hotel, had met all the cruisers, and had gone to the United States Special Interests Section to get clearance to sail into the United States as crew on DOS DIABLOS. The Special Interests Section is a sort of embassy without an ambassador down Avenida 5 on the Embassy Row in Miramar, once Havana's posh suburb.

"They turned me down, the bastards. They said I have permission to fly into America, but not to arrive by boat."

"Why? If I was ever stuck in Cuba I'd head right for Marina Hemingway. Half the people here are looking for crew. You could go anywhere in the world, easily to Key West."

"I haven't a bloody clue. The people in government, of course, never have to explain anything. There was this huge line of Cubans trying to get out; I waited for two hours."

"Why are you in Cuba in the first place?"

She jammed her hands into her hair and tugged in frustration. "Well, I need a little holiday from this person . . . I thought traveling would be an answer. I went to Guatemala, to Mexico and then I just sort of decided to come to Cuba. I had no hotel when I arrived. The Cubans wanted to know where I was staying and they put me into this hotel. After two days I said I would stay two more days and they raised the rates. When I asked them why, nobody could tell me. What a strange place this is."

"How did you land here at the marina?"

"Well, I live on the seacoast. When I'm unhappy, I go to the wharf."

"Unhappy about what?"

She tucked her knees up, embraced them, and planted her chin. "When I called 'him' and said I was ready to come home—that was from Mexico—he told me not to hurry. He said I should take my time, take as long as I wanted."

"Not a good sign."

"No. So I thought I would just sail to America; have a good adventure, anyway, now that my life seems to have turned to this pile of dung. Just keep going."

"I'm sorry. Maybe you should just get on DOS DIABLOS and worry about it when you get to the other side. I think they want to stop in the Tortugas to dodge the electronic surveillance and pretend they are coming in from Central America or across the Gulf."

"I don't want to take that risk."

"So, what's next?"

"Oh, I don't know. I'll become a wharf tart, I suppose."

Two hours later Rebecca vanished as suddenly as she had appeared.

5 Tracking Papa in Old Havana

"Look, look," the old man said in Spanish, "this is something for you." In his right hand he was holding a collection of Cuban coins, neatly organized on a four- by six-inch piece of cardboard and displayed behind a piece of plastic sandwich wrap; one of those rare attempts at merchandising I had seen here. But it was the crisp new currency in his left hand, clutched against a copy of *Granma*, Cuba's newspaper, that caught my eye. It was the lure of the souvenir that made me buy a three-peso bill for $1, seven times what it was worth.

The three-peso bill of the National Bank of Cuba carries the likeness of Che Guevara. Fidel, some said, had always been jealous of Che's charismatic appeal among the people and was concerned that his comrade-in-revolution might be a threat, might replace him. So, after giving him domestic assignments in banking and in the cigar industry, Fidel sent Che to Angola and Bolivia—where he finally was killed.

For tourists, pesos were vanishing, and I wanted one of those Che three-peso bills. The American dollar is the coin of the realm in Cuba, but there is an odd double standard. Cubans are paid by the government, and buy things, in pesos—and in dollars when they can get them. Foreigners buy in U.S. dollars, and only occasionally will they be able to find a place that accepts pesos. Farmers' markets might deal in pesos, but the open air markets trading in crafts and art and knickknacks have prices posted "USD": United States Dollars.

I had not seen a peso before because no one wants them. Even though they are officially declared to be at par with the dollar they trade on the street at 20 pesos per dollar, sometimes offered by men who approach with a wad of money counted out to be traded at today's street rate for a $1 bill. The system creates inequities and hardships because some things simply cannot be bought for pesos. A college professor or the doctor who checked us in at the marina is paid the equivalent of $20 a month, in pesos. A waiter in a tourist restaurant can make U.S. $60 a day in tips. Professionals are driven to abandon their training to wait on tables or become prostitutes. A Cuban friend told me the most popular news anchorman on Cuban television, the Dan Rather of Cuba, makes $15 a week and rides a bicycle to work.

My three-peso bill secured, I returned to my mission: tracking Hemingway.

I was standing at Havana Harbor, Morro Castle behind me and to the north, trying to figure out just where the white, rattling VW bus from the Marina had dropped me. I unfolded the map on an ancient stone wall, part of the moat at the *Castillo de la Real Fuerza* that loomed in front of me. Built in 1582, it is the oldest of the four forts that guarded the harbor. At the top of the tower is a bronze weathervane, the figure of a woman holding a cross and a palm tree. She is La Giraldilla, the wife of Governor Hernando de Soto, whom she replaced when he left to conquer Florida. The weathervane image is the symbol of Havana, and I had seen but not noticed La Giraldilla almost daily because she is also the logo on the Havana Club rum bottle.

My destination was Obispo Street, and I found it just a block away across Plaza de Armas, a wooded park with fountains and gardens surrounded by rack upon rack of books for sale at a perpetual secondhand book fair: Che Guevara's diaries and letters, Fidel's thoughts, Jane Franklin's book on America's covert war on Cuba, books on cigars, old and worn leather volumes on arcane scientific subjects.

Havana began to work its charm. Cuban music spilled out of Cafe la Mina, where, at 2:30 in the afternoon, couples sat in the shade of palms and canopies making a transition from coffee to *mojitos*, the concoction that lubricates Havana evenings: two ounces of white rum, half a lime, a generous sprig of mint, a teaspoon of sugar all crushed together and topped off with ice and club soda.

Obispo Street is a good place to track Hemingway. I headed southwest, on the trail. To my right on the far side of the plaza was the dignified, serious *Palacio de los Capitanes Generales*, a facade of ionic columns supporting nine arches. Spain ran Cuba from this building for 400 years. It was the home of 65 Spanish governors and the residence of Uncle Sam's governor during the American occupation of Cuba after the Spanish-American War drove the Spanish out. Now the Spaniards are being welcomed back with open arms as leading investors in Cuba's tourism infrastructure. The Palacio is now the Museum of the City of Havana. A peacock was strutting about in the interior garden plaza, sounding like a man being tortured. In front, the street was torn up and workmen were laying down what I thought were cobblestones, but on closer examination proved to be black bricks of treated wood, set into leveled sand with the end grains up, replacing rotting wooden cobbles.

Ahead on Obispo Street was the hotel Ambos Mundos, rising before me in a happy shade of rose pink, five stories plus a roof garden, where people could be seen pointing out landmarks from their vantage point. Hemingway stayed off and on at the Ambos Mundos for $2 a night, beginning in 1932 when he and Joe Russell began

123

to slip over to Havana from Key West to drink and fish and chase women. Now rooms at the Ambos Mundos cost from $55 to $100, but they are still small and dark.

Joe's boat ANITA and later PILAR would dock in Havana Harbor at what is now part of the renovated Sierra Maestra #2 terminal, a short walk from the hotel. Pauline and the boys would visit for brief periods during these Cuba visits from 1934 to 1937, and everyone stayed at the Ambos Mundos.

The Ambos Mundos is a very civilized hotel, built in 1920 and recently completely renovated. A piano player in a formal black dress smiled at me as I came into the high-ceilinged lobby bar, a room that whispered "linger here with me a while." I passed through the lobby, where prints and watercolors by local artists were spread out for sale on a low table, and headed for an elevator out of an old French movie, a black steel cage with a door that expands and contracts into diamond shapes. Its operator was a handsome young man in a white shirt and respectful demeanor.

"I would like to see Señor Hemingway's room."

"Of course, please step in."

We rattled to the fifth floor as I thought, "I'm in a Peter Sellers *Pink Panther* movie set."

Esperanza Garcia was about 34, attractive, businesslike, and she was either telepathic or I looked hopelessly like a tourist. She interrupted her conversation with two of the maids and smiled at me. "You are here for the Hemingway room." It was not a question, simply an observation.

"Yes." I did look like a tourist, I realized. Only tourists wear shorts on the street in Havana.

"There is a charge of two dollars."

"All right."

She introduced herself. Esperanza means "hope" in Spanish.

She led the way to Room 511, in the northeast corner, where a wooden plaque announced that the room had been set aside in honor of the memory of Ernest Hemingway. Room 511 is sparse and gloomy and preserved just as it was in the 1930s: plain white walls, a small mahogany bed in an alcove to the left, and a writing table with a black portable Royal typewriter—this one in a glass case—just like the one I had seen in Key West. There must be a cottage industry somewhere based on locating old Royal portable typewriters to lend authenticity to "Hemingway Wrote Here" places. We had entered the room past a collection of photos, memorabilia and books behind glass in a bookcase. It was basic hotel furniture, circa 1930. I studied the transom over the door, looking for clues to a Hemingway mystery.

Then Esperanza pushed open the shutters that went from floor to ceiling; the sunlight poured in along with the distant beat of *son* music from Cafe la Mina down the block, and I understood why Ernest Hemingway liked this corner room. It looks out over the Spanish Colonial skyline of Old Havana, the flowers and fountains of Plaza de Armas down the street, and the back of the *Palacio de los Capitanes Generales*, a wall of stone and iron grillwork. Beyond was Havana Harbor and the stone fortifications around Morro Castle, and below us was Obispo Street. But the entire view is not the view of Hemingway's day. A new building to the left has blocked much of the view of the old skyline. It looks like a high school from the 1950s and is occupied by the Ministry of Education.

Hemingway's own description doesn't mention the Palacio: "The rooms on the northeast corner of the

Ambos Mundos in Havana look out to the north over the old cathedral, the entrance to the harbor and the sea, and to the east to Casablanca peninsula, the roofs of all the houses in between and the width of the harbor." He was writing a story for *Esquire* about marlin fishing off Havana.

Esperanza, very businesslike in her crisp white blouse and dark blue skirt, began her well-rehearsed tourist briefing. "In this room, beginning in 1934, Ernest Hemingway wrote some of his best known works, *For Whom the Bell Tolls, The Green Hills of Africa, Snows of Kilimanjaro, The Short Happy Life of Francis Macomber.* He later had a house outside of Havana, Finca Vigía. He won the Nobel Prize in 1954 for *The Old Man and the Sea.* In 1961, in Sun Valley, Idaho, Hemingway committed suicide."

Not all perfectly accurate, but good enough for tourists. Esperanza was a bit generous about the work Hemingway had accomplished in this room: *Snows of Kilimanjaro* was for the most part written in Key West, and *For Whom the Bell Tolls* was probably started in the Ambos Mundos in 1939 after he left Key West, but Hemingway was using the hotel as a mail drop and front while he worked on the book in a room at the Sevilla Biltmore a few blocks northwest. In 1939 he was supposed to be looking for housing for himself and Martha Gellhorn, who was wrapping up her duties as a war correspondent and spokeswoman for the Spanish Loyalist cause. When she arrived in Havana in April she found him in the Ambos Mundos bar with no housing prospects in sight, so she took over and rented Finca Vigía east of Havana for $100 a month. The book was finished there.

I wondered how much Esperanza knew about some of the other creative activities that had gone on in this room, and couldn't resist asking. "I have learned that while he was here he had an affair with a young American woman named Jane Mason, and he claimed she once climbed in over the transom there in her eagerness to see him. Could you tell me about that?"

Esperanza's English collapsed. It was a dirty trick, and I felt ashamed. The transom was a pane of glass set in molding. It doesn't open now; maybe it did once. Pretty, petite, hell-raising Jane Mason who loved to drink, fish and shoot pigeons with the boys could barely have squeezed through that transom. Jane and her husband, Grant, whom Hemingway called a "wealthy twerp" in a letter, were friends of the Hemingways.

Jane was the real-life inspiration for Margot Macomber in *The Short Happy Life of Francis Macomber*, and for Helene Bradley in *To Have and Have Not*. Like Margot Macomber, Jane Mason had once been paid for "endorsing, with photographs, a beauty product which she had never used," Pond's face cream.

Grant Mason, one of the founders of Pan American Airways, ran Caribbean operations out of Havana. In those years, Pan Am clipper seaplanes touched down in Havana Harbor, and people traveled routinely between Key West and Havana by boat and ferry. Grant and Jane had a business reason to travel back and forth. Pan Am was born in Key West in the late 1920s. Pan Am's first offices at 301 Whitehead Street are now Kelly's Caribbean Bar, Grill & Brewery, owned by actress Kelly McGillis.

Grant and Jane were married when she was 18. She had frequently been treated for unhappiness, although at the time her husband thought she just wanted attention. They lived in a mansion in the fishing village of Jaimanitas west of Havana and near what is now Marina

Hemingway. The beach at Jaimanitas, a Hemingway favorite, was probably as close as he ever came to his namesake marina.

Jane Mason was young and beautiful; today she would have been called manic depressive. She captivated most of the men who met her. Hemingway's brother Leicester wrote of her: "Her grave beauty had a madonna-like quality accentuated by a middle part in smoothed-back blonde hair. She had large eyes and fine features." A friend, however, told a writer: "Jane Mason not only drank a bit, she was one of the wildest, hairiest, most drinking, wenching, sexy superwomen in the world . . ."

Pauline and Ernest were returning to New York from Paris on the *Ile de France* in the fall of 1931 when they met 22-year-old Jane Mason, who was traveling alone. Pauline was seven months pregnant and was going to Kansas City to have her second child; she was hoping for a girl this time, a "little Pilar."

Hemingway went to Havana the following April aboard Joe Russell's ANITA to work and discover marlin fishing while the Key West house was undergoing renovations. When Pauline joined him she checked into a second floor room at the Ambos Mundos and called Jane Mason. Jane and Grant Mason introduced the Hemingways into Havana cafe society and visited them in Key West. In 1932, Jane and Ernest became fishing partners, and then more, and Pauline, back in Key West, began to get uneasy. Pauline started dyeing her hair blonde to be more attractive; more like Jane Mason.

After Key West and Wyoming, Hemingway returned to Havana in the spring of 1933 and reconnected with Jane Mason. Pauline arrived early in May after sending a letter to Hemingway: "Am having large nose, imperfect lips, protruding ears and warts and moles all taken off before coming to Cuba. Thought I'd better, Mrs. Mason and those Cuban women are so lovely." At the end of May, Jane Mason was driving her Packard to Jaimanitas with two Hemingway sons in it when she ran off the road into a ravine, and the car overturned. Although no one was injured, Jane was shaken.

A few days later Jane Mason jumped or fell from a second floor balcony at the Jaimanitas mansion and broke her back. Grant Mason hired a nurse and packed his wife off to New York for treatment, where she was hospitalized for five months. Hemingway went off on a long European holiday followed by a safari in Africa, the basis for the Africa stories yet to be written at the Ambos Mundos and in Key West.

Hemingway told his mother that Jane had broken her back in the car accident, but a sad macho attempt at humor took over when he discussed the incident with John Dos Passos and said, "She really fell for me."

After PILAR was delivered to Miami in 1934 a three-day spring trip to Havana spun into months. Later in 1934, at Hemingway's invitation, Jane showed up in Bimini on the Mason's boat, but she was already interested in someone else and did not stay long. Back at Bimini in July 1936, over drinks at the Compleat Angler Bar, Pauline Pfeiffer introduced Jane Mason to Arnold Gingrich, the editor of *Esquire*, whose advance had allowed Hemingway to buy PILAR. Gingrich began to see Jane secretly in New York. Eventually the Masons divorced and Jane and Arnold were married. Old photos show Jane Mason at the Key West house with Pauline and other friends after the Hemingway divorce in 1940.

A change of subject was in order, and I pointed to a photo of the man who had been in charge of PILAR, Hemingway's fishing boat. "Gregorio Fuentes?"

"Yes, he is still alive and living in Cojímar. He is 101 years old and still tells stories about Hemingway."

Gregorio was a hero among Cubans, but he was becoming very confused and his nephew managed him like a rock and roll star, charging $10 for "consultations" on his years with Hemingway as, in Papa's words, "the pillar of PILAR."

I thanked Esperanza, gave her two Tootsie Pops for her kids, and went up to the roof garden. Three musicians played guitars under the teak-colored lattice that screened out the overhead sun. The attentive waiters, palms and the comfortable white wicker furniture create a gracious island among the rooftops and cathedral towers. Hemingway would sit here at the rooftop bar with his drink and watch the night slip down on Old Havana.

This day, a group of Canadians were sipping coffee, talking about the United Nations, and a young tourist couple whom I had photographed at the Plaza de Armas was wondering what I was doing here, again with a camera. The young man looked hard at me, puzzled and concerned. Was I following them? Spying? Secret Police? Let them wonder. Intrigue is part of Havana's essential energy.

No vehicles are allowed on Obispo Street, but it was swarming with pedestrians as I headed the nine blocks from the Ambos Mundos to El Floridita bar, the most famous of Hemingway's Cuban watering holes. Late in the morning, after wrapping up work on the current manuscript, dressed in faded khaki shorts, a cotton shirt and moccasins, a Hemingway still in his early thirties would head for El Floridita like a man on a mission. In these years before the gray hair and beard, he sported a little Clark Gable moustache. Hemingway would arrive around eleven, have a couple of daiquiris, leave at noon and return at five to have more daiquiris.

But another bar, Cafe Paris, sidetracked me. A band was playing and I was drawn to the music, the crowd watching and spilling out onto the street, and a shapely young woman in a skin-tight aquamarine jump suit. I pushed toward the doorway and the young woman's friend, not nearly as shapely but in equally tight red and white striped pants, looked at me with a curious smile.

"*Alemán?* German?"

"No, *Americano.*"

"*Sí.*" She poked the one in the jump suit. "*Americano.*"

There was no hostility, no tight-lipped resentment about an embargo, just curiosity about America and things American. The bartender was clearing the doorway of non-paying spectators and I stepped back out into the street. A young, black woman with a baby in her arms and a child of about six at her side was coming toward me. Her clothing was worn thin, and hung on a thin, stooped body. She was perhaps 20. She looked at me with desperation in her eyes, cradling the baby in her arms.

"You want boom-boom with me?"

She took me by surprise. "No, *señorita*, I'm sorry." I had, for a moment, forgotten about this side of Cuba.

"But I have no money," she cried. The youngster, who was carrying a plastic grocery bag containing what appeared to be all her possessions, looked at me as if I had just behaved very badly. They moved on into the bar, where the woman went from table to table. No takers. I fished into my backpack and pulled out a bar of soap, which she and the baby urgently needed to use. I intercepted her when she came out. Now the woman in the aquamarine jump suit was carrying the baby. "*Señorita*, sell this." She accepted it with eyes that looked already dead, and moved on. Those eyes were seeing the end of the road, and I was shaken.

I told myself I could not save every poor person in Cuba, and I had seen plenty of poor people in Mexico and Colombia and Hong Kong and Manhattan. So I turned my frustration toward someone else and angrily wished I could put the United States Congress into T-shirts and shorts and let them walk 10 blocks up Obispo Street to meet the Cuban people. The embargo would have to end if there is any soul left in politicians. The embargo crushes the wrong people. Fidel still has his Mercedes, and there is no new Fidel out in the mountains to stage another revolution, if that is the goal of the embargo.

On October 28, 1954, Hemingway's home in San Francisco de Paula, Finca Vigía, was swarming with well-wishers after it was announced that one of Cuba's favorite sons had won the Nobel Prize, primarily for *The Old Man and the Sea*. He made a brief speech to the crowd.

"As you well know, there are many Cubans. But as in ancient Gaul they can be divided into three parts: those who starve, those who subsist, and those who eat too much. After this magnificent (and bourgeois) repast, we indubitably belong in the third category, at least for the moment."

So, I was not the first to confront the bitter truth about Cuba, but it seemed unnecessarily bad because of the embargo, the latest turn of the screw after a century of invasion, intervention and intrigue.

As I headed up Obispo Street, the two women in the tight outfits now honed in on me in a playful way. The

Walking down Obispo Street in Old Havana is the easiest way to meet friendly Cubans.

larger one was trying to explain something to me in Spanish and by gesture, rubbing her fingers on her arms. Based on what I had heard and seen before I pieced it together. She wondered if I had any ointment or salve, a hot commodity in a place abundant with doctors but without adequate medical supplies. The favorites are

Cuban woman.

133

the three antibiotic ointment blends, various mixtures of neosporin, polysporin and similar ingredients. I dug into my backpack and came up with a small tube of toothpaste and, for Miss Aquamarine Tights, a Tootsie pop.

Sweets are a big hit in Cuba, and I had brought a supply of pops to use as a reward for photos. Most sugar is exported. In Spanish, I would ask: "With your permission, a photo of you? I would like the people of North America to get to know the people of Cuba." The reward was rarely necessary, because a photo was interpreted as a form of flattery. After all, when is the last time anyone cared enough, or was able to, take a photograph of the average Cuban? At the sight of the camera, some Cubans would strike poses and ask to have their pictures taken. I was always happy to oblige.

We walked in the same direction, but not together, because at every street corner a uniformed member of the Ministry of the Interior was casting a suspicious eye on those who had too much contact with tourists.

The women drifted off into the crowd and I meandered forward in the direction of El Floridita. Sections of the street were blocked off for construction projects; the buildings were in bad need of repair. Looking overhead I could see cracks and broken sections in the overhangs, a dangerous portent of decay for people walking below. A black and yellow Western Union telegraph sign hung out over the street, but there could have been no Western Union presence here for nearly 40 years. I began looking for a photo shop to buy film. The only likely shop, a store where you had to buy things for U.S. dollars, displayed a mixture of goods that ranged from clothing to cameras, television sets and radios, one or two of each item. But no film. In Cuba, if you need something and see it, you buy it today. Tomorrow the supply could end for months.

"*Señor*, would you like a good cigar?"

I had heard this before, and would hear it a hundred times again. A good bargain on a cigar that would, as John Dupee observed, give you a hernia while trying to drag on it hard enough to keep it lit. But the pitch was always the same: "My brother (mother, sister, cousin) works in the Cohiba factory and I can get you a very special price."

Cuba produces 160 million hand-rolled cigars a year, but walking the streets of Havana it seems that most of the production must go out the back door with employees. As the guard at the marina had warned, most of these "Cuban cigars" are counterfeits from Jamaica or Mexico but are sold in the street with the labels and boxes of famous Cuban brands. Cuban Customs confiscated 530,000 of these fakes in one year in the late 1990s, and Cuba is not their only destination. *Cigar Aficionado* magazine estimates that 80 to 90 percent of the Cuban cigars sold in the U.S. are counterfeit. Organized crime is moving in, using cigars as a means to launder money.

"I'm not a smoker," I said. That usually sent them off. There were two of them, guys in their mid twenties, smiling, aggressively friendly, doing the Cuban hustle that allows them to survive day to day.

"What would you like? We can get anything for you."

"What I really need is some film."

"Polaroid?"

"No, for a thirty-five millimeter camera." I had not mastered much Spanish grammar, but if you know how to say numbers, you can buy anything and usually get anywhere.

"Okay, follow us."

In most of Latin America I wouldn't follow anyone anywhere, but this was Cuba, one of the safest places in Latin America. Everyone is being watched, and since the end of the Soviet Union tourism has grown to be the largest and fastest growing industry in the country, producing two billion dollars a year. Developing tourism is a national strategy, and no Cuban wants to mess with Cuban strategy. Crime is not tolerated, and in a place where you cannot assume due process under the law, the idea of being arrested is terrifying. In preparing for this trip, I had read books about people who were jailed for 20 years simply on suspicion, and about the techniques for controlling dissidents by cutting off a foot: political amputations do slow people down. There were dark tales of people being stood on the cliffs with their backs to the sea and shot; let the sharks clean up the mess and the evidence.

I followed the two young men without seeming to be following them, a polite thirty yards behind so as not to attract the attention of the lads with berets and billy clubs that stood on every corner. They would have done nothing to me, but we were, after all, going through a new "initiative" against violent crime, pimping and prostitution, and too much interaction with tourists and journalists who filed critical stories by fax.

To my left I spotted El Floridita restaurant and I was tempted to take a tack and head for a daiquiri, but I followed the guys hoping that this would be worthwhile. They led me off to the right and into what had been, before the revolution, *Manzana de Gomez*, a massive department store covering the entire block. Now in little shops people are selling whatever they can find to sell until it runs out. We passed a T-shirt shop and went into a place that defies any American description of a store. It sells "stuff": Che Guevara T-shirts, odds and ends of things, nothing organized to the degree that you could categorize it. We made our introductions. Jorge and Rene explained my needs to the shopkeeper in Spanish and from under the counter came a role of Kodak "Elite" slide film. I was back in business, and bought all he had in stock: two rolls for just under $11. Then I traded an 8mm video tape for a third, which sent an employee on a 10-minute trip somewhere to replenish the stock. We discussed my need for Che Guevara T-shirts (thin, $6), which was minimal, and I went back to the street wondering what was in this for the two boys. Nothing, at least not from my end.

"This is where the Bacardi Rum headquarters used to be," Jorge explained, pointing across the street. The entire building was framed in scaffolds and under renovation. It was becoming beautiful, a stunning art deco building decorated with ceramic tiles and, at the top, near-naked nymphs. It now houses government offices; Bacardi fled to Puerto Rico. The building across the street, Harris Brothers, was at the midpoint in its facelift, half dirty gray, half pastels. In fact, much of Old Havana, which was falling down ten years ago, is undergoing a massive renovation that I had not noticed until now. It was not that evident on Obispo Street, but in Old Havana buildings were being transformed from crumbling gray to sparkling pastels.

We stood for a moment on the sidewalk as the stream of bicycles, motorcycles with sidecars, 1950s American cars running on Russian parts, and military vehicles ran past.

"There is a new initiative about crime and prostitution and dealing with tourists, true?"

"*Sí.*"

"Do you worry that when you talk to me the police will catch you?"

"No, you just have to know how to talk to them."

"Good. See you later."

El Floridita bar beckoned from the corner just a half block away, a low, salmon pink building with a shiny metal overhang above the sidewalk. It looked a little like a 1950s diner. A gray-haired doorman in a red tuxedo coat and black bow tie swung open the glass door for me and I stepped into the socialist-run Hemingway industry.

El Floridita is fancier today than it was in the Hemingway years, when it was privately run. It is now a socialist vision. The walls are covered with a flowered, pastel wallpaper, not the stark white from the old pho-

El Floridita, Hemingway's most famous hangout in Havana.

tographs. To the far left a bust of Hemingway looks over the scene, and below the bust, against the wall, is Papa's favorite spot. The bar stool is roped off: no one can sit on this hallowed ground. I did find a spot between Papa's bar stool and a group of young Canadians who were downing daiquiris, which were invented here years ago by the then owner, a former barman named Constantino Ribailagua, who was called Mr. Constante.

The wall behind the rich mahogany bar is dominated by a mural of Havana Harbor viewed from the sea, with a square rigger entering the harbor past Morro Castle. It is flanked by black and gold columns. On the far wall, red drapes frame the doorway separating the bar from the dining room.

Every seat at the bar was taken, all of the nine round red tables in the bar area were occupied. Cameras flashed. Video cameras hummed. Everyone was drinking a daiquiri and looking around expectantly, waiting for something to happen. Perhaps Papa would be beamed down and materialize in the corner seat, which would have scared the hell out of me perched on the next stool. Perhaps Errol Flynn would come swashbuckling through the red-draped door, although this was such a young crowd I doubted they could remember him unless they had studied the photo that hung behind me on the wall. It was a shot of Errol Flynn and an aging Papa in animated conversation at El Floridita in 1960, a year before Hemingway's death. Old timers at El Floridita remember Flynn as not being very trustworthy in paying his debts, but Hemingway always paid his bills before he went on a trip, and added a 20% tip for the staff.

But today nothing special was happening. There was the usual constant churning at the entrance where

Inside El Floridita. Hemingway's corner stool under the bust and photos is roped off, but these tourists from Toronto soak up the ambiance along with daiquiris which were invented here.

people would stick their heads in the door—entire tour bus loads sometimes—to inhale a brief essence of Papa, and head back out. The scene reminded me of Chevy Chase and his four-second appreciation of the Grand Canyon in *Vacation*.

A daiquiri at El Floridita costs $6, more than half the monthly salary of the average Cuban worker and more than the price of a bottle of three-year old Havana Club. Food prices are more outrageous. A shrimp cocktail appetizer is $15, and entree specials like the *Papa and Mary* seafood dish and *Gregorio's Favorite* ranged from $22 to a high of $42 for lobster thermidor. That morning I had paid Carlos $2 for a fresh lobster tail. I had tipped him with three fish hooks and two metal leaders. He was pleased; they were worth more than money.

The young Canadians were in my line of fire for a photo of the Hemingway bust. While I asked for their okay to be in the shot, we chatted about how an American gets into Cuba. They questioned me about my interest in Hemingway. They were from Toronto.

"You know," said one of them, "Hemingway worked in Toronto, too, as a newspaper reporter."

"Yes, at the *Star*."

"You know where we go out drinking in Toronto, our favorite place?"

"Let me guess."

"Hemingway's. Of course it didn't exist when he was there."

While Hemingway is sincerely revered in Cuba, along with Che and patriot José Martí, the value of the Hemingway legacy and legend in Cuba did not begin to crystallize until about 1965. El Floridita is the most popular and best known element of Cuba's Hemingway industry, but for many years after the revolution it was an abandoned shell. Finally, it was torn down. Canadian journalists visiting in 1990 found just a hole in the ground and a crew busily trying to reconstruct the building to open in time for the Pan American Games. It has been reconstructed to a luxurious condition from photos of the period and the memories of employees.

It began its life as a bar in 1819 as the *Piña de Plata*, the Silver Pineapple, a rustic combination store and tavern: the typical *bodega*. It became La Florida during the time the Americans occupied Havana between 1898 and 1902—that name is still in the stone at the top of the building—and eventually the more familiar El Floridita. In the 1930s and 1940s, merchants and politicians and society personalities would gather at noon in places like this to discuss events and business. That was El Floridita of Hemingway's time.

Ernest Hemingway, who favored dives where fishermen and rascals hung out, would have hated El Floridita today. When he first started frequenting El Floridita it had eleven broad doors open to the street, but it could be closed in with the gray metal doors like garage doors that roll down from above. The good dives in Havana still operate this way. But in 1948 or 1949 the neighboring Pan American bar installed air conditioning and the cool air sucked the customers away from El Floridita. An ancient barman told a reporter in the 1970s that "Everybody said the drinks we prepared here were delicious, but the heat was unbearable. We had great four-bladed fans rotating on the ceiling, but the draft they created mussed the ladies' hairdos."

Hemingway remained loyal to El Floridita despite the heat, but the loss of business prompted Mr. Constante to grudgingly install the air conditioning. Hemingway didn't like it that much and Cuban Hemingway biographer Norberto Fuentes suggests:

"He may have been influenced by the fact that the installation of air-conditioning required putting up cement walls to enclose the place. It was well known that Hemingway loved open spaces and liked the possibilities offered by all those open doors.

"On occasions when he had to settle problems with his fists at the bar, the absence of walls gave him more freedom of action and the opportunity to throw his opponent into the street.

"After the air-conditioning system was installed at the Floridita, Hemingway did have one or two encounters; but it was never the same again, because he had to go outside to fight and by the time he reached the street he was no longer angry."

A bartender told Fuentes, "He was like an oak, he

knocked down whomever he hit." It was his way of "advising" noisy troublemakers. As his fame grew and his affinity for El Floridita became well known, he was increasingly plagued by tourists seeking autographs and he spent more time at Bodeguita del Medio.

Today El Floridita is the cornerstone of Cuba's Hemingway industry. Like almost everything, it is run by a branch of the government. I began to see the connection as I wandered around the bar room to look at the other photos. Photos of Hemingway and Fidel laughing together hang in all these Hemingway locales, giving the impression that the two were great pals. But all the photos were taken on the one occasion when the two men actually met, on May 15, 1960.

Hemingway sponsored an annual fishing contest and Fidel, quite legitimately, won a trophy for catching the biggest marlin of the day. Fidel was supposed to have come only to present trophies, but he joined the fun and fished while Che Guevara, on the same boat, buried his nose in Stendahl's *The Red and the Black*. The photos of Hemingway and Fidel together were taken at the trophy presentation by Osvaldo Salas, a photographer for *Granma* who was essentially Fidel's official photographer during those years. Later, his son Roberto joined him.

In 1948, A.E. Hotchner, who would become a Hemingway biographer and friend, was sent to Cuba to interview Papa, who suggested meeting at El Floridita.

"At that time the Florida (that was its proper name but everyone called it Floridita) was a well-lighted old-fashioned bar-restaurant with ceiling fans, informal waiters and three musicians who wandered around or sat at a table near the bar. The bar was of massive, burnished mahogany; the bar stools were high and comfortable, and the bartenders cheerful, skilled veterans who produced a variety of frozen daiquiris of rare quality. On the wall there were several framed photographs of the Hemingways drinking La Florida's most publicized product—the Hemingway daiquiri, or Papa Doble. Requested by most tourists, a Papa Doble was compounded of two and a half jiggers of Bacardi White Label Rum, the juice of two limes and half a grapefruit, and six drops of maraschino, all placed in an electric mixer over shaved ice, whirled vigorously and served foaming in large goblets. I sat on a stool at the Obispo Street end of the bar in the corner under the framed photos, and ordered a Papa Doble."

Another Hemingway pal, Gary Cooper, who played Robert Jordan in the film *For Whom the Bell Tolls*, spent New Year's Eve at El Floridita with Papa in 1951, captured with their entourage and admirers in a photo just behind Hemingway's bar stool. The two men had become friends. In April 1961, Cooper was being ravaged by stomach cancer and Hemingway had been admitted for the second time to the Mayo Clinic in Rochester, Minnesota, where he had been undergoing electroshock therapy. Cooper, in terrible pain from his stomach cancer, was visited by Hemingway biographer Hotchner, who had also been to see Hemingway.

"Papa phoned a couple of weeks ago. Told me he was sick, too." Cooper spoke in short bursts, battling back the pain. "I bet him that I will beat him out to the barn."

A few minutes later he sent a message that will forever remain a mystery. "Please give Papa a message. It's important and you musn't forget because I'll not be talking to him again." Cooper was holding a crucifix and touched it to his cheek. "Tell him . . . that time I wondered if I made the right decision . . . tell him it was the best thing I ever did." Cooper had visited Hemingway and Mary Welsh at the Finca and the three talked all night about his personal problems.

Cooper did beat Hemingway out to the barn, he died ten days later. Two months later Hemingway was dead, too. It was quite a group that hung out at El Floridita at one time or another with Hemingway: Spencer Tracy, Marlene Dietrich, Ava Gardner, Barbara Stanwyck and Robert Taylor were among the Americans but there was also a number of well-known Latins involved. There is nothing left of Hemingway in El Floridita, only the old photos. It is too fancy, too commercial, too bloodless. Tourists like me hang out here now, not rascals and whores like Honest Lil, the good-hearted hooker from *Islands in the Stream.*

I left and walked next door to the Zaragozana restaurant, one of the great Havana restaurants during the forties and one of Hemingway's favorites. A barman in white shirt and black bow tie standing outside advised me, "Very good *mojitos,* very good." As late as the 1970s it was in ruins, but now, with its long sweetly-curving mahogany bar, it is more inviting than El Floridita. It was empty; nobody knew the story. But there were five places that allowed Hemingway to sign his dinner check on credit: El Floridita, La Terraza in the village of Cojímar, the Basque Center, the Bodeguita del Medio, and the Zaragozana restaurant.

The sun was diving toward the rooftops as I turned back around the corner onto Obispo Street. For today's man in Havana there is one more important thing about El Floridita. Next door on the second floor, through a separate entrance on Obispo Street, is the *Casa del Ron,* the House of Rum. Glasses and paper coasters are set up at a small, polished wooden bar set into the wall, waiting for visitors to try free samples of the bottles opened behind the bar. The Casa is stocked with almost every brand of rum produced in Cuba, and although the prices are not as low as in other places, the selection is the best. I sampled the rum, but did not buy, and returned to the street. Prices for Havana Club were better at Marina Hemingway, and I would not have to carry it far.

"*Señor.*" An old man beckoned to me. I thought he wanted me to buy a slightly ragged edition of *Granma*, the national newspaper mouthpiece of the revolution.

"I'm sorry," I said in rough Spanish, "but I'm not able to read Spanish."

"No," he said pulling a three by five card out of his pocket. He pointed to the words carefully printed on the card, separated by a horizontal line: Pen/*Pluma*. To make his point he reached into his shirt pocket and pulled out a pencil stub less than an inch long. He was begging for a pen or pencil, hoping to trade the only thing he had to bargain with, the newspaper of the revolution. I quickly made the trade, defying the U.S. embargo once again, handing this "enemy" the ballpoint pen in my pocket. He thanked me and vanished into the crowd. Not ten minutes later, while I was sitting on a park bench changing film, the elderly woman next to me made the same request. Socialism has, in Cuba, created a very high level of literacy, estimated at 98.5 percent. I sighed and wondered: Is it better to know how to read and beg for a pen and understand your circumstances, or is it better to be illiterate and in the dark and assume your condition is nothing unusual?

I glanced at my map of Havana and decided to take a different route back to the waterfront, down O'Reilly

School children. The colors of school skirts or shorts
identify the education level. Cuba has a high literacy rate.

Street, then over on Cuba Street to see Cathedral Square
at sunset, and back to the fort.

Cuba Street quickly became one of my favorites. It
is a residential neighborhood of people living jammed
together in beautiful but collapsing sixteenth-century
colonial homes and apartments. Where one family lived
in a house before the revolution, there is now a family
in each room of the house. Those hoping that Cubans
will rise up against Castro should bear in mind that if
the people who fled the revolution should return to
claim their property, thousands of people, perhaps hundreds of thousands, would be out on the street. Not
much of an incentive for revolution.

I stuck my head into a doorway where a tangle of
electrical wires and meters would have shocked an
American housing inspector into unconsciousness, and a
woman invited me in to take a look around. The beautiful tile floors had been torn up and rivers of dirt ran

down them. In a central courtyard, laundry hung drying on ornate ironwork 300 years old. A boy, the woman's son, told me twenty-seven families lived here. He was polite, clean and cheerful.

Along crumbling, faded Cuba Street the evening meal was being prepared behind open doorways; music drifted out, I could see figures dancing, and there was laughter. Cubans have a happiness gene that transcends socialism.

Before the light failed completely I paused to take a picture of a young girl of about nine in a red jacket. She dodged behind the door every time I raised my camera, so finally I put it away. Then she stepped out into the street and made an "O" of the thumb and index finger of her left hand, and through the "O" she pumped the index finger of her right hand, beckoned to me, and pointed up a dilapidated staircase. It was the gesture of the world's oldest profession. I walked on, drained, wondering who exactly was for sale up those stairs—the child, the mother, a sister?

It was dark when I reached Plaza de Armas and plunked down on a park bench to wait for the VW bus. The booksellers had folded up their displays and gone for the day. The street lights illuminated shadowy trees and fountains and a statue of a Cuban hero. In the dim light four boys were noisily playing baseball, and I moved over to watch them. They had the moves down pat, probably seen on television somewhere. The batter stood with arched back, cocky, defiant, the bat a few inches off his shoulder, ready. His bat was a piece of lath scavenged from a collapsing historic building. The pitcher sized him up, wound up and pitched, but the ball wobbled oddly. It was a hit, and it rolled toward my feet. I saw that it was not a ball at all. It was a small plastic bathtub duck. They had no ball. But the batter ran the bases and there was shouting and protests and laughing; it didn't matter about the ball. It was the game that mattered.

I liked this place, Old Havana, and the resilience of the people. I felt at home in the park on a warm evening with the shadowy statue of some unknown hero watching over it. I had learned that a stranger must be very careful in Cuba. If you are not careful, Cuba will break your heart.

6 | *Cuba Libre*

Ernesto

We were speeding through the rural, gently rolling countryside east of Havana headed for Cojímar, the run-down fishing village that was the locale for *The Old Man and the Sea*, the place where Hemingway had docked PILAR. As in Havana, clusters of people hitching rides stood along the side of the road. Two men on a cart drawn by a bay horse were hauling vegetables to market. They waved to us. Unlike the horse-drawn carriage rides for tourists in Havana, this was daily transportation.

My driver, Ernesto, was taking a risk by hiring himself and his brown VW Golf out to a tourist, but his job had vanished along with the Soviet support for Cuba.

Ford taxi. The Cubans are proud of their classic American cars and often support them by working as black market taxi drivers.

He spoke good English and, he said, better Russian. He had trained in Russia for five years. But now it had all been for nothing, and he was making $30 to help me find Hemingway's haunts and support his wife, son and daughter. The government operates taxis and licenses some people to drive tourists around by the day, but Ernesto was not licensed. Private cars carry a *particular* identification on the license plate, and the hitchhikers gazed inside at the foreigner in the passenger seat with puzzled looks.

The first few days at the marina I could rent a car and driver by standing outside the little supermarket and shops at the head of Channel 2. Drivers would approach, "Taxi, taxi?" having first passed through security at the entrance to the marina. But things were changing daily. Cubans may at first have nodded at the "special initiative" Fidel had declared, yawned and ignored it, but no more. I had found Ernesto by sitting down with the concierge at The Old Man and the Sea hotel. She set up the meeting by phone.

Ernesto was quiet and cautious, sizing me up.

"What do they do, those people who stand on every street corner in the uniforms of the Ministry of Interior? In the U.S., the Interior Department takes care of the national parks and things like that."

Ernesto pondered the question, trying to frame a diplomatic answer. "They are looking and watching."

"They don't smile very much."

Ernesto burst into laughter and pounded on the steering wheel with the heel of his right palm. "No, they don't. They are very single-minded people."

"Do they have lists of who the people are?"

"They talk into those little radios they carry. The lists are in the computers. We have identity cards."

152

"Can you get into trouble for driving me around?"

"I haven't in the past. There is a new initiative."

"I read about it in the paper before I came, the *Miami Herald*. It is against pimps, prostitution, crime that involves violence, journalists who file critical stories by fax."

"They are also watching for people who spend too much time with foreigners."

When we reached Cojímar, Ernesto parked a block back from the waterfront and gave me directions to La Terraza restaurant—a Hemingway hangout with fishing pals—and to the Hemingway Memorial that had been erected by the local fishermen.

"I will walk this way for a little while," Ernesto said, heading in the other direction. "When you are ready just come back here, I'll know where you are."

Cubans know, by some means that Americans try to guess, where it is safe to be seen with a tourist and where it is not. Casual, quick street encounters didn't attract much attention, but business negotiations did, especially prostitution. Cojímar didn't look like a place for concern. It is a poor town, consisting of blocks of connected single-story apartments with iron grates for doors. The single door enters directly into a tiny living room, beyond that are a small kitchen and a bedroom somewhere out of sight.

Esperanza at the Ambos Mundos was correct. Gregorio Fuentes, Hemingway's "pillar of PILAR" still lived here at 209 Calle Pesuela. For cash, "consultations" could be arranged through La Terraza restaurant. Without question, Gregorio had been a skilled seaman. He tethered PILAR to safely ride out a hurricane, navigated through the tricky shallows around the Cuban Keys, understood the sea and the fish, and claimed to be the first

Hemingway's bust in the fishing village of
Cojímar, where *The Old Man and the Sea* was set.

to tell Hemingway the story about the old man losing a giant marlin to the sharks, although it was a familiar story to fishermen. He was now 101, and his stories repeated so many times were becoming inconsistent. I wanted to meet Gregorio Fuentes; he was a seaman to admire and respect even without his connection to Hemingway. But I simply could not buy into this part of the Hemingway industry, it was a tragic side show at the Hemingway carnival.

The sea was tossing whitecaps at the end of the street. To the left was a circle of white wooden pillars, raised on a stone base, and beyond it an ancient stone fort. Inside the rotunda of pillars is a tall pedestal holding a bronze bust of Hemingway smiling and gazing forever out to sea in the direction in which PILAR was moored and past the beach where the old man launched his sailing skiff and went out farther than ever before to fish the deep Gulf Stream. This is the Hemingway Memorial, erected after "the American's" death in 1961. The poor fishermen of Cojímar had no money to buy materials for the bust but they wanted to honor the man who told the world of their difficult lives. After a meeting at which there was much drinking each contributed a propeller or bronze boat fitting. The sculptor was so touched by this gesture he melted the material down and created the bust pro bono. I could vaguely make out the shape of a fishing boat on the beach, to the right of Papa's gaze. To the left of the fort was a stone wall on top of a ragged stretch of stone and coral. Spray from waves driven by the north wind chilled the back of my neck as I hiked along it to see if there was another possible marina site in Cojímar. There was none.

I strolled back toward the fort, called El Terreon. Nervous Cubans built it in 1643 to guard against the possibility that invaders could land forces here and establish a foothold before attacking Havana. The fort overlooks the beach, commanding control of the one place along this shore where a landing party would not face surf pounding against rock and coral. The fort's defenders fought bravely but failed to stop the English Navy in 1762 when they put ashore to capture Cuba for King George III. A Cuban flag flew over it now and men in green Army uniforms were walking along the top between the rounded towers. This was a small military post, but why here? No wonder Ernesto didn't want to accompany me.

A bus had stopped in front of the fort. German tourists were taking photos of the Hemingway Memorial. They were on the Hemingway Trail tour, another offshoot of the Hemingway industry.

A few blocks east, near La Terraza restaurant, Ernesto reappeared at my side. At one time a scale hung from a gnarled tree next to the restaurant, and here Hemingway and the other fishermen would weigh their catches. The old fisherman in the book and his young friend would come here to La Terraza in the morning to drink their coffee, and in the evening, after the fishing, for a beer. They would talk of the American baseball players like the great DiMaggio that Cubans admired so much, and wish they could take them fishing. In the book it is a simple place populated by simple fishermen, and some laughed at the old man because he had gone 84 days without taking a fish. But like a good Hemingway character, he was battered, not defeated, and there was still fire in his eyes.

In the sixties, La Terraza had fallen into decline, but legend says Fidel himself ordered its renovation in the early 1970s and now it is a way station on the Hemingway Trail. It is about the only reason anyone would have for coming to Cojímar. A Cubanacán tour bus was parked out front.

Ernesto and I slipped into a side door. A couple sat at the bar nursing drinks. Hemingway knew how to pick good, high-ceilinged, mahogany bars. A counter in the front sold uninspired T-shirts and other Hemingway memorabilia but the selection was poor compared to what was available at Sloppy Joe's in Key West. In the back, a pale yellow dining room with tables set in white and red linen overlooked the sea. It was almost lunch time, and sliced Cuban bread was already set out. Photos of Hemingway and Gregorio Fuentes line the walls, most of them related to fishing or PILAR. There was the Papa and Fidel shot again. A German woman was making a video of the pictures. At the end of Hemingway's book a tourist looks out of these windows and sees below the skeleton of the 18-foot marlin, the rest lost to sharks. The old man had lost his catch, but he persevered.

At La Terraza the specialty is seafood and the prices are more down to earth than El Floridita: soup $2, seafood entrees in the $6 range; lobster, $10; lobster thermidor, $12, and the house special, *ranchito de mariscos*, "a combination of lobster, shrimp and fish elaborated in red seasoned sauce and garnished with steamed rice," was $11.

Cubans can no longer afford to eat here, but out front was a small wooden booth under the restaurant's overhang that sold rum, cigarettes, trinkets and snacks, and Cubans were lined up.

We followed a sloping walkway down to the beach. Two steel 18-foot open fishing boats were on the beach, one red, one white, both derelicts; the fish had been fished out or fallen victim to pollution. There are no fishermen in Cojímar any more. The beach is littered with bottles and tires and the plastic flotsam that lives on forever.

Cuban women, Cojímar beach

The beach ends at the Cojímar River where a small marina is tucked behind a low pedestrian bridge leading to a peninsula and a park. Young men lounged on the wooden deck of a small white cabin cruiser. The remnants of large pilings and small jetties suggest that a much larger marina once stood at this end of the beach. This is where PILAR lived. No one but Gregorio would remember exactly where, more than 40 years back. A steady flow of people moved back and forth, many stopping at a shed that sold food.

The iron bridge was a small mechanical draw bridge, and the only sign of fishing was one dark man baiting a net crab trap with a thin fish skin and dropping it into the current below the bridge.

Ernesto paused and looked out to sea. "It is not like in Hemingway's time. No fishing any more. It has become famous for other things. This was the place for the raft people to push off and catch the Gulf Stream and ride it to America. It is close here."

That explained the military outpost at the fort. They were watching the beach to stop rafters. "I saw some of those rafts several years ago, washed up on the beach near Stuart, Florida. There was not much to them, and the Gulf Stream is rough. I wonder how many pushed off and were never seen again. I have a good boat, but when I cross the Stream I think about what lives out there."

Ernesto stared out to sea. "I would not do that," he said, emphasizing the last word, as if he had given it serious consideration along with other options. "By now, the sharks must have developed a taste for Cubans."

We turned back toward La Terraza, past the derelict fishing boats, toward the town that climbs a low hill away from the sea. As we climbed up the sloping walkway a man on a bicycle in the uniform of the Guardia Frontera did a double take and then braked to study us.

When he was safely behind, I said, "Checking you out."

"Yes. And you."

We did not look back. We knew he was talking into his little radio.

Back at the marina I tipped Ernesto $5 and gave him a supply of soap and shampoo for his wife, and a hardball for his son. He rubbed his thumbs over the ball, his eyes welling. "Oh, thank you, man." The ball had cost $2 in the K-Mart at Marathon, and I silently wished I had spent a little more to buy one that said "made in America" instead of "made in China."

The Sailors

Day by day the streets were changing, and so was the marina. Two Americans in their fifties strolled down the canal in the company of two young, attractive, brightly dressed Cuban women. By chance, I was coming up out of DREAM WEAVER's cabin, and said hello.

"We're going to be sailing in the Tampa to Havana race this spring; we thought we'd come over and check out the marina facilities."

"Are you off a boat?"

"No, we're vacationing over in the Yucatán and we flew over. These are some Cuban friends of ours. Actually, they're friends of our friends in Mexico. This isn't quite what it looks like . . . you know."

He made the introductions. "We're staying at the Plaza hotel and the girls came over this morning to show us around Old Havana. In an hour and a half we were stopped and they had their identities checked four times."

"There is a new initiative being enforced."

"I guess there is."

Tomás and Charlie at Sunset

In the evenings the sailors strolled back and forth between boats; the powerboaters setting up camp on deck chairs moved onto the concrete wharf, drinking and swapping stories with each other. I was returning from Havana, thinking vaguely about the bearded man in front of La Bodeguita del Medio who panhandled me for a dollar with the promise that he was going to shave and get a job. Excellent English. An academic, I guessed, but something had gotten the best of him: poverty, despair, rum. I gave him a disposable razor I had with the goodies in my backpack, and he reacted as if it was a sign from God.

I chatted my way through the first knot of sailors. "I've been in Cuba before," a burly American told me over Cristals, "but I wouldn't want our friends here to know that. The circumstances were quite different. Those were the days when I thought it was up to me to save the world from communists." He would say no more, except that it was on the other side of the island. The Bay of Pigs is on the other side of the island.

Tomás and Charlie were in the cockpit of ROSINANTE, taking in the evening air and dockside chatter. "Jesus, man," Tomás exclaimed as I approached, "you freaked us out this morning."

"We thought you were the friggin' CIA," Charlie added.

I had been taking snapshots of the boats from the

other side of the channel, wearing sunglasses and a baseball cap, and I had seen the two freeze and stare at me until I waved and took off the cap.

The boat boys claimed mysterious people, agents, slipped in and out of the marina and photographed the boats. Five boats in a row were flying American flags, and ROSINANTE was flying a Key West flag as well. We were not exactly keeping a low profile. Men in small Russian-built Ladas with diplomatic plates frequently cruised the docks, but I had never seen them take pictures. The Cubans didn't need to take pictures of us; they knew where we were every minute.

"Didn't mean to scare you. It does get a little creepy, everybody watching everybody else all the time."

"You aren't kidding. When we came in the other day, we were maybe ten miles out, the marina hailed us by our boat's name. There was nobody around. We hadn't been on the radio. How did they know the name of the boat?"

I shrugged. "Submarines, maybe. Or maybe their people talk to our people."

"What's going on in Havana?" Charlie asked.

"More cops checking more people."

"Tell me about it. Look where the guards are tonight."

During the first few days, the marina security guards were constantly on the dock, often offered and taking a beer or a glass of rum and making trades—a snorkeling mask my kids had outgrown for the guard's sunglasses; I had sat on mine. Those days were ending. Now they kept back from the docks and peered into cars that had already been cleared twice: once through the guarded gate at Avenida 5 and again through a security guard at a speed bump on the road between the channels.

And, of course, no longer did the *jineteras* knock on the hull and come aboard to party. No Cubans were allowed on boats except for certain ones who were somehow approved to work. It frustrated the old Cuba hands like Tomás.

"Man, this is getting serious," he complained. "This is completely different. When I was here in 1996 it was wide open. The *chicas* would come down the docks, it was a parade until you saw one you liked. Now Cubans are afraid to be seen with tourists. Fidel is peeing in a lot of people's rice bowls. I don't see those big sports fishing boats here that used to make the run from Florida. Boaters talk to each other. Word gets out."

We were going from being residents of a guarded gate community to being inmates in our own institution.

In Old Havana the watchers and lookers were now actively checking the identification papers of young women and rummaging through the backpacks of the teenagers. Tourists were left alone. In fact here at the marina the music—most of it American—raged on at the swimming pool 60 yards away, and the Cubanacán tour buses came and went daily with fresh loads of Canadians, Germans and British people. In the evening we could see them being entertained in the Masai restaurant by the lovely dancers in the skimpy traditional outfits of bikini pants and bright red blouses with puffy sleeves. Later the dancers would come out in street clothes to be picked up in government vans, and members of the band went home on motorbikes. First thing after breakfast, the tourists were whisked off in their buses for the tour of the day. Cuba is a stage set for tourists, but backstage life is different.

Johnnie

A small red motorcycle stopped on the road and a handsome young man walked down to the boat.

"Hi, I'm Johnnie. I hear you were looking for me." His English was perfect.

"I have a package for you from some friends of yours in Key West." He remembered them. He poked through the contents. "This is great, just in time. I didn't get any sleep at all last night, my son cried and cried. He has allergies. When you get back, thank them for me. Do you need any work done on your boat?"

"No, I'm on a tight budget."

"Need the bottom cleaned? Look." He pulled out his wallet and showed me his scuba certification card. "NAUI certified." NAUI is the National Association of Underwater Instructors and certifies scuba divers.

"No, I hauled in Key West and had it cleaned. How did you get such good English?"

"I just worked at it. It's the future."

"You would make a very good capitalist if you ever leave Cuba."

He was a hard-working, engaging young man, and people trusted him.

"I know. I have a lot of American friends. I just got a letter from a guy who came here on a boat who asked me to keep an eye on his girl friend. He's afraid she'll get mixed up with some guy. Can you believe it? How does he know I won't go after her myself?"

"Is she Cuban?"

"No, American. Flew in from the Bahamas. I wouldn't go after her, but that's a crazy thing to ask. American women like me. I try to be charming." Johnnie wasn't shy.

"What's all this security about? It seems to get tighter every day."

"It's the trial, man."

"What trial?"

"You don't know about the trial? Do you have a TV on board?"

"Sure." I plugged in the little 5-inch black and white TV. The last time I tried Cuban television it was Scooby-Doo cartoons in Spanish.

While other Cubans were staying away from the boats, Johnnie climbed aboard without a moment's hesitation. "That's your TV?" Johnnie burst out laughing. "That little thing? Turn on Channel 6." He shook his head. All Americans must be expected to have 24-inch color TVs and a satellite dish. In fact, the boat across the channel did have a direct broadcast satellite dish bolted to the concrete pad.

A man in a robe was making a statement. "What's this all about?" I asked.

"The Salvadoran who blew up the hotels is on trial. This is the prosecutor. He's asking for the death penalty. The trial has been going on for six days; this is the last day when they sum it up. It's incredible. One guy was a double agent: Agent 44 for the guys in Miami and agent Felix for the Cuban Secret Police, do you believe it?" He laughed. "It's like a movie."

It was a dirty little scenario of Cuban-American intrigue and terrorism, reported in *Granma* and carried live on Cuban television, for the anti-American propaganda value. Raúl Ernesto Cruz León, a Salvadoran under arrest in Havana, confessed that in 1997 he was in the hire of a man named Francisco Chavez. The Cuban government says Chavez is connected to the Cuban American National Foundation (CANF), a Miami-based organization of Cuban exiles. The newspaper *Granma* reported that León confessed to six bombings: the Nacional, Capri, Triton, Château and Copacabana hotels and the Bodeguita del Medio. On September 4, three hotels were bombed within an hour, including the Copacabana, where an Italian tourist was killed. That night, the Bodeguita del Medio was bombed. Over five months beginning in April 1997, other bombing targets included the Ambos Mundos, the Sevilla and Plaza hotels. Three people were injured by the bombs, most of them concocted with C-4 plastic and at least two of them put together by León while he stayed at the Ambos Mundos. He was paid $4,500 per bombing, according to his testimony reported in *Granma*.

The objective was to destabilize the tourism economy by scaring off the tourists and to lead the government to believe there was an uprising from within, possibly by operatives in the military.

Another Salvadoran was awaiting sentencing for hotel bombing while León went to trial. Otto Rene Rodríguez Llerena was convicted of placing a bomb in August of 1997 at the fancy new Meliá Cohiba hotel, one of the Spanish investments in Cuba. On his way back into Cuba in 1998 he was arrested at the airport carrying plastic explosives, clocks and batteries, which he was supposed to deliver to "Juan Francisco Fernandez Gomez." *Granma* was reporting that Juan was a double agent for both CANF and Cuban State Security, and he was busy unraveling alleged connections between the bombers and CANF. Llerena was paid $1,000 and travel expenses for the bombing. The prosecution was also requesting a death sentence for him.

The CANF describes itself as an "independent, non-profit organization dedicated to the re-establishment of freedom and democracy in Cuba." The Cuban government connects it to the CIA.

Johnnie summed it up. "Who knows how many more of those guys there are around, or what they'll do next. That's what this is all about."

It struck home. I had been in at least half those targets in the last few days. I watched Johnnie wave and head home on his motorbike, wondering how much of what Johnnie saw and heard on these boats went straight to Cuban State Security.

Other Cubans said it was not just about the trials, Fidel was nervous. There were rumors that 7,000 new policemen were coming on duty, many of them from out in the country, poorly educated, briefly trained and pressed into duty. "We must have a factory somewhere that turns them out," a Cuban told me, shaking his head.

Jack

He was walking toward me along the dock wearing a T-shirt that said "Marblehead, Massachusetts." I smiled, nodded, said "Marblehead."

He looked me up and down and saw boat shoes, shorts, a tan, the generally worn and grubby countenance of a boat person. "You off a boat?"

"Yeah, right here." We were next to DREAM WEAVER. "Vermont."

"No kidding. I'm a liveaboard in Marblehead." He pulled out a Polaroid snapshot of a 34-foot sailboat. "This is my boat. I just flew over from Mexico to see what this place is like. I thought I'd sail back with somebody if I could find a spot as crew. I was looking for a red catamaran named DOS DIABLOS; I heard they need crew."

"They did need crew. It's a guy and his wife. He's maybe seventy, and they wanted a third hand to go to the Dry Tortugas, then the Keys. But they took off yesterday."

"What are your plans?"

"I have a crewman coming in day after tomorrow. We're going to hang around a few days and then head back to Key West."

"Any chance of catching a ride?"

"I'd have to talk it over with him. Want a beer?"

"No, I don't drink, but I'll come aboard to talk."

His name was Jack O'Leary, and he wore his graying hair pulled straight back into a short ponytail. He was a trim and solid fifty-something, with a Marine Corps globe and anchor tattoo on his left forearm. He said he lived on his boat and ran a painting contracting business, serving the Marblehead carriage trade.

I had visited Marblehead, but only briefly. "My daughter-in-law is from Marblehead. Her dad is a lawyer there and her mother works in the boat business."

"Oh, really. It's a great little town." He did not ask for their names. "I live on Dock C."

"How do you like Cuba?"

"It's strange. The minute I got into the airport they wanted to know where I was staying. I was just going to find some hotel. They want to know where you are all the time."

"I know. How long have you been here?"

"Almost three days."

"Let's walk over to the cafe and get a cup of coffee; I don't have much in the way of soft drinks."

We sat at the counter of the Boise cafe and had strong Cuban coffee.

"So where are you staying now?"

"I'm staying on a boat on Channel 1, a converted fishing trawler called EVANGELINE."

A red alert ran down my spine. "I know that boat; it's kind of hidden behind the warehouse. How did you land there?"

"Oh, I just walked down the dock and spotted them for liveaboards. I mean, once you are one, you can always spot one. I asked if they had a bunk and they did."

"What do those guys do? I saw some Cuban women on board the other day and that's the only boat around here that can pull that off." The boat might have been just another cruiser, but a sailor had told me about a boat at Marina Hemingway that never left and was full of what he thought were Drug Enforcement Agency agents posing as Canadian sport fishermen. EVANGELINE matched that description, but I couldn't understand why Fidel would tolerate the presence of U.S. agents. Granted, he was anti-drug to the degree that he had one of his leading generals executed in 1989 for being mixed up in drug trafficking, but allowing the Drug Enforcement Agency to camp out in Marina Hemingway seemed like a stretch.

"Yeah, for whatever reason the Cubans don't bother them about that. They've been here like three years, so maybe they've worked it out . . . you know, somebody gets a few bucks. They're getting out, though. They're going to sell the boat to some Canadian."

"Why?"

"They think it's going to change here. The good times are over. Fidel is nervous. They know the scene. There are like five or six thousand new cops on the streets. Some of these are really stupid, illiterate. They train them a little, but not much. Like, they don't know how to handle situations with tourists. These guys say that if you have a Cuban woman with you, keep her ID card in your pocket, and if they try to check her ID, hold on to her arm and get right in their face. They don't know what to do. They aren't supposed to mess with tourists."

"All the women are scared."

"They should be. There is a hell of a housing shortage with all these new cops around. If they can bust a girl for prostitution, right or wrong, the girl goes to jail and the cop gets her apartment. Then the government hires her out to the hotels as labor, chambermaid, cleaner, whatever. She gets paid $15 a month. The government charges the hotel management $130 a month. Nice system."

"How do you know that?"

"The guys on the boat."

I hesitated a moment. "I heard those guys are with the Drug Enforcement Agency."

Silence, then, "I don't know, maybe they are. Look, I'd like to sail back if you can use an extra hand. I'd like to take some cigars back."

"With three it gets crowded in a 32-footer. And I'm not taking anything back, no cigars, nothing. They can seize my boat and fine me $200,000; it's not worth it."

"They're just trying to scare you."

"They've succeeded."

He shrugged it off. "What brings you to Cuba?"

"I wanted to see it before it changed. Now was the time. I definitely did not want to be here when Castro goes out and the government changes. I think there will be an outbreak of machete trauma going around. A lot of people want to be in charge, including some people in south Miami, the ones who used to train in the Everglades."

Jack picked up the check. "Don't worry, you would

be fine. The Marines at Guantánamo know exactly how many Americans are in the marina here. First sign of trouble, the helicopters will come in and the Marines will establish a perimeter around the marina and around that U.S. Special Interests Section down on Embassy Row. Americans will be lifted to Guantánamo in no time."

"Maybe, but the boat would still be here. What makes you think that would happen?"

"I was in the Corps. I put people on helicopters from the top of the embassy when Saigon fell. We were the last ones out. We know you're here."

We? Jack was still in somebody's Corps. He came by in the evening, briefly, to have a look at the big party being thrown for racers in the Transcaraïbes race from Martinique to Havana, said "I'll catch up with you later," and vanished.

Avenida 5

One of Fidel's residences is on Avenida 5, the Embassy Row between the marina and Havana. It is no secret; a sign out front says so. Like Saddam, Castro moves from house to house without any particular pattern, typically traveling in a convoy of three Mercedes—no one knows which one he is in—flanked by Land Rovers full of guards, the security entourage made up of a trusted inner circle. The first week in Havana, our white VW shuttle bus sped along at a steady clip as it went back and forth into town. Then it started to slow almost to a crawl as it approached *El Comandante*'s house, resuming speed when well past it. Oh well, another Cuban mystery.

One of the responses a few sailors had made to the curtailment of female Cuban company on board was renting an apartment or room in a private home at a cost of $15 to $30 a night. In fact, some yachtsmen were forgetting about sailing to Cuba and simply flew down to find a room or apartment in Santa Maria or Playa del Estes east of Havana, where the beach action was fast if you could compete with the hordes of prowling Italians and Germans.

There is risk to the Cuban landlord in these special times because the principal function of the Committee for the Defense of the Revolution (CDR) is to keep a watchful eye on neighbors and turn them in for slightly better public housing. But the money was just too tempting. Kevin, one of the three sailors on WIND LINE, soon moved into a room in Sante Fe, the community outside the marina, and took daily Spanish lessons. He, the skipper Jake, and the Alaskan fisherman Kodiak, wanted to blend into Cuban society and meet young ladies. Jake spoke Spanish very well, but Kodiak was struggling and also signed up for lessons. They took to hanging out in the disco in Santa Fe but without much luck. Cuban girls were becoming increasingly nervous about being seen with foreigners because the police were now clearing the women out of entire bars, lining them up in the street and inspecting identity cards. However, the sailors from WIND LINE did spend time with their Cuban landlords and language instructors.

Kevin and I were bouncing along in the white VW, heading for Havana, past the towering Russian Embassy building that looks like a sword plunged into the earth, slowing to a crawl for *El Comandante*'s house.

"I wonder why they slow down here now," I said softly to Kevin, not really wanting to raise the issue with the driver.

"Later," he said without looking at me.

After walking past the old fort a dozen times—

Castillo de la Real Fuerza at the foot of Obispo Street—
we decided to go inside and look around. Display cases
held elegant ceramic art, the first Cuban art I had seen
that I really wanted to own. We climbed to the top of
the fort, a stone's throw from La Giraldilla, where an old
man in a Panama hat played his guitar, danced, and sang
Guantanamera, a ballad to a woman from Guantánamo
sung by "a sincere man." We were alone, out in the open.
From the hilltop across Havana Bay in Casablanca a
granite statue of Christ larger than the one in Rio
opened its arms in our direction.

Kevin picked up the conversation. "This is what I
hear from my Cuban friends. About a week ago Fidel's
motorcade was coming out of the house. Two guys on
motorcycles came speeding up and didn't slow down
when they saw the cars. The guards jumped out and
shot them."

"Shot them?"

"Dead."

"Is that true?"

"That's the story that's going around. The Cubans
say it's true."

"There have been lots of cases of guys on motorcycles being assassins, so I suppose guards have a reason
to get jumpy. But imagine if it was a couple of guys like
us on rented motorbikes, guys who don't know the
game."

Kevin laughed. "Wouldn't they be embarrassed! Of
course, we'd be dead."

"Slim consolation. We'll never know if that really
happened. We won't read about that in *Granma*. That's
the one truth about Cuba: you never know what's true."

7 | *Dictators and Mobsters*

In a place where few people have anything, being resourceful is the key to survival. The Cubans most travelers meet are selling something, usually illegally. They will have a business card even if it is typed individually on the back of a cut-up cereal carton. The cards say things like:

PRIVATE HOUSE. PRIVATE CAR.
TOUR IN HAVANA OR SOME PLACES.
EVERYTHING YOU NEED
or
TOURIST GUIDE AND REPRESENTATIVE
OF CIGAR FACTORY:
FLUENT IN ENGLISH, KNOWS CUBA FROM A TO Z,
TRAVEL COMPANION AND MORE

Telephone numbers are often listed, but it is common that the phone will belong to a generous neighbor and the person you are looking for is not there, but can call you back. One of these "anything you want" operatives brought a supply of slide film to the boat, for which I reimbursed him, adding for his effort a supply of toilet paper, shampoo and soap. In Cuba it is always a good idea to establish the terms of the transaction very specifically, but lucky indeed is the fellow who completes a transaction with a Cuban that does not have a surprise at the end.

Even so, striking up a friendship is not a bad idea; these promoters know their way through and around the Cuban system and know where to find things. No need to look for them; they will find you in places like Cafe Paris on Obispo Street. Manuel found me in Plaza de Armas, and he turned out to be a treasure.

"Good afternoon, are you a Canadian?" was his approach, and I thought it was going to be a cigar hustle, but then realized the English was too good, too precise.

"No, I'm an American."

"Really?" he was surprised. "Are you looking for someplace special? I'm a professor of history and perhaps I could help show you around." He asked for nothing.

Manuel was in his late forties, with long, straight graying hair that would be combed straight back except that it fell across his cheeks making him look like a French poet or a temperamental violinist. His brown V-neck sweater was worn very thin. Manuel was a man of intellect and dignity, virtues which must be exceedingly difficult to sustain in Cuba.

I almost said no, because there was always a hustle somewhere down the line, but will forever be grateful that I said, "As a matter of fact, I'm looking for two places. I'm looking for a square near the waterfront

Sloppy Joe's dates back to the 1920s. It is soon to be restored.

174

where there is a fountain and a bar named Cafe de la Perla de San Francisco; and I'm also looking for another place that has to do with Hemingway, Sloppy Joe's."

"The square is not far, only a few blocks. I'll walk along with you. The bar is not there any more, but I can show you where it was. The fountain is there, the Fountain of the Lions." Manuel inquired about my quest, my interest in Hemingway.

"Hemingway's book *To Have and Have Not* opens in the square. I just wanted to see it."

"There are other Hemingway places along the waterfront. I can show you where he docked the boat when he was in Havana."

We walked along the cobbles on Mercaderes Street, past the shop at 115 called El Navegante, where you can buy nautical charts of all Cuba and every kind of map imaginable. The House of Cigars that Dupee never got to visit was across the street.

"I don't understand the situation at the time of that book; what all the shooting was about down here in la Perla."

The book begins with Harry Morgan's description:

"You know how it is there early in the morning in Havana with the bums still asleep against the walls of the buildings; before even the ice wagons come by with ice for the bars? Well, we came across the square from the dock to the Pearl of San Francisco Cafe to get coffee and there was only one beggar awake in the square and he was getting a drink out of the fountain. But when we got inside the cafe and sat down, there were the three of them waiting for us."

The three Cubans want illegal passage to Key West in Harry's boat, the QUEEN CONCH, a thinly disguised version of Joe Russell's ANITA. The conversation has political overtones about "when things change" in Cuba. Harry refuses. The three Cubans walk out into the square and are promptly involved in a shootout with a guy carrying a Thompson submachine gun and another with a shotgun. The three are killed, the windows are shot out of la Perla, Harry and his first mate are hiding behind the bar nervously nipping from the bottles. Hemingway's books have a lot of Tommy-guns in them.

"That was the time of the revolutionaries against Machado. In the book the revolutionaries go to Key West to rob a bank to support the revolution." His specialty was Cuban military history. Manuel, I would discover, not only knew every building in Old Havana, he knew what stood there before. His wife was a researcher involved in the restoration of Old Havana.

It began to fall into place. On his way through Cuba to Africa in 1933 for the safari, Hemingway had witnessed a shootout in the streets. The following year when Hemingway brought PILAR to Cuba he had on board Arnold Samuelson, an aspiring young writer from Minnesota who served as a crewman while Hemingway coached him on writing. A Cuban named Alfonso filled Arnold with stories of bombings and shootings he orchestrated as a member of the ABC, a revolutionary group trying to oust the President, General Gerardo Machado y Morales. Alfonso bragged of having blown up a general by intercepting a pair of new boots being delivered to him and planting a bomb in the package.

Manuel the historian filled in the blanks. The shooters Hemingway had seen and written into the book were very likely operatives of *Partido de la Porra*, government death squads that helped to squash dissidents. Machado had created this organization and the *Sección de Expertos*—secret police specializing in torture—to support his presidency, which had evolved from elected official to dictatorship. He employed a police force of 15,000. His presidency followed a familiar political pattern that began after the Spanish-American War when Cuba first struggled to create a republic after centuries of Spanish control and U.S. economic influence.

First there was the honeymoon. During Machado's presidency it was the period from 1925 to 1927 when the economy was good, a highway was built from Santiago to Havana as part of a big public works initiative, and people were again employed after a sugar crash in 1920.

Then came the period of disillusionment, usually caused by blatant corruption, a collapse of sugar prices, or both. Machado's problems began in 1927 when he extended his own term to six years, and barely coerced support from his political allies for his 1928 election. Then the Great Depression hit the United States, and Cuba's sugar economy collapsed, taking most other sectors with it.

The third stage was characterized by strikes and violence, predictably with a government response of repression. Political parties, some new and some dormant, returned to the scene with new causes. For 30 years, the political scene had been dominated by figures who played a role in the Ten Years' War against Spain. In the late 1920s new groups were forming and the old guard did not want them to gain a foothold. The generation born into the notion of Cuba as a republic was coming of age, and they tended to be more radical: students, the middle class, intellectuals, labor unions, communists, the ABC among them. They had strong ideas about what a Cuban republic should be, and would not be disenfranchised by the old guard. The ABC comprised

mostly intellectuals, professionals and students organized into clandestine cells.

These new political forces were rising as the economy was falling. Strikes were orchestrated. In March
1930 when 200,000 strikers paralyzed the economy,
Machado responded with arrests, torture and assassination. Warfare broke out in the countryside, where revolutions always begin in Cuba, as armed bands burned
cane fields and ambushed trains and small military outposts. Urban terrorism in the form of bombings and
sniping was introduced by radical groups.

The final stage of this dance was the U.S. intervention aimed at protecting American investments in Cuba,
and they were huge. The intervention sometimes took
the form of gunboats and marines; at other times political maneuvering put hand-picked candidates into
office, several of them Cubans educated in the United
States.

The pattern from honeymoon to U.S. intervention
was repeated five times between 1903 and 1930. Our
right to intervene had been built into the Cuban Con-
stitution, along with perpetual ownership of Guantánamo. This time an astute man named Sumner Welles
was appointed ambassador to Cuba. The situation was
in chaos, but his appeals for military intervention were
denied. The new president, Franklin Roosevelt, had
promised a "good neighbor" policy in Latin America.
Like a love affair, America was passionate when it wrestled Cuba, Puerto Rico and the Philippines from Spain
at the turn of the century, launching Teddy Roosevelt
up San Juan Hill into the presidency, but by now Cuba
had become the tiresome mistress who again and again
threatens to commit political suicide.

Still, the stakes were high. Cuba was torched and

bankrupt after the Ten Years' War ended with the Spanish-American War, ripe for an infusion of cash. In 20 years, American investors had put $200 million into Cuba and acquired major or controlling interest in sugar and tobacco production, railroads and other transportation, utilities and banking. A reciprocity treaty bound Cuba's major export, sugar, to one market, the United States. And the treaty had contributed to making Cuba a one-product economy.

Welles managed to convince Machado to resign one year early, but Cuba was sliding toward revolution so rapidly that would not be soon enough. He cut a deal with leaders of the Cuban army to usher Machado out of office. Machado had made himself rich while protecting U.S. interests in Cuba, although his tactics were compared to Mussolini's. Now he had outlived his usefulness. He fled Cuba in August 1933, supposedly with a suitcase full of gold in his hand.

He was succeeded by Secretary of State Carlos Manuel de Céspedes, who began his term in a Cuba buried in depression, the middle of the traditional political cycle. He did not last a month, and one of the people responsible for his demise was an Army sergeant, Fulgencio Batista.

If Americans ever get to take a cruise boat to Cuba, and land at the rambling yellow Sierra Maestra ship terminal, their first taste of Havana will be the elegant little Plaza de San Francisco and the Fountain of the Lions. The fountain has a carved stone base about 20 feet across from which rises a pedestal adorned with four reclining lions. Above, on a carved column, is a basin from which small streams of water cascade. A Cuban mother and daughter were sitting on the base eating popcorn from cones made of rolled-up paper. This cobblestone gateway to Old Havana has been completely restored.

Manuel pointed to a building opposite the terminal. "La Perla was there, but it was torn down in 1953, two years after the owner died. He never promoted the connection to Hemingway. Maybe he never knew it. There was a small hotel with maybe a dozen rooms, the cafe and, of course, the bar." The building that had replaced it looked much older than 1953. It is made of stone and has five tall arched portals, behind which are ten stairs leading to five tall wooden doors. The first floor looks like a commercial building, but the stories above have balconies and tall French doors leading onto them, suggesting residences.

"Hemingway spent a lot of time down here. There is another place not famous at all. I'll show you."

"The book talks about Donovan's bar and the Cunard bar."

"They were here on the square. They are gone too. Donovan's was a rough place full of sailors and women looking for sailors."

I followed Manuel along Avenida del Puerto, which changes names at every curve, past a beautiful stone cathedral that defined the south end of the square. "This was the church and convent of San Francisco de Asis back in the early 1700s. Religious parades would start here, the stations of the cross. It is now a music conservatory and museum. You should come for a piano recital, it is quite lovely and they are held every week."

Restoration had come too late for some of the buildings along the avenue. One had simply collapsed, leaving nothing standing except the interior framing and the four stone columns that had been the ground floor facade. A hillside of rubble rose up the wall of the adjacent building.

"Here is the Dos Hermanos, the Two Brothers." The single-story ivory colored building had large green awnings over tall, wide doors and windows, each with a metal garage-type door that could be rolled up. A band—two guitars, a drummer, a singer—was performing near the front door as we walked in. A long mahogany bar ran off to the right, the young barman was dressed in white shirt, black tie, black vest. A few Cuban couples sat at the simple wooden tables. The cream-colored walls were decorated with old photos of Havana in inexpensive frames. To the left behind the bar was a small kitchen and the rest rooms. This was a real place; the way the Floridita once was.

We sat at a table and ordered beers. "I like this place."

"A few tourists come in, usually people who find it when they come exploring off the cruise ships."

The singer smiled at us mid-song when we paid attention to her. "This kind of music is called *son motuno*, the rhythm is like the rhythm of riding a horse. This is a folk song about a farmer. He is coming into the market with his horse, and he is singing, 'I'm going into town; today is my day', like his lucky day, you know?" The irrepressible Cuban optimism.

"Cuban music is being discovered in the U.S. It is becoming very popular." The next number was different.

"This one is about a man and a woman, and it says, 'Hear me, Conchita. Taste me; savor me.' What do you think of Cuban women?"

"They're beautiful. They radiate energy, fun. They look you in the eye and tease."

"Have you gotten to know any?"

"No."

"You will. Cuban women are not shy."

"The ones that I see out and around are awfully young."

"It doesn't matter."

We meandered like tourists back along the avenue toward the Malecón. Manuel pointed at a two-story building that seemed to float above the waters of Havana Bay on invisible piers. It was brightly painted in cream and orange, but crumbling around the edges. "This is where Hemingway kept his boat when he was in Havana." The sign out front said Los Marinos and offered karaoke, snacks and ice cream. I was certain that in another life it was the Club Nautico. PILAR often anchored across the bay in Casablanca, but Club Nautico was a yacht club that sponsored sport fishing tourna-

Now a snack bar and hangout for young people, this building on Old Havana's waterfront was once Club Nautico, the yacht club where Hemingway kept his boat.

182

ments and provided Hemingway and others with a spot for short-term docking.

An incident took place here that nearly ended the Hemingway/Mary Welsh marriage. In May 1950, Mary was entertaining a guest from America and had invited her on board PILAR for lunch. PILAR was docked at Club Nautico and Hemingway was to meet them there at noon. They waited for an hour, and finally Hemingway showed up tanked on daiquiris. He had with him a Cuban friend, Roberto Herrera and, in Mary's words "Havana's youngest, prettiest whore, whom he had nicknamed Xenophobia. I couldn't blame the shy, ignorant girl for accepting his invitation to share our good food, but fury burst inside me at Ernest's insolence and arrogance in making Bea (Guck) and me wait so long and at his shoddy manners toward Bea. She generously murmured she thought the ploy amusing. She had never seen a designated whore before, and Ernest had contributed to her education."

Mary fumed for two days, then wrote Hemingway a scathing letter in which she told him she was leaving him. The two had a peculiar practice of arguing via letters and notes left on each other's work tables. She wrote, "In 1944 . . . I thought you were a straight and honorable and brave man and magnetically endearing to me . . . although I was suspicious of your over-drinking . . ."

She wrote he was "gay and charming and sturdy in spirit . . . when you are not drunk," and of his "petulant irritability, protecting your steel-bound ego, if your rectitude or infallibility should be questioned."

She added that the marriage was a failure and she was leaving. Hemingway talked her out of it and kept her busy with the projects at Finca Vigía which she so

Lovers on the Malecón. In the background is Morro Castle and the entrance to Havana Harbor.

enjoyed. He had counseled the young Samuelson that to deal with women was "to be tender when you least feel like it."

It was a beautiful afternoon to be strolling along Havana Bay with Morro Castle ahead of us. A young couple was sitting on the seawall, wrapped up in each other, kissing, their bicycle leaning against the wall. In the distance, curving off to the left, was the Malecón, with its fading 300-year-old colonial buildings of pink and peach and lime green, many covered with scaffolding signaling restoration. In the United States they would be million-dollar properties overlooking the sea, but here it was all dilapidated public housing where faint lightbulbs glowed through cracks around shuttered windows after dark and people lingered mysteriously in doorways.

Immediately to our left across the avenue was the public crafts market, a village of canopies and umbrellas selling everything from crocheted dresses to mass produced paintings of Che. Two young men who miraculously still had all their fingers operated the drink concession, hacking the top off coconuts with a half dozen whacks of the machete and driving a plastic straw through the pulp so you could drink the cool coconut water inside, then eat the meat. A mountain of ravaged coconuts grew beside their booth.

We angled away from the waterfront and back into Old Havana at the beautiful Music Museum, an early twentieth-century mansion that houses instruments and exhibits on Cuban music. A huge pink bus pulled by a truck tractor rambled past. It seemed to sag in the middle, giving it humps fore and aft. "We call these *camellos*, camels. During the Special Period we had a huge transportation problem. These will carry more than 300 people if everyone is standing up."

Off to the right was another statue of a Cuban hero, General Maximo Gómez, hero of the Ten Years' War. Gómez and his horse, cast in bronze and placed on a large pedestal, are a landmark along the Malecón and waterfront.

Looming ahead beyond a broad walkway was a building that looked like the love child of a liaison between a wedding cake and a Disneyland castle. A dome rose from the center and each corner supported an ornate tower. Huge windows faced us, the sea, and Morro Castle behind us. This former presidential palace was the home of General Machado and a few of his predecessors dating back to 1917. It was constructed to be the seat of the provincial government, complete with interior design by Tiffany & Co., but became the Cuban White House. Its last occupant was Fulgencio Batista, the man who ran Cuba himself and through puppet presidents for most of the years between 1933 and the moment he fled before Castro's forces rolled into the city on January 1, 1959. He was a happy partner of the U.S. Mafia, which was running prostitution and gambling in Havana under the management of Meyer Lansky. Every night a bagman representing Señora Batista would make the rounds of the casinos collecting 10 percent of the profits. When Batista and his family finally fled the country, eventually settling in Spain, he had built up a nest egg estimated at $300 million.

Batista grew up in poverty, born out of wedlock to a cane cutter father—his grandfather was a Chinese indentured laborer—and a black mother at the east end of Cuba. He joined the army, learned stenography, and was promoted to sergeant.

He rose to prominence when he organized a protest for better wages and housing for army non-commissioned officers. He became head of the country through a series of events that could have belonged in a Gilbert and Sullivan play: The Accidental Revolution. When the non-coms presented their demands to officers, the officers walked out and went home, leaving Batista and his mutineering cronies in charge of Camp Colombia in Havana. In a strange partnership born of revolutions, student radicals urged the mutineers to seize the government, and so they did, tossing out Céspedes. A military *junta* was set up.

But these were tricky times; every other faction in Cuba lined up to oppose the new government. Old political parties were disenfranchised, and so were new ones like the ABC. The old military leaders under Machado suddenly were complete outsiders, despite the deal they had cut with Sumner Welles that said they would be taken care of for ousting Machado. Businessmen feared economic collapse. The students who had been partners of the army in the revolution were pushing for broad, experimental social change. Sumner Welles was sending messages hinting that communists were taking over and military intervention might be necessary after all. To stabilize the situation, a junta member, Ramon Grau San Martin, took charge and within weeks Sergeant Batista promoted himself. He skipped a few ranks and became a colonel and commander of the army, essentially taking control of the government.

The astute Sumner Welles soon cast himself in the role of Batista's coach and advisor, concluding that Batista was the only player in Cuba who represented authority. Grau was tilting toward communism. By January, Batista had ousted Grau and replaced him with long-time liberal Manuel Mendieta, who was recognized by the United States five days later. But radicals from within Grau's government formed a new political party and set off down the familiar opposition path of strikes, sabotage, bombings and assassination.

In the spring of 1935, a general strike signaled another crisis. The government of Mendieta declared martial law, occupied the university, outlawed unions, arrested and tortured some strike leaders, assassinated others, and set up firing squads to deal with dissidents. The harsh measures crushed the strike and the armed opposition, but was so repressive it also brought down President Mendieta.

Not to worry: the political vacuum was filled by Fulgencio Batista and a series of puppet governments that ruled until 1944, when Grau returned to power. Batista was on the sidelines until 1952. His comeback was planned in Florida at a meeting with the mob at his

Daytona Beach home. Meyer Lansky had a home in nearby Hollywood. When it became clear he could not win the election if he ran as a candidate, Batista organized a coup, dismantled congress and canceled the election. One of the candidates for congress in that canceled election was 25-year old attorney and baseball fan Fidel Castro. The Hemingways were headed for Club Nautico and PILAR the morning of March 10 when they began to run into soldiers on the road. They heard the news on the radio. Few shots were fired, but the St. Petersburg to Havana yacht race sailed unwittingly into the coup and one racer turned back when shots were fired across the bow.

Batista's return to power marked the blossoming of the mob's Havana enterprises: gambling and prostitution. Batista began a reign of brutality and repression supported by the United States. He was not, after all, a communist.

After 1959, the old presidential palace had too many memories for Fidel Castro and his revolutionaries. One

The former Presidential Palace, now the Museum of the Revolution.

was a 1957 attack by student commandos on the palace, aimed at Batista. The government had been tipped off; the rebels were slaughtered. After Castro took charge, the palace became the Museum of the Revolution. It does not have particularly nice things to say about the United States government and the CIA; an area of the museum devoted to them as well as Batista is called *El Ricón de los Cretinos* (the cretins' corner).

Out back, in an open plaza, is a collection of recent military hardware scattered around a glass-enclosed building. Manuel pointed to a twisted tangle of aluminum that could once have been shaped like a cigar. Next to it was a small Soviet-built ground to air missile.

"That was the engine of one of your U-2 spy planes," Manuel explained, "and the missile is of the type that shot it down. It is said that one night Fidel was in the Russian tracking station to watch the U-2 fly over. It was in 1962, during the missile time. They taunted us. The Russian said that to shoot such a plane down it was only necessary to engage it, and he demonstrated how, and to push a certain button. Fidel said, 'You mean like this?' and he pushed the button. Down came the plane."

"What happened to the pilot?"

"I don't know. Behind the missile is an American-built plane from the Bay of Pigs invasion."

I said what I felt. "That was a very stupid thing for us to do."

Starting it at all went too far, it was planned by the wrong people, and having been started, it did not go far enough to win. I said no more about it, and neither did Manuel. Our governments could fight like dinosaurs; we did not have to join in. In the end, his decisions may have gotten John Kennedy assassinated for not going all the way in getting Cuba back for the Mafia. And the

Cuban survivors of the invasion became the core of the U.S. Special Forces operating in Latin America; they trained the soldiers who tracked down and killed Che Guevara in Bolivia.

The invasion was planned by the Central Intelligence Agency and approved by President Kennedy on the assumption that it would look like an operation conducted by Cuban exiles and the United States was not involved. Yet on the night of April 17, 1961, the first person on the beach with a group of Cuban frogmen was an experienced American soldier, Gray Lynch, and the first shots fired on the Cuban shore were from his Browning automatic rifle, propped up on the bow of an inflatable boat. Ironically, he fired at guardsmen in a Jeep, who had turned their headlights on the invaders, thinking a fishing boat was trying to come in over the coral reef, and it should be warned off. The reef had been identified as "cloud reflections" when the U-2 spy plane photos were examined by the invasion planners, but the landing craft carrying the invasion brigade—Brigade 2056—grounded on it before reaching shore. One thing after another went wrong, and finally the invaders were left on the beach to fend for themselves when it was decided that bringing in air cover for their retreat could reveal U.S. involvement. President Kennedy clearly had not been fully briefed on the details. He commented that the invaders could "take to the hills" around the bay, but the area is surrounded by swamps. Those taken prisoner were later ransomed.

In the glass building behind the weapons is *Granma*, a 38-foot wooden luxury yacht that brought an exiled Fidel Castro and 81 others back to Cuba from Mexico in a disastrous voyage that concluded when it was shipwrecked in Oriente Province on December 2, 1956. They had come prepared to launch a revolution, but an uprising in Santiago de Cuba timed to coincide with their "landing" had only served to tip off Batista. In an ambush on December 5, Batista's Rural Guard killed all but 16 of the revolutionaries. The survivors included Fidel, his brother Raúl, and Che Guevara. On New Year's Day 1957, the rebel army consisted of about 30 men. Two years later Fidel's army seized Havana and mobs of jubilant Cubans stormed the gambling casinos and tossed the slot machines and roulette wheels into the streets.

Over the course of two years, Fidel's guerilla war moved through torched cane fields and demolished police and military outposts from the southeast to the northwest. He once commented that he had learned about guerilla warfare from reading *For Whom the Bell Tolls*. The revolutionary rhetoric of the time focused on forging a democratic republic; there was no discussion of socialism or Marxism. The U.S. government supplied arms to Batista, but there is evidence that the CIA was funneling funds to Castro, and the pillar of PILAR, Gregorio Fuentes, claimed that Hemingway was using PILAR to run guns to the rebels. Hemingway had run-ins with Batista's musclemen at Finca Vigía; he had no love for Batista.

The mob-run gambling casinos are gone, but the hotels are still there, all brightly refurbished and showing no signs of being bombed. When Fidel realized in 1991 that he was holding a very poor hand indeed he declared that foreign investors could own 50 percent of new hotel properties and run them on their own.

The Russians were pulling out, Noriega had fallen in Panama and his political soulmates in Nicaragua had collapsed, too. As a communist, it was getting lonely . . .

hardly anyone left to declare "solidarity" with except Vietnam and maybe a few backwater nations in equally bad shape. After 300 years of trying to throw the Spanish out of Cuba, Castro welcomed Spanish hotel investment with open arms. Spain is the biggest investor in hotels in Cuba. Reports in *Granma* speak in glowing terms of Spain's continued interest in Cuba. And billboards along the Malecón announce the visits of dignitaries who have money to spend.

Fidel may be painting himself into a corner. Tourism was the only card left to play, but it has its risks: propaganda only works as long as it is consistent with the experience of those being propagandized. At some point, they are able to decide for themselves between the truth and the poop. Cuba has educated its people and has now exposed them to foreigners who are not the demons they are supposed to be. Except for the Russian embassy and rattling Russian cars, every sign of Russia has vanished. Cubans love things that proclaim "made in America."

"Have you been to the hotel Sevilla?" Manuel asked.

"No."

Tourists from around the world, except the U.S., now stay in the hotels where the American mob's casinos once thrived: The Nacional, Capri, Comodoro, Deauville and Sevilla-Biltmore. The fanciest, Habana Riviera, cost the mob $14 million and opened only three weeks before Castro marched into Havana and closed the casinos. By June, key mob figures had been arrested and kicked out of Cuba.

The little bar off the lobby of the Sevilla is a gem, done in colorful tiles with a ceiling that soars to the top of the building. It feels like a place to get into good kinds of trouble with an exotic foreigner. The walls outside the bar are lined with old black and white photographs of long-dead customers. Gangsters get equal billing with politicians, movie stars and opera singers.

Without hesitation and despite the fact that security people in blue blazers were standing around watching, ready, their hands folded in front of them as if in church listening to a liturgy, Manuel led the way to the elevators and up to the roof garden. I had to keep reminding myself that nobody really cares if you belong here or not unless you are toting a bomb or look terribly out of place or are a *jinetera*. These are the "people's" hotels, the government owns everything.

The roof garden was not yet open for the day, but from the promenade around the top floor we looked down upon Old Havana. It is a city to love, not only because her architecture elicits wonder and surprise and sadness with the turn of every corner, but because it offers a palette of intrigue, mystery, passion, music, laughter, and celebration. Like its women, it is not shy. Like its women, it teases with the promise of sensual pleasures. Betrayal here, if survived, would be forgiven. It is in the nature of some places.

The tree-lined Prado stretches out below toward Morro Castle and the sea, a wonderfully civilized promenade, tile surface glistening in afternoon sunlight, the Champs-Elysées of Havana. A black woman in tight pants, a bandana wrapping her hair, walks through a patch of sunlight, shoulders back, full of herself, looking life and passers-by squarely in the eye. These Latin women do not look at the sidewalk when a man approaches, they look him in the eye, and then study his shoes as if his footwear holds dear secrets.

Strolling the Prado.

What will become of this place when Fidel is gone? I did not feel one bit guilty about wanting to keep American business out. No one has survived us intact. I hoped I would never see Colonel Sanders' stylized image beckoning from a storefront on the Prado, and there is plenty of vacant space. I asked Manuel who would replace Fidel.

"No one knows. Someone in the Cabinet. There are qualified people."

It would have to be someone who could turn Cuba from an isolated communist state increasingly shunned by its neighbors for human rights violations into a respected player in the global economy. Cuba would probably go the way of Russia into confusion, corruption and chaos, and that would be a tragedy. Maybe it would even repeat its familiar cycle. Honeymoon, corruption, collapse, disenchantment, strikes and violence and then what? The U.S. no longer had a constitutional right to intervene, only Guantánamo remained protected.

"Sloppy Joe's", said Manuel, shaking me back to the real world.

"Yes."

"Only two blocks away, up the Prado."

We lingered on the Prado watching the lovers and the children, even a pair of teenagers on in-line skates, and walked slowly up the sloping promenade toward Central Park.

"I have a question," I said to Manuel. "I have seen images of three men everywhere: José Martí, Che Guevara and Hemingway. But not Fidel."

"He forbids it. He has said that the revolution is not about one man, it is about all men."

"But the others?"

"The others are dead. That is different. When Fidel is gone, his image will be like theirs."

We turned left onto Animas Street, the block behind the Sevilla, and Manuel pointed to a crumbling, faded pink three-story building wrapped in wrought

A pensive Cuban woman watches the world go by from her crumbling balcony overlooking the Prado.

iron balconies being used to dry laundry. It was at the corner of Animas and Agramonte. The facade, a series of arches, ran out to the street and the sidewalk was beneath the overhang. The walls were stucco with a four-foot high run of brown, patterned tile along the base, and broad openings were covered by the roll-up metal shutters. The sidewalk was tiled in mottled rose, and set into the tile in a darker shade was "Sloppy Joe's."

"How long has it been here?"

"Since the 1920s. It was closed some time in the 1950s. It was dangerous. The floor is collapsing, but it will be restored soon."

I peeked through a crack and could see a high-ceilinged room, what appeared to be a bar running along the wall, a wood-paneled column in the middle of the room. I could imagine it opened up, tables spilling out onto the sidewalk.

"How do the restorers know what it was like 40 years ago?"

"There is a huge book from the period, with photographs and illustrations of many of the buildings in Old Havana. It is used, and whatever can be found in archives. I have heard there is another Sloppy Joe's in Key West."

"Yes, owned by a friend of Hemingway's named Joe Russell. Did he own this one, too?"

Manuel shrugged. "I don't know. It was a place where tourists came, and Hemingway, until the 1950s, but his favorite was El Floridita and after that the Bodeguita del Medio. But there were many places, places like Dos Hermanos."

"What are the plans for it?"

"My wife is working on the drawings right now. It

Cubans are gregarious and curious about foreign visitors. These boys followed us around while we investigated Sloppy Joe's.

will be renovated in less than two years, maybe one and a half years. The next time you are in Cuba you can come to Sloppy Joe's."

"Then I will buy you a beer. But for now, let's walk over to that little street between El Floridita and Central Park and I will buy you a beer there."

We walked up the street past the Plaza hotel and Manuel pointed to a passing car. "A 1956 Chevrolet. My family had one of those. We had new Chevrolets every few years then."

We sat with our cans of Cristal in the little plaza with the beer stand between El Floridita and Central Park, where Martí's statue towers next to the Cuban flag. Manuel explained how each month his family was entitled to a ration of rice and beans and soap and cooking oil. A woman came to our table and gave us her card, offering an apartment to rent. Manuel put on his glasses to read it. The right lens was cracked diagonally across the center. A beggar came along and I gave him a wooden pencil. We talked until dark. Manuel, the professor of history, said nothing bad about Castro.

And I bit my tongue and did not ask the question that was on my mind. If Che's biographers are correct, there was a plan in place to pull Che Guevara out of Bolivia in 1967. Che was in desperate straits, racked with diarrhea to the point where he had to be carried, weak, low on supplies, being hunted by the Bolivian army. But the order never came from Fidel. Did Fidel think a dead martyr would be more useful than a charismatic potential competitor?

Instead, Che was captured and locked up in a dingy school at La Higuera, a backwater village in the high plains of southeast Bolivia. Pappy Shelton and twenty Green Berets were not far away, training these soldiers. The order came down from the Bolivians to execute Che and cut off his head and hands to confirm identification.

The soldiers drew lots; the task fell to Lieutenant Mario Terán. He drank some Scotch and went into the room. Che was surprised he was to be executed, but he said that killing one man would not stop the revolution, and he asked his executioner to let his wife know he wanted her to marry again. Che was only 39. Terán shot him and the body was taken to the laundry room at the hospital of Nuestra Señora de Malta. He was cleaned up and photos were taken, including some by a Cuban CIA agent. The officer in charge refused to cut off his head, at least in part out of respect for another military man. The body was buried near the runway of the airport at Vallegrande. A memorial has been erected in Bolivia,

198

but Che's family refused Fidel's plan to build a mausoleum in Cuba.

So for many years, back there in the Museum of the Revolution, tucked away out of public view and preserved in formaldehyde, were Che Guevara's surgically removed hands. His remains now rest at the memorial in Bolivia.

8 | *Hemingway at Home*

Ernesto turned off the main road through San Francisco de Paula onto a short uphill street. Hemingway's home is on a hilltop in a modest, unremarkable community of single-story bungalows and simple open-air shops and restaurants. The street narrowed into a gated driveway that wound upward through towering trees and blossoming red bougainvillea. Two young women at the gate collected our entrance fee: $ 3 from me and 3 pesos from Ernesto.

The girls and Ernesto chatted in Spanish and he told me what to expect.

"You can take photos anywhere outside, but if you take pictures in through the windows, it will cost $ 5 for every photo. No one is allowed inside."

"Let's talk to somebody up there and see if we can't get a better rate. That's outrageous." It was half a month's pay per shot by Cuban standards.

We drove up the hill and parked at a small lot flanked by a tiny gift shop and an administration building that looked like it was once a garage for the Chrysler, Buick and Lincoln convertibles, and Mary Hemingway's yellow Plymouth. The house was still out of sight.

Finca Vigía, Hemingway's "lookout" farm, is nine miles east—and commands a view—of Havana and the sea. It had its lookout designation long before Hemingway arrived and had a tower constructed behind the house. The Spanish built a small wooden fort and tower where the house now stands, part of a heliographic communications system. The finca was Hemingway's home for more than 20 years, longer than he stayed anywhere else, from 1939 when Martha Gellhorn rented it, to July

25, 1960 when Hemingway and Mary Welch took the ferry to Key West, leaving Finca Vigía fully staffed, expecting to return.

A Frenchman, Joseph D'Orne Duchamp, who operated a real estate business in Havana, had owned the Spanish-style villa since the 1920s. A few expensive homes were built in San Francisco de Paula then, when it was believed that the village would blossom into a classy residential area like Miramar. It never happened and most of the Hemingways' neighbors were blue collar workers: a tinsmith, a streetcar mechanic, a worker in the Hatuey brewery in a nearby town. The Steinharts, who lived in the even more elegant, but out of sight, house next door were the exception. Frank Steinhart Jr. owned the Havana trolley company. For whatever reason, Hemingway created another one of his "gangs" out of neighborhood kids and delighted in leading them in firecracker and stink bomb attacks on the Steinharts' house while they were entertaining. After the revolution the house became a government-run school.

Ernesto spoke with a parking attendant who pointed toward the administration building. "We'll talk to somebody up there," Ernesto said.

The woman in charge, the assistant curator, met us outside and listened to our plea for a better rate with her mouth turned down at the corners. "It is not possible," she said in English. I spoke of the great publicity value of the stories I would write about Finca Vigía, avoiding the obvious obstacle of Americans being forbidden to come to Cuba as tourists.

"It is not possible," she repeated, and added something quickly in Spanish to Ernesto.

"She says she does not make the regulations and there are a lot of people around watching."

She turned to me. "But I will walk up with you." She began to describe the history of the finca, and finally we rounded the curve in the driveway and the white building emerged from behind the palmettos and bougainvillea in the center of the circular driveway.

"There is something missing," I said. "There was a large ceiba tree up there on the patio, the one that is described in *Islands in the Stream*, and I have seen it in the old photos."

She looked surprised. "The roots had gone under the house into Mary's room and were doing damage. We had to cut it down, but we planted a small ceiba in its place."

"Yes, that tree was causing trouble, heaving tiles in Mary's bedroom. Hemingway and Mary argued about the invasive ceiba in the 1940s. He opposed pruning the roots, she went ahead and was having them cut back when Hemingway surprised the covert operation and raised hell about it. He opposed pruning anything."

She looked at me for a moment and smiled. "You don't need me to walk with you. But you should come back for the Hemingway Colloquium. It's in July. Do you want to take pictures inside?"

"I don't know, I haven't seen inside yet."

"Let me know if you do." She returned to her office.

A tumultuous lifetime was jammed into the 20 years at Finca Vigía, made even more fascinating by the nature of the man and the nature of the times: an egocentric writer afraid of losing his macho powers, covering World War II as a correspondent, changing wives midstream, staging a Nobel-prize-winning comeback, surviving two plane crashes in Africa, living through the Cuban Revolution and finally leaving Cuba behind forever.

203

When Martha Gellhorn joined Hemingway in Cuba in 1939 he was still married to Pauline Pfeiffer, but the marriage was beyond repair. Martha secured the run-down but promising Finca Vigía for $100 a month rental. She used the place to decompress from her assignments as a lecturer on behalf of the loyalist cause in the Spanish Civil War. Ernest immediately went fishing; Marty began cleaning up the place, using her own money, just as Pauline had done in Key West. Hemingway approved of her efforts and moved in. They shared household expenses fifty-fifty, except for liquor, which was Hemingway's expense. Independence and physical courage ran deep in Martha Gellhorn. Hemingway continued using the Ambos Mundos as his mailing address for a while and gradually let his publishers know he was spending his time at a house on a hill where a breeze always blew.

In September, Hitler started his march across Europe and by November, Marty had taken an assignment from *Colliers* to go to the Finno-Russian border to report on Russian ambitions there. The war at sea was under way; her ship approaching England sailed through German mines bobbing in the water and bodies floating face down in lifebelts. She arrived in Helsinki in time for the first Russian bombing. Hemingway had been staying as a guest of the publicity people at the new Sun Valley Resort in Idaho since September, part of the time with Marty, finishing *For Whom the Bell Tolls*. He extended his stay.

He returned to Key West hoping to spend Christmas with Pauline and the boys, but she was deliberately gone and he took the Buick to Havana on the ferry. Marty was completing the writing of her *Colliers* assignment in Sweden and was held up in Europe so it was a lonely Christmas for Hemingway, but finally everybody returned to the finca, including the three Hemingway boys. Marty won them over as best friends, and on November 4, 1940, the divorce from Pauline was final after almost a year of wrangling over terms. On November 21, Hemingway and Marty were married in Cheyenne, Wyoming. The couple went off for a honeymoon at the Lombardy hotel in New York. They returned to Cuba for Christmas and a few days later closed on the finca—purchased December 28,1940 for $18,500 out of a $100,000 royalty check from Paramount Pictures for *For Whom the Bell Tolls*, which starred Hemingway's hunting pal Gary Cooper. Some 180,000 copies of *For Whom the Bell Tolls* had been sold in addition to the film rights. Hemingway wanted—and could afford—to kick back and fish, and drink and play, and perhaps create a daughter.

Martha, however, wanted to see the Orient and was on assignment to write about the defenses of Hong Kong, Singapore, the Dutch East Indies, and the Sino-Japanese war. Hemingway humored her and went along, soaking up experiences and writing a few magazine stories. They spent almost no time in Cuba, and were sipping daiquiris in a bar outside Tucson, Arizona on December 7 when they learned of the bombing of Pearl Harbor.

Hemingway earned over $141,000 in 1941, savored his success, but did little serious work. Over the next few years he fumed about his income taxes and said his contribution to Mr. Roosevelt's war was paying for it.

In 1942, Marty stayed out of the war except to write articles about submarine warfare in the Caribbean for *Colliers*. When she was away she missed him and feared being dumped, but when she was home she scolded

him for not bathing—she fondly called him The Pig—
or embellishing his deeds to prop up his self-image, or
drinking too much. When her mother visited and Hemingway kept them waiting for two hours, she stormed
into the Floridita and dragged him out.

Hemingway played at warfare. In order to conduct
intelligence operations and ferret out Nazi Fifth
Columnists in Havana, he recruited a gang of Spanish
noblemen, sportsmen, bartenders and wharf rats to
keep their ears open. He set up headquarters in the
guest house at the finca and had an official code name,
the Crime Shop, but he called it the Crook Factory. He
obtained permission to have PILAR designated a Q-boat,
a Nazi submarine hunter.

By the end of the year Martha was back home and
the fighting began. Marty called Hemingway's U-boat
hunting a "lot of rot and rubbish" when she saw it consisted mostly of drinking, talking, throwing hand
grenades at seaweed and Tommy-gunning flocks of
birds. She accused him of doing it all so he could get
rationed gas to go fishing.

They also fought about his drinking, including an
episode when she insisted on driving him home from a
party in Havana. He cursed her and slapped her with a
backhand. She responded by slowing the Lincoln down
and running it into a ditch and tree, leaving him to walk
home.

By the spring of 1943 he was off submarine hunting
for months at a time and she was managing the house
and working on another novel. He returned in July to
find a Marty wishing for the good old days in the late
1930s, but also with a new assignment to cover the war
in Europe for *Colliers*. She urged him to come over and
recreate the working arrangement they had during the

Spanish war, and told him to do something serious instead of play acting at submarine chaser out in PILAR. Late in 1943, Marty ran into Dr. José Luis Herrera Sotolongo, Hemingway's friend and personal physician, on the path to the house. "I'm saying goodbye to you, Doctor. I'm leaving for Europe and I won't come back to the beast," meaning Hemingway. She left behind an angry Hemingway.

Hemingway followed her to Europe, basking in the attention awarded a famous novelist returning to his craft as war correspondent and orchestrating a typical Hemingway piece of one-upmanship. He signed on as a correspondent with *Colliers*, and under the rules for the U.S. Press Corps, a magazine was allowed only one frontline correspondent. Martha was bumped. Hemingway flew to England, but Marty was told women weren't allowed to fly. She set sail for Europe on a shipload of dynamite to cover whatever she could find behind the frontlines.

At the White Tower restaurant in Soho Hemingway ran into Irwin Shaw, who was with a documentary film crew, and his female companion, a feature writer for *Time*. Her name was Mary Welsh, and the two connected.

When Marty arrived after 17 days at sea she found out from reporters that Hemingway was in the hospital with a gashed head acquired after a party when the car in which he was riding ran into a water tank while negotiating streets that were blacked-out because of the bombings. She searched him out in the hospital. He was holding court, with champagne and whisky and gin in rich supply, a potentially lethal prescription for a subdural hematoma. She both ridiculed and raged at his behavior. He expected sympathy and attention.

The last time they saw each other was in March 1945, at the Dorchester hotel in London. The conversation was brief, and about divorce.

Hemingway, desperately lonely back in Cuba, had sent for Mary Welsh following their romance in Europe. Mary was about to become the new mistress at Finca Vigía. As Ernesto and I approached, it seemed just as Mary Welsh, writing in *The Way It Was*, described it in the spring of 1945 when she arrived from the airport with Hemingway in his Lincoln convertible—he freshly scrubbed in a white *guayabera*.

"Inside the finca's wooden gate we drove through a bower of scarlet flowers, up a little rise and half around a circular driveway from which rose a prodigious tier of broad old stone steps, with an enormous tree growing out of one rise. The house seemed to have grown gradually out of its hilltop. Its roof and a projecting terrace were laden with flowers and the air smelled of plants growing. I thought of Jane Austen and Louisa May Alcott and country vicars' manses and fell instantly in love.

'A ruin', Ernest said.

'It's beautiful. It's wonderful.' Afternoon sunlight was brightening the inside, making the house look hospitable through its open doors and windows."

The foliage has grown since the 1940s and 1950s, but it is just the same in a spooky way. The house and grounds step back in terraces. The main entrance terrace, where the ceiba tree stood, is nine steps above the driveway and to the left is a higher and separate terrace that wraps around the living room, Hemingway's corner bedroom, and on around the back of the house.

Instead of Papa, Mary, Ramon the cook, Pancho the house boy, or Boise the cat, drifting through the rooms of the finca are women in uniforms of blue blouses and black skirts guarding the inside, while a bus load of German tourists circles the outside, peering into the windows.

Another little portable Royal typewriter is propped up on the bookshelf in Hemingway's bedroom. This one probably is the real thing, since everything in the finca has been preserved just as it was found, right down to the booze bottles next to the favorite easy chair in the living room and the white visor on the bed. Hemingway wrote standing up, sometimes on the typewriter but usually in pencil, typically shirtless and in baggy shorts held up by the thick leather belt with a silver buckle—inscribed *Gott Mit Uns*—taken from a dead German soldier.

Writing was hard work for Hemingway and writing 500 good words was a day's output, with the working day beginning around 6 a.m. and ending at 11 a.m., when fishing and drinking began. He used a good writer's trick: never stop for the day when you are written out; always quit when you know what the next sentence will be. Then, the next day you can mark up the work from the day before to get back into the stream, and you will know exactly where to go because the next thought has been germinating all night.

Finca Vigía is smaller than I expected it to be, smaller than the Key West home, all on one floor, with one room rambling into the next through wide doorways. It is a comfortable, pleasant place looking out at gardens in all directions. It contains 9,000 books, and safari trophies: the leopard skin in the library, the gazelle head on the wall over the typewriter, a lion skin on the floor of the sitting room. The front door opens into the 38-foot-long sitting room. To the far left is

Hemingway's small bedroom, and to the far right is the bedroom first occupied by Martha Gellhorn and later by Mary Welsh Hemingway.

The house is only two rooms deep. Behind Hemingway's bedroom is the bathroom, where, next to a scale, Hemingway's records on his weight and blood pressure are scratched on the wall in pencil. A doctor who was treating Mary for a fever took Hemingway's blood pressure in 1946 and found it to be 215 over 125, and Papa said he could hear a swarm of bees above the roof. Drinking was curtailed briefly, but overweight and high blood pressure became long-standing problems.

Next to it is a guest room with two twin beds where, on bare mattresses, the permanent guests were a collection of cats that numbered in the high fifties, all named,

Hemingway greeted movie stars, matadors, a Nobel Prize committee, Batista's soldiers and a vast collection of friends and admirers at this front door of Finca Vigía, his home near Havana.

who caused the place to always smell like cat. Then there is the library lined with book shelves so tall a rolling ladder like those found in libraries is at the ready, and finally the dining room and kitchen.

What parties that dining room saw. Thursday nights brought together a half dozen people who had a connection to the International Brigade in the Spanish Civil War with Hemingway: Dr. Herrera, who had been a battalion surgeon, his brother Roberto, Juan Dunabeitía, a Basque who was called Sinsky and skippered a tramp steamer, and Father Don Andrés, nicknamed the Black Priest, who had been banished from Spain for being on the wrong side of the war. They joked, drank wine, reminisced and sang songs of the war and the International Brigade.

Out front, next to the circular drive, was a bungalow built to house the visiting Hemingway children and other guests. This white *casita*, or little house, was a home away from home for movie actors and actresses, stars of the literary world both writers and publishers, the world's best bullfighters, and at times the lovely young Adriana Ivancich, her widowed mother Dora and brother Gianfranco.

In back of the house is the three-story tower constructed under Mary's direction in 1946 to give Hemingway a proper work space on the top floor, to offer the cats a residence other than the smelly guest bedroom, to provide additional space for guests and a workshop, and to furnish a private rooftop where Mary could sunbathe in the nude. It commands a view over Havana from the top story, which was intended to be a place for writing but was rarely used except when Hemingway worked there to escape house guests. Today it is set up as a work room with a mahogany trestle table standing on a lion skin rug, bookshelves nearby, but no black Royal typewriter in sight. The preferred writing spot was the bedroom bookcase where Hemingway could hear the sounds of daily life going on at Finca Vigía.

After spending much of 1945 decompressing from the war and recuperating from a car accident near the finca that severely cut Mary's face and injured his leg, Hemingway began to work on *The Garden of Eden*. The life of a successful writer could now be savored. His children and friends from the war and Hollywood visited.

From time to time Cuban politics intruded. The year after Mary arrived she was aroused by the barking dogs and she found the bushes around the finca full of soldiers with guns at the ready. Hemingway was gone, but Mary told them to get out. They had their orders, however. They seized all the sporting weapons and ammunition in the house and arrested Mary, but the Hemingway's connections with important Cubans soon got Mary and the guns released.

The presence of guns at the finca and the comings and goings of many Cubans and foreigners made the political powers uneasy, and created rumors of plots. As the Castro Revolution took shape in the fifties the finca was watched closely by a local outpost of Batista's Rural Guard, commanded by a Lieutenant Maldonato who reportedly killed several locals suspected of being revolutionaries, including one of the boys in Hemingway's gang of kids who tormented the Steinharts years earlier. One night a patrol under Maldonato confronted Hemingway at the farm, setting the dogs off. A soldier in the patrol killed one of Hemingway's dogs with a rifle butt. Hemingway had no love for Batista, but whether or not he actively supported Castro's Revolution is not clear. He was a passionate supporter of the loyalists against the fascists in the Spanish Civil War, but by the time he got to Cuba he seemed totally engrossed in his own affairs and avoided politics in favor of writing, fishing, cockfights, boxing, and shooting doves at a shooting club.

And while Gregorio claims that Hemingway smuggled arms for the revolution in PILAR, Mary was on board when they dumped a big load of sporting guns and ammunition into the sea from PILAR so neither side would get them.

In 1946, Mary's divorce became final and Hemingway took her as his fourth wife, perhaps the one who would provide a daughter. The sale of film rights for *The Short Happy Life of Francis Macomber* furnished the comfort of cash. He began to cut down on his drinking and everybody went off to Wyoming late in 1946 for the hunting and fishing. There, in Casper, Mary very nearly died of a hemorrhaging tubular pregnancy and was pulled back with blood transfusions and oxygen. There would be no more Hemingway children. The next year was better, and late in 1948 the Hemingways took off for an extended holiday in Italy, bringing their car with them, and returning to the Italian countryside where Hemingway had been at war and wounded as a 18-year-old volunteer ambulance driver.

One rainy winter day Hemingway and a group of Italian friends went shooting. Tagging along was a newcomer to the sport, a family friend of the host and the only woman of the group, Adriana Ivancich, a month short of her nineteenth birthday. Hemingway would celebrate his fiftieth in July. After the shooting he found the lean, innocent, darkly-beautiful Adriana sitting in front of an open fire, bruised by the shooting, drying her black hair. They chatted, and he broke his comb in half and gave a piece to her. Adriana, her older brother Gianfranco, and her mother became friends of the Hemingways. Adriana also became an inspiration.

Hemingway was feeling that it was time to defend his title as top dog writer and was working on a book that would evolve into *Across the River and Into the Trees*. A 50-year-old colonel returning to the Italian country-side to revisit the locales of his war years falls in love with beautiful, 19-year-old Renata, and in the book they consummate their passion under an olive drab blanket. Hemingway was not going gracefully into his fiftieth year; old friends and enemies had been dying or being killed relentlessly, and he remarked wryly that ". . . people are dying who never died before." Cold winds were blowing through his heart when he created the colonel and Renata. Renata translates as "reborn." The book got bad reviews that hinted Hemingway had lost his gift and his best work was behind him.

I climbed to the terrace near the front door and tried to imagine the electricity that must have crackled through the air when Adriana and her mother came to stay at the finca in October of 1950. Mary Hemingway knew of the infatuation, but Adriana glided along in innocence, although it must have been difficult. While Adriana was around, Mary was treated like a pariah. One night Hemingway threw her typewriter onto the floor, another night he exploded in anger and tossed his glass of red wine into her face. Adriana and her mother pretended they didn't see it. And there was the night when Adriana and her mother were preparing to leave the main house for the little guest house. To prevent their departure, Hemingway seized a rifle, stepped out the front door and shot out the light on the path. I looked at the angle. It was not that tough a shot for a man of Hemingway's skill with weapons. They retired by flashlight. A few days later, Mary called Hemingway to her room and told him she would not leave unless he came to her in the morning, sober, and asked her to depart, and he never did.

But something did blossom during Adriana's visit. Hemingway's writing took off. He wrote a novella he was calling *The Sea When Absent*, part of a trilogy he had been talking about for years that would involve the earth, sea and sky. He was averaging 1,000 words a day, twice his average writing output. Hemingway was astonished by how quickly it had flowed out of him. He told Adriana he was working well because she was there. Early in February Adriana, her mother and Mary flew out of Havana to visit Florida before the Ivancichs began their return trip to Italy, but by then this elegantly simple story of struggle was nearly done. It was the story first told him by Carlos Gutierrez, the man who had preceded Gregorio Fuentes as the pillar of PILAR. It was about an old man who caught a marlin that was eaten by sharks. It was eventually called *The Old Man and the Sea*. Hemingway's career was *renata*.

Hemingway had to be argued into publishing a work he thought was too short to stand alone at just 26,500 words, but finally he relented. *Life* magazine ran the novella in its entirety on September 1, 1952 and overnight it found its way into more than 5 million hands. He had rejected the design for the book's dustjacket, and asked Adriana to come up with something. Her simple design of five shacks, three fishing boats and the sea became the final dustjacket artwork for the book, published September 8.

In 1953, Spencer Tracy came to Cuba and plans were made to turn the book into a movie. The book earned Hemingway the Pulitzer Prize, an honor he almost didn't get to savor.

That fall, the Hemingways went on assignment for *Look* magazine on an African safari. The *Look* assignment and other travels took them out of Cuba for 13 months. In January 1954, Hemingway and Mary walked away from two light plane crashes just two days apart and he was in fact reported dead. He quipped that Mary had never seen an airplane on fire before and was particularly impressed to find herself inside one. On the first flight, the pilot of their Cessna had been blinded by a flight of ibis as they circled Murchison Falls to take pictures. The plane snagged an abandoned telephone wire and crash landed, resulting in minor injuries to Mary and Hemingway, although Mary went into shock and Hemingway could not find her pulse.

They made their way to Lake Albert where they found a bush pilot and an old De Haviland Rapide canvas-covered biplane that had been searching for them. The plane bounced along an abandoned airfield on takeoff, lifted and then crashed, and slowly began to burn. Although Hemingway bluffed and blustered for the press, he had been badly injured—head and kidneys in particular—and never fully recovered. Unable to get out of the plane after the second crash, he used his head and shoulders to butt open the door—a head that had suffered extensive damage in war, auto crashes, fishing accidents and other mishaps of an adventurous life. It was his tenth concussion. Not only was his head bleeding, clear cranial fluid leaked out behind his left ear. He was seeing double and his hearing came and went sporadically. His lower intestine collapsed, he had a ruptured liver, spleen and kidney, a crushed vertebra, sprained right arm, shoulder and leg, and first degree burns. He told reporters, he never felt better, and "My luck, she still holds." In truth, he never recovered from the injuries.

But it was not the plane crashes that dominate the book on these safaris, *True at First Light*. It includes sections on Hemingway going native: taking a young native wife named Debba from the Wakamba tribe and hunting a leopard with a spear.

He was far from recuperated in October when he received the Nobel Prize and the resulting onslaught of reporters and well-wishers. He used the Nobel money to pay off overdue loans, and eventually presented the medal to the *Virgen de Cobre*, Cuba's national saint, to be kept at the shrine of Our Lady at Santiago de Cuba.

In the middle and late 1950s Hemingway worked hard on the safari pieces for *Look* and the *True at First Light* book. Spencer Tracy and the film crew arrived to shoot *The Old Man and the Sea* and Hemingway was hired as a technical consultant, which led to searching for huge marlin off the coast of Peru. He and Mary then went to Spain. His intention was to update *Death in the Afternoon*, his 1932 book on bullfighting. But *Life* magazine got wind of his activities and convinced him to write a long, two-part series called *The Dangerous Summer*. During the Spanish trip Mary thought he was behaving oddly, and she returned to Cuba ahead of him. He returned to write the *Life* articles and had trouble accomplishing something that had been his writing credo—leaving things out. The manuscript ran to 12 times the length it was supposed to be, and he called Hotchner for help in cutting it back. Hotchner found the Hemingways an apartment at 1 East 62nd Street in New York.

On July 25, 1960 they caught the ferry to Key West, leaving the house fully staffed and expecting to return and resume their normal life. The Castro Revolution's practice of seizing private property as well as occasional burglaries at the finca prompted Mary to deposit Hemingway's unpublished manuscripts and other valuables into her bank. A year later to the week, Hemingway was dead.

He traveled to Spain for more work on the manuscript and sent letters to Mary in New York saying he was feeling terrible. He had begun to fear inconsequential tasks, and suspected he was being investigated by the FBI and the IRS. Instead of Cuba, Hemingway went to the Mayo Clinic in Rochester for treatment of high blood pressure and mental problems. He was registered under an alias, but gradually the story leaked out. At Mayo, he underwent electroshock therapy. Hotchner's last photos of Hemingway at the finca show a shadow of the man most people remember as Hemingway.

While post-revolutionary Cuban writers talk of Mary giving Finca Vigía to the people of Cuba according to the terms of Hemingway's will, it was appropriated like private property everywhere was being appropriated: Mary was left all Papa's property in a will read in Idaho after the funeral. When the Cuban foreign ministry called a few days later asking who should receive a contract making the finca the property of the Cuban government, Mary responded "I'm not sure I wish to give you our finca." By 1961 U.S. citizens had to have permission from both the U.S. and Cuban governments to travel to Cuba. She negotiated with the foreign ministry to obtain permission to return to the finca to rescue manuscripts and paintings, and burn many letters in accordance with

Hemingway's written wishes; letters from Scott Fitzgerald, Gertrude Stein and James Joyce among them. With the permission of the Cuban government, she recovered 30 to 40 pounds of original and unpublished manuscripts from safe deposit boxes in Banco Nacional de Cuba. She wrote:

"Except for a few nicks in the white plaster outside the house, from Castro's militia mistaking each other for enemies and banging away, the finca retained for me its timeless quality of muted tranquility and hospitality."

She wanted to remove seven paintings that Hemingway had given to her as gifts, but ran into the Cuban bureaucracy and a regulation forbidding export of art. Then one day Fidel called at the finca. At dusk, Mary was waiting when Fidel Castro and nine soldiers arrived in three purple Oldsmobiles. He toured the house, sat with Mary's permission in Hemingway's favorite chair, viewed Havana from the work room at the top floor of the tower, and said, "I will help you with your pictures." As he left, he noticed the little guest house and promised, "We will leave that untouched, for your use when you may return."

Mary gave severance checks to the staff. She met with Gregorio Fuentes to arrange the fate of Hemingway's most prized possession, PILAR, and left Cuba.

Mary Welsh Hemingway oversaw the publication of most of the writing that was published posthumously: *A Moveable Feast*, about the Paris years; *Islands in the Stream*, an autobiographical fiction about the Bahamas and Cuba; *Dangerous Summer*, an expanded version of the bullfighting articles Hemingway wrote for *Life* magazine, and *The Garden of Eden*. Her rule for publishing these works that Hemingway never had a chance to finally polish was to cut and edit, but never to allow anyone to add anything. In 1999, *True at First Light*, written at the finca about the African safaris of the early 1950s and edited by son Patrick Hemingway, was published to commemorate the centennial of Hemingway's birth. Mary traveled the world, hunting and fishing and writing, returned to Africa to salute Kilimanjaro on Hemingway's birthday. She died November 26, 1986, at age 78.

Adriana Ivancich received more than 2,000 letters from Hemingway and married twice with his best wishes and blessing. At age 53 she published her memoirs, *La Torre Bianco*, and hanged herself from the limb of a tree on her farm at Capalbio, Italy.

9 Finding Pilar

A footpath winds down from the finca through a tunnel of palms to the rectangular blue concrete swimming pool, dry and empty today except for a young German woman seated on the steps swimmers once used. She was looking into the pool, smiling distantly, perhaps imagining Ava Gardner swimming here in the nude when she stayed at the cozy white *casita,* or Hemingway and Mary swimming their morning laps and having poolside cocktails with movie stars and bullfighters. The path continues downhill to PILAR, blocked up on the hard, sheltered under a wide roof and surrounded by a raised wooden walkway: black hull, green decks, bright red waterline stripe and rosy pink bottom paint. The transom still says:

PILAR

KEY WEST

FLA

It is a miracle PILAR survived at all. When Mary Hemingway settled her affairs in Cuba she turned the boat and all the fishing equipment over to Gregorio Fuentes with the suggestion that he use or sell the fishing gear as he wished, but he should take PILAR out and scuttle her in the Gulf Stream. Gregorio could not afford to maintain the boat—one of the Hemingways budgeting sessions revealed PILAR's expenses were higher than those of the finca—and PILAR became the property of the government. For a while, she was a government work boat, and eventually Mary learned she was on display on the lawn of the finca, "poor thing."

PILAR was more than 25 years old in 1961 and had operated in tropical waters all her life. She had been

The author and Hemingway's boat PILAR at Finca Vigía.

re-decked, re-planked, and re-engined over the years.
Today PILAR is tidy and trim, but without outriggers and
the normal clutter of a busy sportfishing boat. Fishing
the Gulf Stream was a Hemingway passion and tons of
marlin and other sport fish had been hauled in over the
stern. She had been a writer's sanctuary from frustration
and fame, a submarine chaser, the scene of many parties
involving some of the most famous people of the day,
but above all she was a fishing boat.

Hemingway, Captain Bra Sanders of the Key West
Mob, and Pauline went up to Miami early in May 1934,
to retrieve the newly-delivered boat and bring it back to
Key West. Charles Thompson pulled some strings that
allowed Hemingway to keep the boat in the Navy yard
at no charge. Soon a dinghy named *Bumby* was added,
the nickname of Jack Hemingway, Papa's first son, with
Hadley.

Within months of delivery PILAR made her first trip

to Cuba. Hemingway signed on a captain of the Key West-Havana ferry to handle navigation, and also had on board the aspiring young Minnesota writer Arnold Samuelson as night watchman. Hemingway found the young man willing, but slow and clumsy at sea, and full of questions. Hemingway later noted, "If any more aspirant writers come on board the PILAR let them be females, let them be very beautiful, and let them bring champagne."

PILAR was built by Wheeler Shipyard in Brooklyn on a stock hull—hull number 576—with a few custom features requested by Hemingway. It has an ornate chrome plate on the bow—the flying W of the Wheeler Shipyard—reminiscent of hood ornaments of the day. PILAR is 38 feet long with a beam of 12 feet and draft of 3½ feet. It was built of white cedar over closely-spaced, steam-bent white oak ribs and powered originally by an 80-horsepower Chrysler marine engine with a backup 40-horsepower Lycoming. PILAR had a top speed of almost 16 knots, and cruised at between eight and 10 knots. Two cabins below could sleep six people.

She has a roomy 12- by 16-foot varnished mahogany cockpit with cushioned seats along each side. The custom features were designed to make fishing easier: a built-in stern fish box, a stern cut down 12 inches and equipped with a roller to make it easier to haul fish over the back, and the second engine for trolling and emergencies. On the first trip to Cuba the fishing was done from a pair of wicker lawn chairs that skidded around, but soon afterward a proper fighting chair was bolted into the cockpit.

The rhythms of the Gulf Stream and the marlin dictated Hemingway's calendar all the way back to 1932, when Joe Russell first introduced him to fishing, and particularly after 1934 when PILAR was always standing by. The season for marlin is the middle of April to the middle of August, and it was then that Hemingway would be found in Cuba, in the early years living at the Ambos Mundos hotel. The season started, Hemingway claimed, with the white marlin, then the immature striped marlin with stripes that faded with death, followed by the black and striped marlin together, the big ones, and finally in July the huge black marlin, which were old and stupid. Hemingway also claimed there were days when the Gulf Stream reversed itself and the current flowed from east to west.

After Hemingway had a light breakfast—fighting big marlin in the hot sun on a full stomach was to be avoided—PILAR would head out of Havana Harbor with its stern ice chests loaded: bait on one side, beer and fruit on the other. The alligator pears were served for lunch with a squeeze of lime and salt and pepper. In the early years Carlos Gutierrez was always on board and later it was Gregorio. The rest of the crew would be friends and children or family or no one else. Bait was set out—one- to three-pound cero mackerel or kingfish—usually on the surface to attract fish that were up top feeding, while the old Cuban fishermen in their skiffs would be fishing deep with handlines in 40 to 70 fathoms. The best conditions were when the prevailing northeasterly trades were blowing and the Gulf Stream was running strong in its easterly direction at five knots. Then the marlin were out feeding a quarter of a mile to four miles offshore, traveling from east to west against the current.

In *Marlin off the Morro*, one of the *Esquire* letters that helped to pay for PILAR, Hemingway explained that, "If such a fish (an indifferent one) swims with his pectoral fins tucked close to his sides, he will not bite. He is cruising and you are on his course. That is all. The minute a marlin sees the bait, if he is going to strike, he raises his dorsal fin and spreads those wide, bright blue pectorals so that he looks like some great, undersea bird in the water as he follows."

At the time, the largest marlin brought into the Havana market weighed almost 1,100 pounds gutted, head and tail cut off, flanks cut away. He carefully studied and wrote about the marlin, the sharks, the habits of the Gulf Stream, and all that he encountered in PILAR's ramblings along the coast of Cuba and to Bimini in the Bahamas, preparing to write the major sea book that would include *The Old Man and the Sea* and *Islands in the Stream*, but have one more section. He brought scientists out to support some of his observations about the Gulf Stream. Very likely his happiest days were aboard PILAR, learning about the Stream and searching for giant billfish in the company of friends and family. Favorite destinations were the cove at Bacuranao, Bahia Honda, Cayo Megano de Casigua, and Puerto Escondido.

Pauline Pfeiffer and Martha Gellhorn did not share Hemingway's passion for fishing and the sea, but Mary Hemingway was a fishing and hunting enthusiast and even competed in fishing tournaments on her own in PILAR's motor tender, THE TIN KID.

Their first trip together on the boat was to a key about 60 miles west of Havana that Hemingway and Gregorio had visited many times. Crescent-shaped and tricky to reach because of surrounding coral reefs, Megano de Casigua was an idyllic setting of palm trees and beaches with only a few thatched huts used off and on by fishermen. Hemingway had named it *Paraíso*, paradise.

Paraíso was a base of sorts during the World War II sub-chasing years. As the marriage with Martha Gellhorn unraveled, Hemingway spent weeks at a time out on the water and finally grew his famous beard to protect his sun-sensitive skin. Like the intelligence-gathering Crook Factory, the Nazi sub-hunting aboard PILAR was a strange adventure.

In 1942, Hemingway, now famous and well-connected, used friends at the embassy to get a radio, hand grenades, bazookas, small bombs and two .50-caliber machine guns on board. He had a permanent crew that included Gregorio Fuentes, a millionaire sportsman named Winston Guest, a Marine Corps gunner, the Basque ship captain Sinsky, and a jai alai player. He occasionally recruited his boys for these adventures, code named "Operation Friendless." Son Gregory dubbed it "Don Quixote vs. the Wolf Pack."

Nazi subs were indeed sinking ships in the Caribbean, and Hemingway's plan for sinking a sub with a 38-foot wooden fishing boat called for either lots of courage or lots of Gordon's gin. Fishermen had reported being boarded by subs looking for fresh food, so Hemingway concluded that PILAR might attract similar attention while cruising the north coast of Cuba. This was the plan: When a sub surfaced to rob them, Hemingway would wait until they were 20 yards away and attack with the machine guns, mowing down deck hands. Then they would drop grenades and bombs into the open hatches. They never did engage a submarine, but sighted a few and came fairly close to one near *Paraíso*, but it motored away from them.

He fleshed out this fantasy in *Islands in the Stream*, in which people and locations in Cuba were very thinly disguised, as was his loneliness for an absent wife.

Thomas Hudson, a painter, with a crew that included some Basques, a marine and a man like Gregorio, sets off through the mangrove keys after the crew of an abandoned German submarine. In the final shoot-out, Hudson tells the men to "have your .50s ready to fire" and they heave bombs made of fire extinguishers packed with explosives. There is, of course, the rat-a-tat-tat of a Thompson submachine gun. Thomas Hudson is severely wounded, slumped at the helm of his boat, light-headed from loss of blood, wondering if he will ever paint again because work is the most important thing and to work you need life.

A loyal crewman says, "I love you, you son of a bitch, and don't die." But Hudson knows he is a dead man. He feels the lovely throb of the boat's engines at 3,000 rpm.

"He looked up and there was the sky that he had always loved and he looked across the great lagoon that he was quite sure, now, he would never paint . . .

'I think I understand, Willie' he said.

'Oh shit,' Willie said. 'You never understand anybody that loves you'."

That is the end of the book. It was published posthumously in 1970.

When I returned to walk once more around the finca I knew I wanted a photo through the bedroom window of the little black Royal typewriter on the book case. But when I actually pulled out the camera and aimed it through the window, anxious Cubans appeared out of the woodwork. I had caused a red alert, and some of the people I had taken for other tourists were now surrounding me. A woman in a white blouse was jabbering on the radio, a handsome young man in a yellow polo shirt was explaining to me in English that it cost $5 for interior photos, a guy with a moustache who must have practiced menacing looks in the mirror every night was doing a very convincing job of it.

Then the curator showed up in response to the radio call, reminding me with a wry smile and a shake of her head that she had instructed me to let her know if I wanted photos. "So, do you want to take pictures inside?"

"Yes." I had come more than two thousand miles at five miles an hour. This was no time to be a cheapskate. I could afford a few dollars to be permitted to lean in the window and shoot a couple of shots, but I was beginning to have a sour taste for Cuba's Hemingway industry.

She led me around to the front, where a door from the vine-shaded terrace leads into the long sitting room, and to my astonishment she unclipped the red rope, and led me into Hemingway's little bedroom for my photo. She took me room by room through the house and sud-

The living room at Finca Vigía is adorned with art work and hunting trophies from African safaris.

denly I was standing next to the favorite easy chair where Hemingway did his reading and sipped drinks from the bottles that still stand on a low table. I had seen it in a hundred photos.

The old photos flashed through my head: the Cuban pals, Gary Cooper, Spencer Tracy and other movie stars of the forties and fifties, Martha, Mary, Adriana, Nobel Prize officials, the great Spanish bullfighters. Here, where I was standing, Hemingway had received word that he had won the Nobel Prize.

There was nothing of Hemingway at El Floridita or La Bodeguita del Medio and even the Key West house sent just faint vibrations from the carriage house studio, but here it was different. I wanted everyone to clear out so I could sit down in the other easy chair with a Gordon's gin mixed with coconut water and a splash of lime, Papa's favorite, as the evening gathered and ask the questions of this man I had come to know across so much time and so many miles. This man had eventually betrayed his women and many of his friends. He could be a wonderful, generous and charming friend, but a mean and petty enemy. He had been so driven by whatever inner demons controlled him that he had become the best character he ever created; the bravest, the most reckless, the most ruthless and the most needy. You could only love a man who viewed life—at once clinically and passionately—as a curious passing parade that should not be taken too seriously because, in the end, it was all ridiculous except how you responded to it. He created a swashbuckling character that no one else could ever play, and when he could no longer play his own creation he "cheated that old whore death" by taking up the shotgun. He was within months of my age now.

The thoughts were rushing through my head like a dream, with no relationship to real time. I stared at the lopsided chair and silently asked Hemingway the questions that I really had been asking myself for much too long.

"So, Papa, now after all these years, how do you finally measure yourself, and when do you know it is too late?"

My answer came then, standing in that room of my ghosts, and I was finally free. The curator was looking at me in an odd way, wondering what was going on. Her right eyebrow arched like a question mark, and I did not know how much time had passed.

"I'm ready." I took a deep breath and a last look around the room, just as I had when I walked out of my home for the last time. I turned to the curator. "He may have been a lot of things, but he could write one hell of a true sentence." As I walked down the steps of Finca Vigía for the last time I wondered what my grandchildren were doing at that moment. I wondered what Dale was doing, and if during my long odyssey she had found someone else. I was done here.

10 | *Havana Nights*

If you stand in Havana's Central Park, with the statue of José Martí behind you and the hotel Inglaterra dead ahead, the Feria Fornos is a short half block down the first street on the right. The Prado slopes gently down to the sea at your far right.

The deal was unfolding around this little wooden table under blue and white striped canopies so close together that in the dark, with a little rum put by, you might think you were inside and not outside, but we were in fact on the back patio of Feria Fornas. It was a bar and cafe full of colorful locals, European expatriates and a few uneasy tourists in search of an authentic Cuban experience. The deal was about to happen. Several deals might happen.

Sitting to my left was the quick sketch artist, the black man who had penned a gruesome caricature of me on Thursday when this whole thing started, and I had rejected it but given him a dollar for an equally bad rendering of Fidel because he had dated it and signed it and it said *Havana*. He had wonderfully expressive eyes like Rochester on the Jack Benny show that I had seen when I was a kid. He had passed out or was taking a nap; his head was resting on the table, using my red windbreaker as a pillow.

Next to him was Kodiak, the Alaskan commercial fisherman from WIND LINE, puffing on a stubborn cigar, trying to keep it lit. He was still convinced the cigar salesman had a brother who worked in the cigar factory: that is why he got such a good deal on these cigars. In his innocent way, he was the one who had set this thing up. He brought me here the first time a few nights ago, and now he was why I had been lured back.

Kodiak was being courted by Maria just to his left, a beautiful black *jinetera* wearing a brown suit jacket and flower print dress, her hair pulled straight back and tied, much classier than the too-tight, too-bright Lycra-adorned street ladies. She was dressed and soliciting in the European style, an attractive companion. She was 24 and had a nine-year-old son. Another *jinetera* had introduced herself all around and plopped down at the end of the table as if she was joining her oldest friends.

To my right, completing the loop, was Paul, a 44-year-old bachelor sailor from the marina off a big boat named CHEYENNE. Paul had the best Spanish by far of all of us and had agreed to handle negotiations. "Kodiak, aren't you going to buy these girls a round of drinks?" he asked.

Kodiak dug for cash and said it would be cheaper if a Cuban bought them because of the double standard, and gave the new *jinetera* a $10 bill for a round of *mojitos*. She said it would be cheaper if she bought them at the upstairs bar instead of the patio bar, and it took us about five minutes to realize that she had taken the $10, bolted out the front door, and was long gone.

Suddenly Marco arrived, all smiles and handshakes. I remembered him from last Thursday night as the guy who sat next to my backpack with the two cameras in it. He was very tall, very lean, black, wearing a short Levi's jacket and jeans, and his nose seemed like it should have been on an American Indian. Last Thursday I had kept a close eye on the backpack, placed it under a light in the center of a table, but it was my wallet that was missing when Kodiak and I had returned to the marina at 3 a.m. and I had reached for it to pay the cab driver. My pocket had been picked. We had not gone with any girls, so the driver's license and half dozen credit cards and telephone calling cards had been lifted at Feria Fornos.

It became clear that Marco was "the man" and he managed everything and everyone that took place on this turf, maybe even the *policía* who were so busy cracking down. Twenty minutes before we had described him precisely to a series of bartenders who, of course, had never seen anyone matching that description.

So far, it had been a peculiar game with great risk involved and not on my part. A Cuban who is involved in credit card fraud can do 20 or 30 years in jail, and U.S. credit cards are worthless in Cuba, as are travelers' checks. Perhaps they could be sold on the black market, or cashed at one of the big hotels, but a Cuban trying to pass a card with the name "Schaefer" on it seemed unlikely. Friday morning I was convinced I would never see any of the contents of the wallet again and had everything stopped before any transactions could take place. I had faxed all the card numbers to my son Kurt in Vermont and asked him to cancel everything, but I did want to get the driver's license back.

I thought the game was over, but it was just beginning. Kodiak had gone back to the Feria on Friday night, and on Saturday morning there was a knock on my boat hull.

"I have something for you," he said, handing me a stack of plastic cards: American Express, Boat US, Kaiser Permanente HMO, Social Security, U.S. Power Squadron, a few others. Except for the American Express, all worthless to anyone but me. The valuable ones were missing. This was bait.

"I'm surprised. I never thought I would see these things again. But the most valuable ones are missing, my Visa card and my driver's license."

"This guy came up to me, very nervous looking, said he recognized me from the night before. Said he was walking along and found the wallet on the street, or maybe on the floor somewhere. Then he said a kid found it and gave it to him. He didn't want the police involved. He said he tried to find you at Marina Hemingway, and he has more stuff."

"He sure does, but I've canceled everything. I'm surprised at the American Express card coming back. Maybe he didn't know what it was."

"He said he wanted us to come back tomorrow night, but I told him no, maybe Monday. I gave him ten bucks for this, but he didn't seem to want the money. He bought me rums with the money. Do you want to go back on Monday?"

"Sure, I want the driver's license and whatever else he has." I was sure the Eddie Bauer wallet was gone, and so was the St. Christopher's medal that Dale had given me when the voyage began. It was tucked into the coin pocket.

We all were here now, and Paul asked Marco, seated at the end of the table to his right, if he had any more of the lost credit cards. Marco opened the bidding by sliding my Mobil credit card in my direction. He asked Paul what it was, exactly. You don't find any Mobil stations in Cuba. I had forgotten it was in the wallet, so this was still good. He wanted $5 for it, and I offered him $2 just to save the hassle of canceling and renewing it; phone calls to the U.S. from Cuba are $3 a minute.

He refused. Marco and Paul huddled in conversation. This odd group was beginning to attract attention from neighboring tables. We looked like a collection of characters from a Humphrey Bogart movie.

"He wants $20 for everything," Paul explained.

I did my best in broken Spanish. "These have no value to me or to anyone else. I have canceled them all. For me, no value, but for you 30 years in the big house. Where did you get them?"

"A scared street kid brought them to me," Marco said.

We were at an impasse. "I'm sorry, but I have something for you for the time you have spent." I slid a used Jimmy Buffett audio cassette across the table. "For you." He looked surprised, then pleased and jumped up and ordered a waiter to put the tape on the boom box that was blaring away in a corner. Then he went out the door and we looked at each other while *Cheeseburger in Paradise* filled the patio. Buffett was coming in a few weeks with a group of American musicians to play with Cuban musicians; the tape was hot stuff.

"That *chica* took off with the money for the drinks," Kodiak realized.

Marco was back with a handful of my credit cards. He pushed them across the table to me. No driver's license but, oops, my Visa debit card for my business account. I had forgotten about that one, too, but decided to bluff it out.

A European at the next table was watching all this with a smile. He caught my eye and shook his head. He looked like he had been around Havana a long time. The *jineteras* weren't even hustling him.

"All canceled. No value." I pushed them back across the table.

He huddled with Paul. "He wants $5 for everything."

"Ask him where the driver's license is."

From the look on his face it seemed he had never seen it. He shook his head in response to Paul's question.

The quick sketch artist woke up, shook his head, and began to sketch Kodiak smoking a cigar. The waiter came over and asked Marco if he could put the regular salsa music back on; he seemed to hate Jimmy Buffet. I agreed to the $5 and handed it over. The deal was done. I'd buy a round of drinks. Marco took charge and took an order for five *mojitos* to the bar.

We drank our *mojitos* while the sketch artist sketched and hustled us, but to no avail. We had hit our hustle tolerance threshold.

"Let's get the bill and get something to eat," I suggested.

When the bill came Paul said. "I paid half that amount for four drinks 15 minutes ago."

"That's the way it's done. It's Cuba. Just like Rebecca's hotel." Rebecca the wharf tart had stayed in her hotel for two nights at $32 a night, and when she extended for two more nights the rate jumped to $44 for reasons nobody explained. In Cuba, there is always a surprise at the end, just when you think things are settled.

Paul told Marco about the *jinetera* who had taken off with $10 for drinks. He looked shocked and angry that anyone could be so dishonest and said to Paul. "You come back tomorrow night and I'll have the $10."

"I have a feeling that if we come back for the $10 it will somehow end up costing us $50," I said.

We began to leave, but Kodiak was growing fond of Maria, who could do interesting things with her pelvic area in rhythm to the music. "I can't stand that much energy," Paul said.

"Wait for me, I'll be back later," Kodiak told Maria and we headed out the patio door while the getting was good, the music of Feria Fornos following us into the darkness. We crossed Central Park and stuck our heads

in the door at El Floridita because Kodiak had never
been inside before. It was getting late and there were
only a dozen people in the bar, most sipping daiquiris.

"I wonder where Hemingway sat," Kodiak said.

"Right over there in the corner, the stool that's
roped off. Sacred ground."

"And they've got a bust of him there. Cool."

We headed down O'Reilly Street for La Bodeguita
del Medio, this time not despite the fact this Hemingway hangout was a tourist mecca, but because it was.
Our experience with the wallet had left us with a han-
kering for simple, straightforward encounters and we
were reluctantly willing to pay $4 for a *mojito* to do so.

Bodeguita del Medio, the little store in the middle
of the block, is a hole-in-the-wall joint painted blue and
yellow on narrow Empedrado Street just a short half
block west of Plaza de la Catedral. The stone-columned
facade of Havana's cathedral is the most photographed
building in Havana. The Bodeguita opens to the street
with two of the roll-up metal doors, the broad doorways
left over from the days when the building was a carriage
house for a mansion next door. Angel Martinez turned it
into a *bodega* in the 1930s and cleverly offered credit to
writers, insuring their loyal patronage and grateful publicity. Hemingway started frequenting the Bodeguita in
the 1940s, often in the company of Paco Garay, a
Cuban customs inspector, and his wife, an American
who exported parakeets to the States. Angel Martinez
recalled Hemingway as a man who was in dread of
solitude and was a difficult guy, hard to take. By the
late 1950s and early 1960s the Bodeguita began to
eclipse the Floridita as the place for visiting celebrities
to see and be seen and scratch their wisdom and autographs on the walls.

The bar at Boguedita del Medio, a Hemingway hangout,
attracts a mixture of locals and tourists.

Today, the clientele is an assortment of Cubans
doing business deals over lunch and tourists rubber-
necking their way through. Sometimes the bar is full of
just Cubans, at other times organized tours stop out front
and the guide describes the Hemingway connection.

Drinkers in the small bar on the right side are somewhat sheltered from the stares of curious tourists by a
wall of wooden spindles. The narrow door is at the far
left, and every time I was there a serious, beefy man in
a white *guayabera* was standing in the doorway watching
things. Once I learned about the bombing here, his role
became clear. I was willing to bet there was a pistol
tucked away under that *guayabera*.

Squeezing around him and turning right we found
Eddy the barman dourly mixing *mojitos* for a noisy international crowd that included two Americans. Mary
and Ken, a young couple from Taos, New Mexico, had

slipped in from Mexico. One wall of the bar is made up of bottles of Havana Club rum, and in the center is a framed sign, supposedly in Hemingway's hand and signature that says: "My daiquiris in El Floridita—My mojitos in La Bodeguita".

Behind the bar is a bright yellow sign that dates back to other days and says General Electric. The walls of the bar and the dining rooms behind it are covered with the signatures and scribblings of thousands of famous, infamous and unfamous people, and many of their photos. Small, cave-like rooms ramble back and up three floors. La Bodeguita is usually dark, hot, airless, a place of simple wooden tables and chairs and bright blue and yellow tile floors. From above, a large portrait of Che keeps an eye on the goings-on below. We squeezed back through the narrow, tiled aisle to the dining rooms, past a tiny kitchen. The authentic Cuban food is the real attraction of La Bodeguita: basic black beans and rice with choices of chicken and pork, prepared simply and well. Simple Cuban food is wonderful, but things get spooky when cooks attempt creativity. For example, the breakfast at the marina offered, for $5, fresh fruit, eggs, coffee and toast, but also five stunning and surprising ways to serve bologna for breakfast, including one involving pineapple. The evening buffet was simply weird in its inventive combinations.

La Bodeguita was a little too quiet, so we continued on down to the waterfront for a good but inexpensive meal of chicken at Dos Hermanos, which was quickly becoming a favorite hangout. Our other favorite dives were the small, open-air courtyard in the Hanoi restaurant on Bernaza Street up near the capitol—good cheap lunch, hot band—and Cafe Paris on Obispo Street a block up from the Ambos Mundos.

Restaurant Hanoi, a favorite of sailors from the marina because of good, inexpensive food and drink and a lively lunch hour band.

Cafe Paris has a band playing in the doorway day and night that snags both tourists and Cubans who want to do some kind of business with tourists. It was on the way to the bus back to the marina and our little groups of sailors would stop in "for one *mojito*" before catching the last bus at 7:30 p.m. Sailors can resist anything but temptation, and usually we would have to resort to our cab money, stashed in a special pocket or sock, to haul us back to Marina Hemingway. At Cafe Paris you can find a car and driver, locate a room or apartment in a private home, be hustled by the proprietor of a small private restaurant who will whisper the cost of lobster while watching for police since it is illegal for anyone except government establishments to serve shellfish, find people who will locate anything you need, and briefly fall in love with a beautiful Cuban or lonely foreign tourist.

Or, you can buy an inexpensive slice of pizza at a streetside window behind the bar. One night we ran into a pleasant young trial lawyer from Minneapolis who had taken a circuitous route to Cuba and was staying at the Ambos Mundos. He had gone to a department store in Minnesota and asked a clerk what to wear in Cuba, and she had decked him out in a linen sports coat and T-shirt right out of an old episode of *Miami Vice*. We had a good laugh about his ability to blend into the crowd, which he agreed was at least as good as ours, decked out in shorts and boating shoes.

When Kodiak, Paul and I finally returned to Feria Fornos the outside gate to the open patio was locked. We knocked and Marco let us in. The place was empty except for Maria, who was still waiting for Kodiak. Marco made arrangements, the two vanished, and Marco directed a lad to hail a cab for Paul and me for our return to the marina. I tipped the kid $1, and then began thinking about the events of the night.

The taxi roared off toward the university and marina beyond, exhaust fumes from a broken exhaust pipe filling the interior.

"Do you think we did the right thing?" Paul asked.

"Leaving Kodiak?"

"Yes."

"I don't know, we practically pushed him into her arms."

"He needed a nudge."

"How much money did he have?"

"He said he only had about $35."

"Good. He'll be all right. You know, that kid who got us the cab? He was hanging around us the other night, too. One story Marco told us was that a kid found my wallet, didn't know what to do, and brought it to him. You know, I think I just gave the kid who picked my wallet a $1 tip."

Paul laughed, "The perfect Cuban experience."

The Road Warrior

Kodiak had become so used to roaming into Havana and the surrounding countryside at all hours—pedaling his little boat bicycle with 20-inch wheels—that he ignored the advice of Cuban friends not to wander around alone beyond the lights of Santa Fe, the village outside Marina Hemingway. Despite our adventure at Feria Fornos, there is very little street crime beyond the kid stuff of purse-snatching, picking pockets and the rare mugging—at least in downtown Havana. Kodiak roamed the countryside, returning at the wee hours of the morning hungry, waking up Kevin and Jake as he banged around the galley cooking up a batch of pancakes.

He had gone into Santa Fe for dinner with the family of his Spanish tutor, and then roamed out beyond the village to get to a more remote bar and disco. After a few drinks he climbed onto his bicycle about 2 a.m. and headed back for the boat along the dark, deserted highway. Suddenly he felt a sharp pain below his left shoulder blade, and a moment later something whistled past his ear. Somebody was throwing rocks at him, and when he looked back he could see he was being pursued by three shadowy figures on bicycles. One had a bag of rocks slung on his handlebars as ammunition. His pursuers were on full-sized bikes, but he tried to outrun them, pedaling for all he was worth. There was no sign of light ahead, and rocks glanced off him as the three riders overtook him. One came up alongside and tried to jam a stick into the spokes. Kodiak put on a burst of speed, but couldn't maintain it for long and the rider came up for another pass. But they had chosen the wrong victim. Kodiak veered toward the rider, grabbed his hair and shook his head so hard he almost fell off the bicycle. The three attackers gave up and peeled off into the darkness. Kodiak returned to WIND LINE and made pancakes. He did not give up his nocturnal rambling, but stayed closer to the city lights.

Chicas

"If we could export our women," the Cuban at the bar at Cafe Paris said thoughtfully and in perfect English, "we would solve our economic problems and all have enough to eat. But we could never do that. We could never give them up." Cubans not only admire their women, they treat them as equals in a game between the sexes that exceeds even baseball in the vigor with which it is played.

Cuban women run the spectrum of colors from vanilla to licorice, and they are not all physically beautiful, but they radiate a magnetic energy, a pure, uninhibited sense of joy about being female. Americans may never understand the Cuban rules of engagement completely, for they are different from what we are used to in the northern climates. Paul, the American sailor who helped with the Feria Fornos negotiations, confessed to being shy about meeting women but had mastered the formula, and confided, "If I tried to do in America what I do here, they would call the police on me. These women like being women. Where I'm from, I'm not so sure that's true. They start by busting your chops."

Without exception, the young sailors I got to know in Marina Hemingway were not interested in meeting *jineteras*; they wanted to meet "a nice Cuban girl," get to know her family, and become as much absorbed into Cuban culture as a foreigner could be, given the fact everyone is being watched all the time. Kevin had already taken up residency in a *casa particular*, a private home in Santa Fe. He and Kodiak were taking three hours of Spanish tutoring a day several days each week simply because they recognized that it would be impossible to assimilate if they could not carry on at least a semblance of a conversation in Spanish around the dinner table.

As for meeting *chicas*, they were going at the game as they would in America, heading for the bars and discos, with their favorites being a joint in Santa Fe because it was nearby, another called Johnny's and from time to time the disco in the hotel El Comodoro.

The chase could become a consuming part of life. While reading in a lounge chair at the pool I listened to a conversation among the WIND LINE crew, two young sailors from France, and a newcomer, a non-sailing Canadian who had simply dropped in to check out the poolside action at Marina Hemingway. Chéla, the master of ceremonies for poolside fun from 11:30 to about 4:30, was hosting a game of "Name that Tune," playing mostly American pop tunes to a somewhat bewildered collection of Argentines, Italians, Germans, and a scattering of visitors from other Latin countries. The reward for naming the tune was three fingers of Havana Club white rum in a plastic cup, no questions asked about age. Just like Vermont. A group of young men from Finland were big winners, but the young Americans were too deeply engrossed in disco lore to join the game and become ringers.

"I was having trouble sorting out the *jineteras* from just the regular girls. I mean how do you tell?"

"Well," the Canadian said, "you just figure it out after a while. Personally, I like the disco at the Comodoro. It's just right. These are not *chicas* from a slum somewhere. They're just average Cubans and their expectations aren't too high. If you hang out at the Meliá Cohiba hotel, you're expected to have big money. The rooms start at $200 a night. Drinks, maybe dinner, $50 to slip to the security guy at the hotel so you can get her in. You're looking at a $300 evening and nothing has happened. And that's just where it starts. I like the Comodoro."

"It's getting harder. A week ago at least somebody would dance with you. Now they're all afraid."

Paul, the man with the formula, had also watched the disco scene and simply shook his head. "They've got it all wrong. Here's how to do it. Go down here to the Old Man and the Sea hotel and rent a car for $60 a day. You can spend that on overpriced drinks in a disco and still not get anywhere. Drive around until you see the most beautiful woman you can imagine, and then just pull up and say 'You are so pretty I just had to stop to meet you. Would you like to go to the beach?' Ninety-nine point nine percent of the time she'll jump in. Where I live, if you did that you'd get snubbed, slapped, or they'd call a cop. You drive out to Santa Maria to the beach for the day, and on the way back you ask her out for dinner. If things have been okay that day, you'll get a date . . . probably not for the same night. Or you'll get a phone number or address. If you're staying somewhere with a phone, she'll call you."

Paul's favorite restaurant for these first dinners, he said, was El Aljibe, the cistern, at Seventh Avenue in Miramar. He said it was the best restaurant he had found in Havana, and he had been there a month when I arrived. The house specialty is roasted chicken in a secret sauce.

"In a few days you'll go out to meet the family. Bring

some rum and food. Bring plenty, these families expand. Set yourself up in a *casa particular*. You have to understand that here, love and sex are not necessarily interrelated. Sex is the only thing Castro can't ration, although he certainly is trying hard."

Fidel's crackdown on prostitution and too much contact with foreigners came as Cuba began to develop an unsavory reputation hinting that it was becoming the Thailand of the Caribbean, a place where foreigners, including pedophiles, could freely indulge their urges. It was a health issue and an image issue. "I think it's about time," an American told me. "The last time I was here I stayed at the hotel Nacional and every night we had to run the gauntlet of prostitutes in front of the hotel, from age 12 or 14 to age 60. I'm no prude, but seeing the children . . . I don't know."

While Cuba has one of the most aggressive anti-AIDS programs in the world—by 1994 nearly every adult had been tested for AIDS, and 12 sanatoriums had been established where patients remain isolated from society but receive treatment at full salary—tourism threatens to send sexually transmitted diseases spinning out of control. Homosexuals can face harassment and they tend to stay underground, but in Cuba, most AIDs cases are transmitted by heterosexual contact. And the old tried and true STDs are still around, a situation aggravated by a shortage of common medical supplies and the reluctance of Cuban males to use condoms.

Months later, Paul stopped in Vermont on his way to Montreal to catch a plane to Cuba to see his girlfriend.

"Did you see that piece in *Cigar Aficionado* magazine where Jesse Helms connected the need for an embargo and the *jineteras*?"

"I did. I wonder who on his staff wrote that for him; who's the *jinetera* expert?"

"What a jerk!"

"I trust our Congress. It will be able to stamp out sex in Cuba by embargo right after it passes campaign finance reform."

11 | *Back into the Stream*

Cristóbal, the high-priced boat repair boy, was exhausted and red-eyed when he slumped down onto the lawn next to DREAM WEAVER. He was wearing a windbreaker over a still-wet diver's short wetsuit. I handed him a Cristal and asked what was happening.

"Man, I'm tired. One of the racers landed on the reef. I had to swim out to him with a line so he could be pulled off. He was freaked out, yelling about his boat."

"What happened?"

"He's all right, they pulled him off. The sea buoy blew off in the norther and he missed the entrance through the reef. It's still rough out there."

I did not want to be in Cristóbal's place, swimming out in that tumultuous surf, or with the race fleet clawing its way along the north coast of Cuba in the norther. The day before, the winds were sending waves against the rocky shore beyond Channel 1 in throbbing, 30-foot explosions of surf. Boats in Channel 1 were holding themselves off the leeward wall by running lines completely across the channel to cleats along the windward side.

He sipped his beer. "Have you seen that big trimaran in Channel 3? He was here a day before anyone else."

"No, I thought the racers were all here in Channel 2."

"Take a look at that one."

They had been straggling in for a day, these racers in the inaugural *Transcaraïbes des Passionnés*, a 1,300-mile race beginning in Martinique and ending at Marina Hemingway with overnight stops along the way. I had visited the trimarans ahead of and behind me. This race had it all: confusion, calms, a cold front, a Coast Guard rescue and a big welcome.

The last leg to Cuba had the racers pounding into a strong norther that sent the sea buoy up onto the shore. Many racers finished at night in a strong north wind, risking a broach coming in over the reef. A temporary marker was set out to replace the buoy and marina staff helped guide boats in through the reef.

"This last part was very rough, very wet," said Jean Marc Muniglia, a crew member on CARAÏBES AIR CARGO, a custom trimaran a few boats ahead of me that looked like a giant yellow water-striding bug. It had just one interior seat, a molded pivoting chair that allowed its occupant to swing back and forth between the navigation station and galley. Anyone else below decks had to be in a bunk. There was a crew of three, and after a few days of resting, partying and provisioning, they would sail the bug back to France. The French seem to own the sport of long-distance ocean racing, they were everywhere in these racing boats.

I was killing time near the boat, waiting for Fritz Horton to arrive as my crew member for the return sail to Key West. An architect and a member of Lake Champlain Yacht Club, Fritz was going to love this. He is an avid racer; his son Andy was part of a Vermont crew of small boat sailors with Olympic aspirations and a good chance of making it.

Directly behind DREAM WEAVER was Udo Gabbert of Martinique in his Outremer 43 trimaran AMC. I walked over and he described the race over beers. Suddenly I heard a familiar voice. It was Fritz. "There you are. The guards said you were over here." He climbed aboard.

Udo was a German who owned a medical supply company in Martinique and was his own racing sponsor. "The winds until St. Martin were moderate trade winds, except for six hours with no wind off Haiti, but on the leg to Cuba a cold front moved in and the winds went up to about 25 knots. In the night we lost our biggest spinnaker. Several boats lost spinnakers. As we came up the coast a 28-foot catamaran was breaking up and the U.S. Coast Guard rescued the crew of four by helicopter."

Forty-one boats started the race—16 monohulls and 25 multihulls—and 33 finished. One boat lost its prop, another hit a channel marker in Marigot because of an autopilot malfunction, others broke up, landed on the reef, had gear failure or just dropped out.

As we returned to DREAM WEAVER to settle Fritz' gear I hinted at things to come. "I gave Fidel a call and arranged to have a little party here tonight in your honor." The normally sleepy marina had taken on a festive atmosphere because of the race. Cubans from the tourist office wandered the docks providing free Cuba Libres—rum, cola and lime—and handing out tourism packages and Havana posters. Television crews and still photographers were covering the finish, and journalist Julia Mirabal Blanco of the Cuban Radio and Television Institute even asked me for an interview to get the American perspective on the race, but I declined.

Best of all was the party being thrown by Club Nautico, the host. Last night there had been an elaborate buffet, rounds of free *mojitos*, a big water ballet in the pool, a hot, fleshly floor show with the big hats and scanty costumes of the Tropicana dancers, and finally a big band and singer Tony Cortez doing Cuban dance music. Everyone at the marina was partying. There might be hunger in the neighborhoods, but it was not showing here. They were going to do it all over again tonight and hand out the race awards. It didn't matter if it wasn't just for Fritz; by the end of the evening he was a convert to *Cubanismo*, trying to learn the Cuban names for the rhythms.

In the morning we meandered up the canal inspecting the racing boats, then went over to Channel 3 to find the big trimaran. Laurent Bourgnon, a professional racer, was aboard the boat he had skippered to a record-setting win of the Route du Rhum race. Then called PRIMAGAZ for its sponsor, it was now called MATOUBA. The huge trimaran, 60 feet wide and nearly blocking the canal, looked like a huge predatory insect created by an Italian designer who believed even killers should have soft, curving lines. On this race it averaged over 16 knots and at times was clocking 27 knots. It arrived in Havana 49 hours ahead of the other first place finishers, and blew out two sails on the last leg. One of the crew members who knew Udo and lived in Fort Lauderdale described the boat as "the greyhound of the sea."

Bourgnon, a handsome guy with tousled blond air, seemed too young to be a world-class racer but, as he made preparations to leave, it was clear his crew held him in high regard. He said that as a professional racer he entered "for fun and relaxation," and did not compete for a position among the other competitors. They were pushing off for an undisclosed U.S. port that sounded like it would be Miami. "We understand the Americans don't like boats that have been to Cuba," he explained. He was making plans for an attempt to break the west to east transatlantic crossing record: New York-The Lizard, England. Fritz and I watched the big tri head down the channel toward the sea. In the world of elite racers, everybody knows everybody and Fritz had chatted with members of the crew who knew friends of his son Andy, who himself was entering that small fraternity.

I suspected that, in his imagination, Fritz was on board MATOUBA, too. "Do you wish you were on that boat for a season?" I asked. Cruisers and serious racers may share their love of sail, but they are worlds apart in motivation. The racer lives on performance and competition, and at the end of a race is happy to park the boat until the next race. Racing is an exercise in controlling dozens of changing variables. The cruiser sees the boat as a magic carpet equipped for habitation, and lives to see what mystery and adventure lies beyond that horizon of crinkly waves. Cruising involves learning how not to go to pieces when things go out of control.

He watched MATOUBA turn out of sight, and said thoughtfully, "Yes, I would like to do that." I hoped just as I was living my dream, Fritz would get to live his. First, however, it was time to show Fritz and Udo Old Havana. We caught the VW bus into town.

Fritz had been doing his homework on the restoration of Old Havana. "They have given a man named Eusebio Leal, the city historian, almost a free hand, top to bottom. His organization picks what is to be renovated, establishes priorities, does the historical and architectural research, manages the architects and construction companies, even selects the businesses to go into the renovated buildings.

"From what I've read, he comes across as this low-key, everyday kind of guy, but you don't want to be on his bad side. Lately they've been getting some criticism because all the focus is on Old Havana because it's a tourist magnet, but other things need attention, too."

We strolled along the north side of Plaza de Armas on O'Reilly Street, hung a right on narrow Oficios, and headed in the direction of the Plaza de la Catedral. We paused to gawk into the tall, wide-open

A policeman tries to sidestep out of the picture while a woman from the Museum of Colonial Art smiles for the camera.

wooden doorway of an abandoned building. A portly man with a moustache was sitting in a chair, reading *Granma*, just inside the doorway. He motioned us inside as if it was his own home and gave us a tour.

It was a former hotel, abandoned for years, with tall arched doors and windows, trenches lacing the floor, a broad interior courtyard two stories high with guest rooms radiating off the balconies, and the faint hint of elegant painted designs on the walls. Birds flew in and out through windows of back rooms overlooking beautiful Cathedral Square. Immediately to the left on the square was the Museum of Colonial Art, where an old woman sat outside in her traditional white costume at a wooden table covered with a lace tablecloth. Across the cobblestone square was the little cafe in front of the cathedral where people lounged under canopies with their *mojitos* and listened to a band play salsa. A half

254

block up from the cathedral on Empedrado was La Bodeguita del Medio. It was a perfect location for a small tourist hotel, and although it looked hopelessly far gone, restoration work had already begun. We picked our way carefully through the upper floors, half expecting that a misstep would deposit us on the first floor 15 feet below. Keystones in the stone arches were propped in place by two by fours wedged against the floor. But once back on the first floor our host showed us where the six by eight wooden floor beams overhead had been replaced. The basic structure was being restored, and sooner or later the entire building would be reborn. "This is where we will stay," I promised myself, "when I bring Dale to see Cuba."

Outside we turned left around the first corner, toward the square, and found the building that houses the scale model of Old Havana, big as two average rooms. It is possible to locate any building you have visited in Old Havana on the model, which looks a little like it is made of yellow and pink Legos.

Fritz, Udo and I prowled the streets, poking our heads into old buildings, pausing for a beer at the hotel Sevilla bar but failing to get into good trouble with interesting foreigners, and finally taking the elevator to the top of the hotel Plaza to a dining room and a roof garden that overlooks the city. It was getting late and the sun was plunging into the sea. Lights came on in the buildings around us. The falling sun raised a shimmering golden river on the sea, burnished a glow from the tiles of the Prado below us, and floodlit the nymphs on the old Bacardi Building. The nearby Harris Brothers Building, which was just beginning its facelift when I arrived three weeks earlier, was now a bold and stunning mosaic of blue and green.

Old Havana was shedding 40 years of abuse; she was being reborn as a stunning beauty. As we stepped back through the rooftop dining room the staff was setting out linens and silver. We paused before pushing the elevator button to look at photos of the elegant, if dictatorial, "old days" in Havana when she was the Queen of the Caribbean. No wonder the Cuban exile community in south Florida could not forget their theme: Havana by Christmas. They would never be immigrants, always exiles. No one can leave Havana forever. Those days had fallen into chaos, Old Havana had fallen into ruin, but the Cuban character had stayed resilient and hopeful on both sides of the Florida Straits. Things were changing. Who could imagine how they would end?

Vanishing Pepes

Except for two things—the engine had failed and the big bookshelf and dining table mounted to the midships bulkhead had ripped off—we were off to a good start back across the Gulf Stream to Key West.

The *pepes* were leaving. Tomás and Charlie on ROSINANTE had received their $50 cruising permit from the Cubans and departed to cruise west and then south along the Cuban coast. Paul on CHEYENNE had found a pretty, perky young Englishwoman to crew back to Florida and was gone. WIND LINE's crew was planning to leave after the Cuban all-star team played their first game against the Baltimore Orioles. The partying American powerboat in our lineup of five Americans had gone a week before. Fritz had to catch a return flight from Key West to Vermont. It was our turn.

I had discovered—for reasons no one could explain and few believed—that from the top balcony of the yellow condominiums just west of the Marina Hemingway swimming pool I could pick up Key West weather forecasts on my little Standard handheld VHF. They were in and out, and full of static, but most important, they were good. No northers coming, although it was getting late in the season for northers. Winds 10 to 15 from the east southeast. No significant weather features on the horizon. This was the window; time to go home. We quickly did the last-minute shopping on shore: with my Treasury license I could bring back $100 worth of forbidden Cuban goods, and among the souvenirs was a bottle of good Havana Club for New Year's Eve. I would bring La Giraldilla to a Norwegian coastal steamer above the Arctic Circle to remind me of palm trees and sunshine, of the year I made my peace with Hemingway, and most of all of Cuba.

As expected, when I paid my marina bill there was a little surprise at the end of the deal. A 10 percent tip had been added to the dock fees—40 cents per foot per night—electricity fees and the fuel. Even so, I had been in the marina for just a few days short of a month and the bill was just $382.47.

Clearing out of Customs was a shorter version of clearing in, but this time the good doctor did not appear. It is important to notify Customs of any crew changes, so right after Fritz arrived we had gone over with his passport and changed the crew list. The Coast Guard was interested in any Cubans we might have stashed away and made a quick check of the cabin and cockpit sail locker. Customs wanted to be sure we left with everything we had brought in. Sailors who bring in bicycles—a good idea—and leave them behind might have to pay a small fee. When a big powerboat appeared around the bend the officials cut short their inspection and quickly cast us off to make room on the dock.

At 2:30 p.m. we cleared the outer entrance to the marina into a choppy sea driven by an east-northeast breeze and took a little water through the hatch at the top of the cabin. We were motorsailing to charge the battery, and I went below to secure things while Fritz took the helm. When I returned to the cockpit the red light signaling an overheating engine was on, and a quick check revealed no water was belching out the exhaust. I quickly turned it off, wondering what damage might have been done. I would let it cool down and try it later. For now we had plenty of wind to keep us moving. Once through the reef the waves settled down into an even pattern.

With the wind favoring northeast we would not be able to hold our course of 20 degrees to Sand Key Light off Key West. But the evening was young and the Gulf Stream was running with us. Fritz went below to stow some gear and soon wound up in a wrestling match with a big, heavy storage unit that had ripped off the midships bulkhead. The unit housed books and computer equipment. When closed, it stuck out about 10 inches from the wall, but when opened up the front folded down to become the dining table and it had been left open as a navigation station. I put the boat on Autohelm and soon we were both waltzing with the heavy unit, which was still attached to the wall by several wires for lights and plug-ins. It was like dancing with an elephant who wanted to lead on a sloping floor that defied our non-skid shoes, but finally we cut the wires and wrestled it into the V-berth. I noticed it had not been through-bolted, but just screwed to the bulkhead. I was glad I was not alone.

The moon, three quarters full, rose early during daylight, so we knew it would set early in the morning while we still could use it. Too bad.

Fritz had all the good habits of a racing sailor. He never stopped watching and trimming the sails, trying to get the most out of them. It contrasted with my more casual "set it and forget it" approach. We talked of Cuba and kids, business and boats, and clicked off our two-hour watches into the night. At 10 p.m. a brilliant green light appeared over the horizon to our east. It seemed to go off and on, or signal.

"We're outside Cuban waters, can't be them looking for rafters."

"Maybe it's our guys, looking for drug smugglers."

I had heard the tales from other sailors. They claimed the Coast Guard would slip up behind you in the dark, running blacked out, and when they were right over the stern they would hit you with the searchlights. Like a deer in the headlights, everybody froze. That was the idea. No time to dump drugs, or Cubans, over the side.

Gradually the wind was clocking to the east and southeast, and we were also getting a ride from the Gulf Stream. In the middle of the night the wind dropped and we slammed around in more waves than wind. We rigged a boom vang and I went below to see what could be done about the engine. It still wasn't pumping water. I closed the through-hull and took everything apart from the water intake strainer—no plastic bag in there—through the plumbing, and finally replaced the water impeller. It spun nicely. No apparent problems. I closed it up and tried it: still no water coming through.

We rigged a whisker pole and ghosted along for a while, but finally it just dropped for lack of wind and I took it in. Dawn came and now our problem was the reverse of the one yesterday when we could not fetch Key West. Without an engine the Stream would carry us past Key West.

"Where will it carry us?" Fritz asked.

"Well, Matecumbe Key, then Miami, eventually Cape Hatteras." I tried to smile.

"Is there a way of getting water into the engine from a bucket or something?" Fritz was standing in front of the engine. The cover was still off.

"I tried everything from the pump down and it seemed fine. But I didn't see if it would pump on the far side of the pump. Pull off the hose and let's give that a try."

Fritz disconnected the water hose on the far side of the pump and I started the engine. The engine chugged nicely with no sign of damage.

"Nothing," Fritz said. I was about to turn it off. "No, wait. It's pumping strong."

"Jam the hose back on."

He reconnected the hose and an instant later water was again spitting out the exhaust.

"A bubble in the system," Fritz concluded. "Maybe when we passed through that rough spot in the reef we sucked in some air and it wouldn't pump."

"The intake is way down, but it's the only thing I can think of." Sand Key Light was off in the distance. We weren't going to drift to the North Atlantic after all. The engine behaved perfectly.

We called A & B Marina for a slip and they alerted Customs. We were tied up by 12:30 p.m. Agriculture and immigration inspectors came to the boat to check us in, and told us we would have to walk down the street to Customs. "They rarely come out for boats from Cuba any more."

I had to go into a Customs office to get the $25 boat Customs sticker—I had 48 hours after returning; most departing boats get it ahead of time. Boats coming back from the Bahamas or even Cuba often call in and get clearance by phone. But don't bet on it. When CHEYENNE called in from Marathon to clear Customs, an inspector was sent out to search the boat. The incoming procedure is random enough so that no assumptions can be made. If Customs wants to get tough—and getting caught lying about a couple of cigars or a bottle of rum tucked in the bilge is one sure trigger—they have lots of legal leeway to do so. They are part of the Treasury Department, which has the mandate to enforce the "trading with the enemy" Helms-Burton embargo.

Fritz and I went into the government building on Simonton Street across from the Pelican Poop Shoppe not knowing what to expect. It was fast, easy and we were something of a curiosity because I had both a license and a letter from a Senator. The papers went off for scrutiny for a few minutes. I left convinced that people who had gone to and come from Cuba legally were rare in these parts.

Fritz's cab for the airport came early the next morning. We had barely known each other before, but an adventure is a bond to treasure for years. It was one of the best parts of this trip, sharing adventures with folks I knew only slightly. Alone again, I replaced the battery charger, through-bolted the storage unit to the bulkhead and continued to explore Key West. It was too expensive to linger long, so I headed out for Marathon only to get pinned down by the weather and spend three miserable days anchored off Christmas Tree Island, a place where I really never wanted to spend any time. While trying to reset an anchor that was dragging at sunset I was boarded by the Coast Guard (they really do sneak up on you) for not having my anchor light lit. They wrote me up for having the Y-valve on the head in the open position. We had not used it since crossing the Stream and I had simply forgotten about it.

For three days it blew out of the east, where I was headed, at 18 to 30, with the current running so strong that I always seemed to be sideways to the wind, always on the verge of dragging, always pitching back and forth. I planned my solo trip back north, figuring on a trip up the Intracoastal Waterway after following Hawk Channel to Miami to see a part of Florida I had not seen, the many bridges notwithstanding, but prepared for an outside run alone if the weather looked favorable: Key West to Marathon, Marathon to Rodriguez Key, Rodriguez to No Name Harbor near Miami, Miami to Fort Lauderdale, Lauderdale to Lantana, Lantana to Peck Lake south of Stuart, and Peck Lake to Vero Beach and my friends, where I had spent Christmas. It seemed like a lifetime ago, but it was now only April.

"You will change," my friend Gael had said thoughtfully at Christmas, studying her dinner plate. The words came slowly, almost reluctantly, as if she was sharing a secret. Sailors usually talk about toilets and diesels, rarely this. She and her husband, Don, had lived on their boat for several years. We three had sailed from the Bahamas to Bermuda, my first and only long ocean sail. "You will come back changed."

Don nodded. "Don't expect anybody to understand. Unless you've been out there, you don't get it. Don't even bother talking to people about it."

Gael added, "When we came back after our first trip our reality for years had been the weather and the sea and the boat and new experiences. I would sit and listen to people talk about life on shore and say to myself: Is this really important?

"And if you plan to go out again after you get back, don't tell anyone. If they know you are leaving again, they start to disconnect or never reconnect."

Good advice. I had changed, discovered exactly what I must do, and knew nobody would understand: it would have to be my secret. That is how it ends. Pilar is found.

I headed out of Key West and east up Hawk Channel. In an hour I saw the round roof of Oceanside Marine and the marks to Boca Chica Channel. It was an easy sail. Off Bahia Honda I saw a sea turtle drifting, looking skeptically at the world. I should find TIGER LILY and vindicate myself. Sue and Robert had left a message on my voice mail: if I wanted to see turtles I should go to the Key West aquarium. The Seven Mile Bridge and the channel under the bridge to Boot Key Harbor were just ahead. By dark, the anchor was down almost exactly where I had anchored in January.

I took the dinghy to Dockside and called Indiantown Marina on the Okeechobee Waterway, where I had been on a waiting list since New Year's week, then I rang Dale.

"I'm leaving the boat at Indiantown. I'm coming home."

"You're not bringing the boat back? What will you ever do in the summer?"

"Mission accomplished. I'm coming home."

"You'll leave the boat there?"

"I'm not quite through down here yet. Anyway, I miss you."

263

Silence for a moment. "I thought once you got out, you might just keep going forever."

"Not this time. Besides, we have plans for Norway."

"You surprise me."

"I found my Pilar. She's not a Latina, but pretty good otherwise. I'll see you in Vermont."

When I arrived in Boot Key Harbor in January I had anchored next to a Baltic 28. A red-bearded young man lived alone on board and he told me he planned to fix up his boat and circumnavigate. The mast was down on deck, there was no rigging, and each morning at 7:30 he motored to the dock in his dinghy, where he kept his bicycle, and rode off somewhere to earn a day's wages as a carpenter. I would see him wheeling around on Overseas Highway on his way back from work, or run into him in the market.

"I've been here since April," he said then. "Every week I do a little more for the boat. Next week I'm going to put the mast up." And he did. The mast went up on galvanized shrouds and stays. "I can't afford stainless," he explained apologetically. Over the next three weeks we chatted, fussed with our anchors in a storm that had us swinging dangerously close to each other, and he hammered and sawed.

By chance I had found a spot next to the same boat. In the morning I noticed a mainsail was hanked on and he was pulling up one of his anchors. I heard him tell a liveaboard friend that he was headed for Key West, where a carpenter could make better wages. I took the dinghy over. "So you're headed out."

"Yep, the first stop is Key West. I've been here a year now and the boat's ready to go."

"I just came up from Key West. The anchorage at Christmas Tree Island was terrible. The current keeps you sideways to an east wind, so you roll, and the bottom is sandy; not very good holding. Be careful if you go in there, there are some shallow spots."

"Thanks, I'll be careful. This will be a test of my sailing skills. First time out."

"Do you have charts?"

"No, just the maps you get in the sporting goods stores." He grinned a nervous grin. "Where have you been?"

"Just got back from Cuba. Checked in at Key West."

"That's great. Some day I'll head over there, too. This will be a test of my sailing skills. First time out," he repeated.

He was going alone. After a year of preparations it was time to push off, time to live the dream. I understood. Oh, how I understood. I wanted to give him a profound piece of advice about my last six months as a solo sailor, to tell him I understood his fear, and that it was justified, because there would be times when he would be in over his head and could lose his boat or even his life, and that despite the risk it was a greater risk to fail to live your dreams. I could tell him how he would change, in stages, and he would never be the same again.

But then tears were forming in the corners of my eyes behind my sunglasses, and I couldn't explain why. It was silly. "Good luck. Safe sailing. The breeze is with you today, and it is not a Friday. Remember, it is bad luck to begin a voyage on a Friday."

I motored away to get provisions. When I returned, he was gone.

Bibliography and Sources

Anderson, Jon Lee, *Che Guevara*, Grove Press, New York, NY 1997

Baker, Carlos, *Ernest Hemingway—A Life Story*, Charles Scribner's Sons, New York, NY 1969

Baker, Christopher, *Cuba Handbook*, Moon Travel Handbooks, Chico, CA 1997

Bellevance-Johnson, Marsha, *Hemingway in Key West*, The Computer Lab, Ketchum, ID 1987

Bethell, Leslie, *Cuba—A Short History*, Cambridge University Press, Cambridge, UK 1993

Brian, Denis, *The True Gen*, Grove Press, New York, NY 1988

Calder, Nigel, *Cuba—A Cruising Guide*, Imray Laurie Norie & Wilson Ltd., St. Ives, Cambridgeshire, UK 1997

Casteñeda, George G., *Compañero, The Life and Death of Che Guevara*, Alfred A. Knopf, New York, NY 1997

Coe, Andrew, *Cuba*, Passport Books, Chicago, IL 1997

Fuentes, Norberto, *Hemingway in Cuba*, Lyle Stuart Inc., Secaucus, NJ 1984

Fuentes, Norberto and photographer Roberto Herrera Sotolongo, *Ernest Hemingway Rediscovered*, Charles Scribner's Sons, New York, NY 1988

Hemingway, Ernest, *Across the River and Into the Trees*, Scribner's Paperback Fiction, New York, NY 1996

Islands in the Stream, Charles Scribner's Sons, New York, NY 1970

The Old Man and the Sea, Charles Scribner's Sons, New York, NY 1952

To Have and Have Not, Scribner's Paperback
Fiction, New York, NY 1996

*By-Line: Ernest Hemingway, Selected Articles and
Dispatches of Four Decades* (William White,
editor), Touchstone, New York, NY 1998

Hemingway Reader, Charles Scribner's Sons,
New York, NY 1953

Hotchner, A.E., *Papa Hemingway*, Random House,
New York, NY 1966

Kert, Bernice, *The Hemingway Women*, W.W. Norton &
Co., New York, NY 1983

McIver, Stuart, *Hemingway's Key West*, Pineapple Press
Inc., Sarasota, FL 1993

Reynolds, Michael, *Hemingway in the 1930s*, W.W.
Norton & Co., New York, NY 1997

Rieff, David, *The Exile—Cuba in the Heart of Miami*,
Simon and Schuster, New York, NY 1993

Salas, Osvaldo and Roberto, photographers, *Fidel's
Cuba: A Revolution in Pictures*, Thunder's Mouth
Press, New York, NY and Beyond Words
Publishing, Hillsboro, OR, co-publishers, 1998

Samuelson, Arnold, *With Hemingway—A Year in Key West
and Cuba*, Random House, New York, NY 1984

Selkirk, Errol, *Hemingway for Beginners*, Writers and
Readers Publishing, Inc. New York, NY 1994

Voss, Frederick, with Michael Reynolds, *Picturing
Hemingway*, Yale University Press, New Haven,
CT 1999

Welsh Hemingway, Mary, *How it Was*, Alfred A. Knopf,
New York, NY 1976

Williams, Joy, *The Florida Keys—A History and Guide*,
Random House, New York, NY 1995

Wyden, Peter, *Bay of Pigs—The Untold Story*, Simon
and Schuster, New York, NY 1979

Additional Sources:

Brothers to the Rescue, *www.hermanos.org*

Cuban American National Foundation,
 www.canfnet.org
 www.cubanet.org

Department of the Treasury, Office of Foreign Assets
 Control, *Cuban Assets Control Regulations*
 (covering travel and trade), Federal Register,
 Vol 60, No. 203, Friday, Oct. 20, 1995, available
 by faxback at (202-622-0077)

Franklin, Jane, *The War Against Cuba*, CovertAction
 Quarterly, Fall 1998

Granma International, Havana, English editions, March
 1999

Granma, www.granma.cu

The Miami Herald, www.herald.com

Murphy, Tim, *Visit Cuba, But With Your Eyes Open*,
 "Cruising World", March, 1997,
 www.cruisingworld.com/timcuba2.htm

Wilson, Mark, The Hemingway Resource Center,
 www.lostgeneration.com/hrc.htm